AF601340

Support for the production of this resource has been provided by the Australian Government Office for Learning and Teaching. The views expressed in this document do not necessarily reflect the views of the Australian Government Office for Learning and Teaching.

2014

ISBN: 978-1-74361-685-7 [PRINT]
ISBN: 978-1-74361-686-4 [PDF]
ISBN: 978-1-74361-687-1 [DOCX]

Acknowledgements

The Blended Synchronous Learning Project has been a collaborative initiative, and it would not have been possible without the inspiring contribution of the following Case Study partners (in order of occurrence):

- James McCulloch, Timothy Kyng, David Pitt and Hong Xie (Macquarie University)
- Joanne Curry (University of Western Sydney)
- Lucy Webster (Charles Sturt University)
- Nicola Jayne (Southern Cross University)
- Scott Grant (Monash University)
- Matt Tilley (Curtin University)

We would like to acknowledge the tireless work of the technical support staff at each of these universities, who helped to make the case study implementations and recordings a reality. Particular thanks also goes out to the students in each of the cases who were such willing and insightful participants.

Immense thanks is extended to our expert and esteemed Reference Group:

- Professor Shirley Alexander (The University of Technology Sydney)
- Professor Geoffrey Crisp (RMIT University)
- Professor John Hedberg (Macquarie University)
- Professor Belinda Tynan (University of Southern Queensland)

Just when we thought we'd considered everything, the Reference Group provided us with wise and illuminating guidance to help us enhance the project.

Finally, thanks goes out to the Australian Office for Learning and Teaching for having the forward thinking to sponsor research and development into the exciting and emerging area of blended synchronous learning.

Matt Bower, Macquarie University
Barney Dalgarno, Charles Sturt University
Gregor Kennedy, The University of Melbourne
Mark J. W. Lee, Charles Sturt University
Jacqueline Kenney, Macquarie University

Executive summary

The Blended Synchronous Learning Project sought to investigate how rich-media technologies such as web conferencing, desktop video conferencing and virtual worlds could be used to effectively unite remote and face-to-face students in the same live classes. Increasingly university students are opting to learn from off-campus, often due to work, family and social commitments (Gosper, et al., 2008; James, Krause, & Jennings, 2010). Often universities will cater for remote students by providing access to asynchronous resources via Learning Management Systems, meaning that off-campus students miss out on the benefits of synchronous collaborative learning such as rapid teacher feedback, real-time peer discussions, and an enhanced sense of connectedness.

As part of this project a scoping study was conducted to determine the types of rich-media synchronous technologies that Australian and New Zealand tertiary educators had been using and why they were using them. The results from the 750 respondents indicated that the use of rich-media technologies for learning and teaching had experienced over a decade of strong growth, with desktop video conferencing used for more incidental small group work, virtual worlds being used for immersive role play and simulation tasks, and web conferencing being used with larger cohorts of students for a great variety of pedagogical purposes. Interestingly, 39% of respondents indicated that they had used rich-media synchronous technologies to unite remote and face-to-face students. Over 600 respondents to the scoping study accepted an invitation to join the Blended Synchronous Learning Collaborator Network, and survey responses were used to identify case study partners.

Seven case studies of blended synchronous learning were conducted in Higher Education institutions across Australia. These encompassed a wide variety of technologies, discipline areas and learning designs, including:

1. web conferencing to develop investment understanding using a collaborative evaluation task;
2. room-based video conferencing to develop understanding of healthcare quality improvement approaches using an interactive lecture and collaborative evaluation task;
3. web conferencing to develop microscopic tissue analysis and interpretation skills using group questioning tasks;
4. web conferencing for participation in statistics tutorials using collaborative problem solving;
5. virtual worlds to facilitate Chinese language learning using a paired role-play;
6. web conferencing to enable presence in sexology using interactive lecture discussions; and
7. virtual worlds for teacher education using collaborative evaluation and design tasks.

The analysis of the case studies was based upon a variety of data sources which included pre-observation teacher-documented case overviews, pre-observation teacher interviews, video and screen recording of the blended synchronous learning lessons, researcher lesson observations, post-observation student survey responses, post-observation student focus groups, and post-observation teacher interviews.

A cross case study analysis revealed an assortment of reasons why many students valued blended synchronous learning. Remote students found it offered them faster access to support and increased their sense of connectedness. Many face-to-face students appreciated being exposed to a broader range of perspectives. Both remote and face-to-face students valued the flexibility that blended synchronous learning afforded, and in many cases felt that it led to an enhanced sense of community. The ability to hold extended discussions and to mutually support one another, as well as having all of the information in one space, were seen as advantages of blended synchronous learning. The technology enabled students to engage in a wider range of activities than would otherwise have been possible, including group writing tasks, diagram labelling exercises, voting activities and role plays. In some cases both remote and face-to-face students reported learning more in blended synchronous learning mode than in their usual classes because of the active learning tasks that the teacher designed and applied. Responses to the lesson evaluation questionnaires across the seven case studies indicated that 74% of face-to-face and 77% of remote students would like blended synchronous learning to be used in other subjects that they studied. Technology reliability and performance was seen as an issue for some remote and face-to-face students and comments from some face-to-face students suggested that the involvement of remote students could at times slow down the lesson or interfere with face-to-face students' interaction opportunities.

Teachers also recognised that there were several advantages to blended synchronous learning, such as the ability to include remote students in classes, field more questions during lessons, and increase the active learning of all students. The technology was seen as a way to facilitate greater contribution by all students, and increase the sense of community amongst the class. However, teaching in blended synchronous learning mode placed high demands on teachers in terms of cognitive load, with the teacher needing to simultaneously manage two cohorts of students, multiple streams of information and the technology, all while teaching the subject matter. Technology performance issues and preserving the quality of the face-to-face experience were also seen as issues when teaching in blended synchronous learning mode.

Blended synchronous learning offers many advantages to institutions. It can provide more flexible access to programs, increase the amount of in-class participation, enhance students' sense of connectedness, and potentially be more financially efficient. However, findings from this study indicate that for blended synchronous learning to be successful, institutions need to provide appropriate technical support, teaching assistance, professional development, and pre-equipped learning and teaching spaces. Additionally, adequate workload allowance needs to be provided to teachers teaching in blended synchronous mode to account for the extra time commitment it requires during preparation.

This Handbook is the main output of the Blended Synchronous Learning Project. It includes a Blended Synchronous Learning Design Framework that offers pedagogical, technological and logistical recommendations for teachers attempting to design and implement blended synchronous learning lessons (see Chapter 14). The Handbook also includes a Rich-Media Synchronous Technology Capabilities Framework to support the selection of technologies for different types of learning activities (see Chapter 4), as well as a review of relevant literature, a summary of the Blended Synchronous Learning Scoping Study results, detailed reports of each of the seven case studies, and a cross case analysis.

Another key output of the project is the Blended Synchronous Learning website (available at http://blendsync.org). It contains video overviews of the case studies, a link to the Blended Synchronous Learning Collaborator Network, and other information about the project including the personnel, publications, and workshops associated with the initiative.

It is envisaged that the outcomes and products of the Blended Synchronous Learning Project will provide guidance to help educators and universities effectively unite remote and face-to-face students in live classes using contemporary rich-media synchronous technologies.

Table of Contents

Chapter 1: Overview

Blended Synchronous Learning in Higher Education

This Handbook is a primary output of the Australian Office of Learning and Teaching Innovation and Development Project entitled "Blended synchronicity: Uniting on-campus and distributed learners through media-rich real-time collaboration tools" (Project ID11-1931). While there are few definitions of blended synchronous learning in the literature, Hastie, Hung, Chen and Kinshuk (2010) define it as the "integration of physical classroom and cyber classroom settings using synchronous learning to enable unlimited connectivity for teachers and students from any part of the world" (p. 10). For the purposes of this Handbook, we define blended synchronous learning as:

> *Learning and teaching where remote students participate in face-to-face classes by means of rich-media synchronous technologies such as video conferencing, web conferencing, or virtual worlds.*

Research clearly indicates that Australian university students are attending university campuses less and are going online more to fulfil their learning needs (Gosper, et al., 2008; James, Krause, & Jennings, 2010). As students increasingly need to juggle the competing demands of work, family and study, the ways in which they engage with Higher Education institutions is changing. The use of technology is playing a key role in this change. While most students still enrol to study on a centralised campus, their studies are supported through a range of online resources – lecture recordings, notes, readings, and so on – that make coming to campus more optional. As students choose more flexible study options and technology-based learning support becomes pervasive at universities, the boundary between traditional campus-based and distance learning in Higher Education is becoming blurred (Dillenbourg, 2008).

Given the changing patterns of student engagement in Higher Education, the tertiary sector is more actively considering how technology can facilitate collaborative interactions between staff and students who are increasingly distributed and dislocated (Herrington, Herrington, Ferry, & Olney, 2008; Lowe, Murray, Li, & Lindsay, 2008; Smyth, Andrews, & Tynan, 2008). Moreover, university educators recognise that in many disciplines, collaborative activities often lie at the heart of engaging and effective learning experiences. These collaborative interactions take a variety of forms and may include an individual student and tutor participating in a deep discussion about a difficult concept, pairs or small groups of student peers discussing problems or creating artefacts, whole-class discussions including facilitated question-and-answer sessions, or tutorial 'papers' or presentations delivered by students in front of their peers.

While enterprise Learning Management Systems have some ability to support some of these collaborative learning activities, such systems are often used for and suited to the provision of resources and asynchronous communication via tools such as discussion forums (Kennedy, 2010; Valcke, 2004). However, rich-media synchronous technologies such as video conferencing, web conferencing and virtual worlds can greatly enhance the educational experiences of university students who are increasingly distributed (Bower & Hellstén, 2010; Dalgarno & Lee, 2010; de Groot, Harrison, & Shaw, 2011; Dede, 2009; Kan, 2011; Koenig, 2010; Stewart, Harlow, & DeBacco, 2011).

Australia's Tertiary Education Qualification Standards Agency (TEQSA) has indicated that students' place or mode of study should not influence the learning outcomes that they achieve (Tertiary Education Qualification Standards Agency, 2013). Given this, blended synchronous learning is one possible way that educators can provide equivalent educational experiences to remote and face-to-face students. As such, there is likely to be an increased need for better and more widespread guidance on the use of rich-media synchronous technologies as Higher Education institutions move to provide more flexible access to engaging collaborative online learning experiences. Increased targets for student participation resulting from the Bradley Review of Australian Higher Education (Bradley, Noonan, Nugent, & Scales, 2008) and the continual upgrade of the National Broadband Network will only increase the need for clear, evidence-based advice in this area.

In this context, the Blended Synchronous Learning ('BlendSync') Project sought to investigate how three specific technology-based tools – video conferencing, web conferencing and 3D virtual worlds – could best be used to support activities that engage Higher Education students and teachers in effective real-time learning irrespective of their location. This project is based on the premise that, in the future, students should be able to seamlessly participate in live face-to-face classes from any location, and that by better understanding the theory and practice relating to the use of rich-media real-time collaboration tools, students will be able to be more effectively united across distributed learning contexts.

Overview of the Blended Synchronous Learning Project

The Blended Synchronous Learning Project ran from October 2011 to February 2014 and consisted of four phases. During Phase 1 the team performed a scoping study of how universities were teaching with rich-media synchronous technologies, which included an extensive review of the literature and also a survey of over 1700 educators from across Australia and New Zealand. From the survey respondents over 600 nominated to be part of the Blended Synchronous Learning Collaborator Network, and throughout the Project this number grew to nearly seven hundred members. During Phase 2 case study partners were selected from respondents to the survey, and case study instruments and protocols were established. The Phase 3 case studies were conducted between July 2012 and August 2013, and consisted of observations and the analysis of seven blended synchronous learning contexts in universities across Australia. The final dissemination phase (Phase 4) took place from September 2013 to March 2014, and involved several blended synchronous learning workshops in capital cities around Australia as well as the production of this Handbook. For more information about the Blended Synchronous Learning Project see the project website at <blendsync.org>.

Structure of Handbook and Intended Audience

As mentioned above, this Handbook represents one of the primary outcomes from this project and aims to provide a detailed overview of the findings and outputs of the project. Chapter 2 provides a background to blended synchronous learning and a brief review of the interdisciplinary literature drawn on by the project team to underpin the project. Chapter 3 provides an overview of the findings of the empirical investigation conducted in Higher Education institutions in Australia and New Zealand as part of the project. Chapter 4 introduces a Rich-Media Synchronous Technology Capabilities Framework. This Framework outlines a way of conceptualising blended synchronous learning designs, and provides support for practitioners who aim to utilise video conferencing, web conferencing and virtual worlds in their teaching. Chapter 5 provides an overview of the case studies that were conducted as part of the project, including the methods and processes used to conduct those case studies. Chapters 6-12 report on the seven case studies completed as part of this project, and act as learning design exemplars as well as investigations of classroom practice. The cross case-analysis reported in Chapter 13 enabled the overall project findings relating to blended synchronous learning design and implementation to be distilled. Chapter 14 summarises key findings, provides recommendations for teachers and institutions, and offers concluding observations about areas of future research and development.

By contributing to the understanding of how rich-media real-time collaborative learning technologies can be most appropriately applied in a range of institutional and disciplinary settings across the Higher Education sector, this Handbook caters to a number of audiences. As emerging collaborative technologies move into the mainstream, the Handbook bolsters the capacity of educators, technologists and university leaders to design and implement blended synchronous learning using the variety of tools at their disposal. In particular, this Handbook may be useful for:

- **Academic and educational design and development staff –** By documenting useful learning designs and case studies, the Handbook helps academic staff and educational designers to understand the potentials (and limitations) of blended synchronous learning, so that they can more effectively utilise technology to enable remote student participation in face-to-face classes. The Rich-Media Technology Capabilities Framework that is provided also supports educators and designers to discerningly select and apply rich-media technologies in order to facilitate collaboration, concept representation and a sense of co-presence.
- **IT management and support staff –** By describing the capabilities, limitations and uses of specific rich-media real-time collaboration tools, the Handbook will assist university IT departments and their managers to decide how to best implement these technologies at their respective institutions. The Handbook will also support them to determine how to more effectively integrate these technologies into the existing infrastructure associated with online learning, and how to better support academic staff in their use of such tools for learning and teaching purposes.
- **Higher Education institutions, leaders and policy makers –** Equipped with knowledge of the ways in which rich-media real time collaboration tools can be used to enhance learning and teaching, leaders and policy makers in Higher Education institutions will be better placed to create policy and make strategic decisions about how to improve students' access to and participation in learning experiences.

Chapter 2: Background Literature and Context

Introduction

This chapter provides a review of relevant literature relating to the design and implementation of blended synchronous learning. It is divided into four sections that address collaborative learning in general, findings from previous studies of blended synchronous learning, tools to support blended synchronous learning, and Learning Design Frameworks.

Collaborative Learning

Dillenbourg (1999) offers a broad definition of collaborative learning as "a situation in which two or more people learn or attempt to learn something together" (p 1-2). While seemingly simple, the definition of collaborative learning has been the topic of much debate among researchers and theorists, particularly the distinction between collaborative and cooperative learning. While beyond the scope of this Handbook, those interested should consider the extensive literature on computer-mediated communication (CMC), Computer-Supported Collaborative Learning (CSCL) and Computer-Mediated Collaborative Learning. Dillenbourg's (1999) chapter, "What do you mean by collaborative learning?" is also a useful starting point.

Despite these debates, educators and educational theorists have, for some time, recognised the importance of social interactions more broadly, and collaboration more specifically to students' learning experiences, processes and outcomes. Contemporary educational theories and frameworks – particularly social learning theories, informed by social constructivism – point to the important role of peer-based interaction, communication and collaboration. Given this, it is not surprising that there is broad consensus among educational researchers about the positive effects of collaborative learning on achievement (for instance see Jonassen, Lee, Yang, & Laffey, 2005; Joseph & Payne, 2003; Slavin, 1995). In the area of technology-mediated learning, Laurillard's (2002) well-known conversational framework suggests that dialogue or 'conversations' between teachers and learners is critical in order for students to reconcile their views of the world with the abstract academic concepts they are required to master. Moreover, Laurillard argues that a range of technologies can be used to support and facilitate this conversation. However, while a number of technologies and technology-based tools offer the potential to foster genuine collaboration, there is no guarantee that simply using them will necessarily improve learning (Naidu & Järvelä, 2006; Reeves, Herrington, & Oliver, 2004). A key take-home message from many empirical studies exploring the value of collaborative or cooperative learning is the importance of designed rather than incidental learning activities (Borokhovski, Tamim, Bernard, Abrami, & Sokolovskaya, 2012).

Blended Synchronous Learning: Advantages and Challenges

Blended synchronous learning – learning and teaching where remote students participate in face-to-face classes by means of rich-media synchronous technologies – has been proposed as having a number of educational and practical benefits. Stewart, Harlow and DeBacco (2011) suggest that rich-media contemporary technologies offer universities new solutions to existing problems, such as preparing students for the 21st-century workplace, attracting students to university (especially underrepresented populations of students) and providing opportunities for expert collaboration. More concretely, providing students with learning opportunities to collaborate in synchronous online environments, accords with evidence indicating better course and program completion rates for students who participate in synchronous interactions with their teacher and peers rather than relying solely on asynchronous communication (Norberg, 2012; Power, 2008; Power & Vaughan, 2010)

One of the most often cited practical benefits of blended synchronous learning environments is their ability to provide greater educational access to students, and in many ways, to provide more equitable learning experiences for students who are geographically isolated or cannot physically attend classes due to other demands in their lives (Norberg, 2012). For instance, blended synchronous learning enables people who cannot be present in person because they are working full time, need to mind children, or are ill, to still participate in on-campus learning experiences (Pope, 2010). Irvine proposes the concept of 'multi-access learning' as one that addresses students' need for flexibility and choice by giving them the ability to select and customise the modality or modalities through which they access classes, regardless of their enrolment mode (Irvine, 2010; Irvine, Code, & Richards, 2013). Blended synchronous learning can allow remote participants to experience an instructor's lesson, ask and answer questions, offer comments in class and generally allow engagement "in a similar manner to on-campus students" (White, Ramirez, Smith, & Plonowski, 2010, p. 35), providing them with both access to knowledge and social interaction (Rogers, Graham, Rasmussen, Campbell, & Ure, 2003).

Some researchers report that students who have the choice of attending face-to-face or remotely often choose to participate remotely, for instance because they can unobtrusively contribute to the lecture discussion via text chat (McCue & Scales, 2007; Vu & Fadde, 2013). Convenience is often cited as a reason for preferring to remotely participate in blended-synchronous learning activities (Irvine, 2010; McCue & Scales, 2007; White, et al., 2010), particularly for students who have a demanding life outside their studies (Pope, 2010). Interestingly, there is some evidence to suggest that regardless of whether students participate remotely or face-to-face, blended synchronous learning can lead both cohorts of students to develop a similar 'sense of community' (Atweh, Shield, & Godat, 2005; Shield, Atweh, & Singh, 2005).

This notion of creating an enhanced sense of community among both face-to-face and remote students participants is one of the educational advantages of blended synchronous learning environments (Lidstone & Shield, 2010). Part of this can stem from the ability to form a larger cohort of students, so that more perspectives can be offered on any particular topic (Rogers, et al., 2003). Face-to-face participants can benefit from the expertise of off-campus students (Stewart, et al., 2011), who in many cases are older and have substantial professional or industry experience to share (McCue & Scales, 2007). Alternately, some academics have found blended synchronous learning can be useful to form community in less structured teaching contexts, such as through out-of-class discussion and cooperative learning in graduate and higher degree research classes (McCue & Scales, 2007; Roseth, Akcaoglu, & Zellner, 2013; Stewart, et al., 2011).

It is worth noting that some face-to-face students have suggested that attempts to simultaneously teach remote and face-to-face students can lead to the teacher being distracted and giving them less attention than if the remote students were not participating in the lesson (Popov, 2009; Rogers, et al., 2003). The technology can also be an imposition for face-to-face students, for instance if they need to speak into a microphone (Rogers, et al., 2003). Attempting to simultaneously cater to face-to-face and remote students can lead to teachers compromising their pedagogical approaches by, for example, 'slide reading' or slowing down their teaching pace (Popov, 2009). Factors such as these can leave some face-to-face students feeling blended synchronous learning modes negatively impact on their experience and learning (Stewart, et al., 2011).

This challenge of blended synchronous learning highlights the demands placed on teachers in successfully creating these environments. Attempting to teach remote and face-to-face students simultaneously can result in a significant increase in the 'teacher effort' required than when teaching in one mode alone (Norberg, 2012; Popov, 2009). For instance it can be difficult to promote seamless interaction between remote and face-to-face students (Stewart, et al., 2011) and teachers may need to spend additional class time and effort encouraging remote students to participate in the lesson (Rogers, et al., 2003). For this reason, it may be necessary to limit student numbers in order for teachers to effectively manage and support the blended synchronous learning experience (White, et al., 2010).

Students' technical skills and familiarity with the communication platform are issues that warrant consideration before attempting to teach using blended synchronous learning approaches (White, et al., 2010). Lack of institutional recognition for the degree of effort involved and cultures that do not encourage risk taking can leave some teachers feeling unsupported in their efforts to innovate with blended synchronous learning (Stewart, et al., 2011). According to Gilbert's (1995) innovation adoption model, this lack of perceived value can reduce the likelihood that the approach is propagated.

A recurring theme amongst the literature is the need for teachers to be organised when teaching in blended synchronous learning mode (Chakraborty & Victor, 2004; Rogers, et al., 2003). One way to manage the load on individual teachers is to employ a teaching assistant who can attend to technology-related problems, respond to student text chat comments, and manage other issues not related to the core aspects of the lesson (Rogers, et al., 2003; White, et al., 2010). It has been suggested that increasing the ratio of teaching assistants to participants may be necessary to minimise disruptions to lessons (White, et al., 2010). Having multiple teachers involved in class discussions can also lead to a richer learning experience for students (Lidstone & Shield, 2010).

Teacher perceptions and the need to provide professional development opportunities present challenges for the growth of blended synchronous learning. As Norberg (2012) notes, "where there is no technology at all, a teacher has to be in the same room with his or her students to build a learning environment ... while those limitations no longer exist technologically, they still exist culturally" (p. 329).

Tools for Blended Synchronous Learning

A wide variety of tools with a range of affordances are available to facilitate blended synchronous learning. Examples include web conferencing systems like Blackboard Collaborate (Spann, 2012) and Saba Centra (White, et al., 2010), virtual worlds like Second Life (Beltrán Sierra, Gutiérrez, & Garzón-Castro, 2012), chat rooms with video feeds (Lidstone & Shield, 2010), and even custom-built systems comprised of tools such as Etherpad, Google Hangouts, Piazza and online forms (Roseth, et al., 2013). On occasions Smartboards and tablet devices have been used with web conferencing in order to increase the capacity of teachers to write notes on whiteboards and slides (McCue & Scales, 2007).

The ways in which these blended synchronous learning tools can be used or structured educationally can, of course, vary. And, the way in which tools are organised, arranged and deployed across modalities reflects their purpose and pedagogical intent. For example, Lidstone and Shield (2010) comment that their 'postage stamp'-sized video feed of the classroom was used as a 'cueing' device to enhance a sense of connectedness for distance students using text chat, rather than as a content transmission and interaction tool (p. 96). More generally, Hastie, Hung, Chen & Kinshuk (2010) present a framework for conceptualising blended synchronous learning configurations in terms of whether teachers and/or students are in the cyber classroom and/or the physical classroom, and the number of participants in each location (groups or individuals). Their nine mode model demonstrates the range of possibilities for blended synchronous learning, from one remote student logging in to a teacher-led small group face-to-face session, to many teachers and many students at many different locations collaborating together via synchronous technologies (Hastie, et al., 2010).

In addition to educational structure or design of the class, the way in which any particular platform performs in terms of functionality and reliability is critical to the success of any lesson (Stewart, et al., 2011; White, et al., 2010). Lags or breaks in audio transmission can, for example, be highly detrimental to the success of blended synchronous learning activities (Chakraborty & Victor, 2004; Pope, 2010; White, et al., 2010). Student bandwidth is part of this concern, and represents a perennial problem in terms of ensuring uninterrupted communication (Atweh, et al., 2005; Shield, et al., 2005). Difficulties with connectivity can lead to teachers choosing low-bandwidth tools such as text chat over higher bandwidth options such as audio and video (Lidstone & Shield, 2010).

Capturing teacher and students' face-to-face discussions so that it can be broadcast to remote students, particularly without background noise, is difficult (McCue & Scales, 2007; Rogers, et al., 2003). If these conversations are not captured with adequate fidelity it will result in remote students not being able to follow discussions, quickly leading to disengagement. Similarly, capturing video feeds as the teacher moves around the class can also be problematic (White, et al., 2010). But in attempting to resolve these issues, care must be taken not to overly modify or constrain face-to-face lesson activities (White, et al.,

2010). All of these factors can lead to a 'transactional distance', which not only refers to the geographic separation of students but also to psychological separation (Moore, 1991).

As indicated in the discussion to this point, rich-media real-time collaboration tools have the potential to provide students, particularly remote students, with enhanced educational and practical experiences in Higher Education. Video conferencing tools (e.g. *Skype*), web conferencing tools (e.g. *Adobe Connect*, *Wimba*, *Blackboard Collaborate*) and virtual worlds (e.g. *Second Life*), are increasingly being used to bring together on-campus and geographically dispersed students. The ways in which each of these tools has been used in tertiary education is discussed briefly below.

Video conferencing

Video conferencing systems allow for synchronous audio and video feeds to be transmitted between sites so that each user or group of users can see and hear the other users. Traditionally in education settings, dedicated room or lecture theatre-based systems were required, and such systems have been used for some time to simultaneously deliver lectures to students based at multiple campuses. More recently, desktop video conferencing applications such as *Skype* (see Figure 1) have become available. These allow live audio and video interactions to occur between remote participants using webcams and microphones attached, which are attached to desktop or laptop computers. Many of these systems have also gradually introduced additional tools such as instant messaging, file transfer and desktop sharing tools, which have brought them closer in functionality to web conferencing systems.

The use of video conferencing is largely underpinned by the premise that "visual signals improve human interaction" (Fullwood & Doherty-Sneddon, 2006, p. 168). Video conferencing can facilitate informal communication, unplanned interactions at distance and a shared understanding between participants (Parker & Joyner, 1995). Stewart et al. (2011, p. 358) argue that "productive learning occurs through conversations among students and faculty who create knowledge together, in real-time, without [necessarily] physically being together in the same place". As with arguments about the value of blended synchronous learning more generally, researchers have noted that students appreciate how video conferencing can reduce commute time, increase real-world skills, and promote a sense of connectedness among overseas students (Kan, 2011; Koenig, 2010). Koenig suggests that when faculty were good communicators via video conferencing and were able to keep students involved, the classes were deemed to be "equally as engaging as traditional classroom delivery" (Koenig, 2010, p. 2). A variety of communicative patterns are possible with video conferencing, including 'voice switching' (a 'free-for-all' situation in which the 'floor' is passed to the person speaking at a given moment) and 'chairing' (where the 'floor' is allocated to an individual by the chair of the meeting) (Parker & Joyner, 1995).

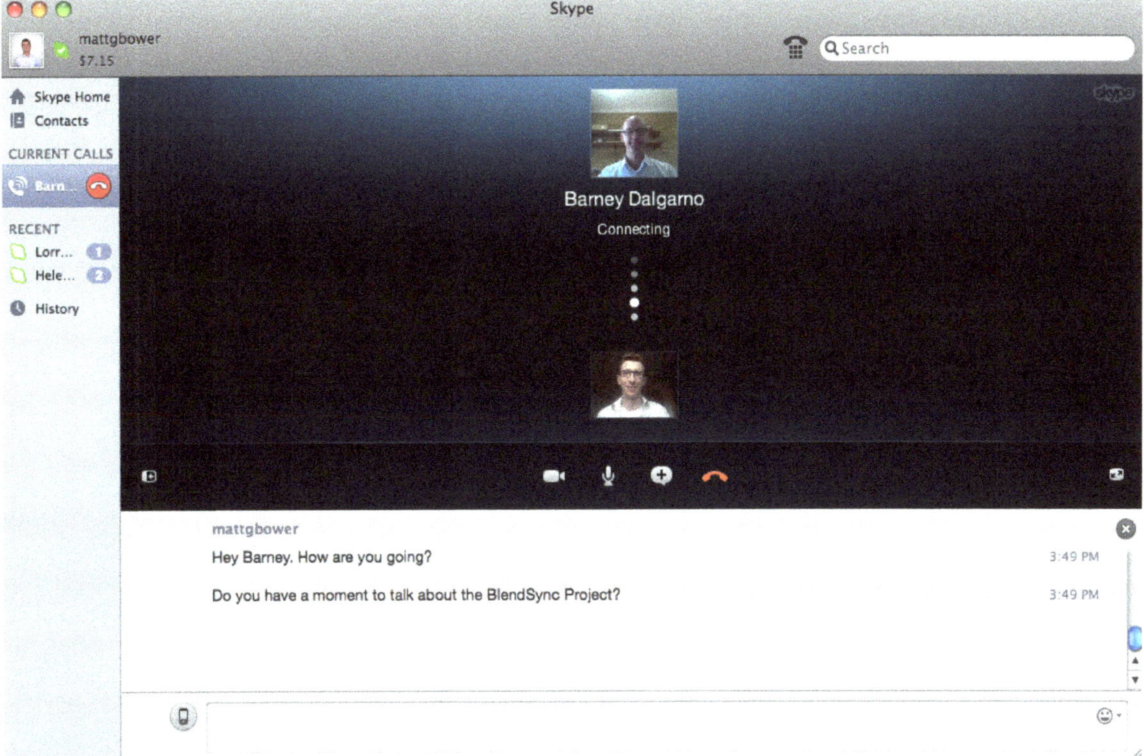

Figure 1: Screenshot of the Skype video conferencing system

Web conferencing

Web conferencing tools allow groups of users to enter a shared online space where they can use features such as whiteboards, screen sharing, chat, voting, file sharing and collaborative authoring facilities together in real-time from within their web browsers (see Figure 2). The functionality employed by the most commonly used web conferencing tools (e.g. *Adobe Connect*, *Blackboard Collaborate)* have begun, in recent years, to be replicated by desktop video conferencing tools (e.g. Skype), so that many of the features of one are now also found in the other.

Almpanins, Miller, Ross, Price and James (2011) describe synchronous web conferencing environments as a 'virtual classroom' and "the digital version of a classroom meeting" (p. 317). Interaction is facilitated through different modalities such as text chat, audio streaming and video streaming (Steed & Vigrass, 2011). Typical functionalities include the ability to display PowerPoint presentations, broadcast webcam video and voice, exchange files, vote, write shared notes, and collaboratively draw on a whiteboard (Bower, 2011). The ability for users to broadcast their screen enables web conferencing systems to considerably enhance the student learning experience (Steed & Vigrass, 2011). Social presence and responses can be facilitated by a variety of emoticons and voting features providing a mix of communication and participant management modes, with multiple group work instances supported by 'breakout' rooms (Todhunter, 2008).

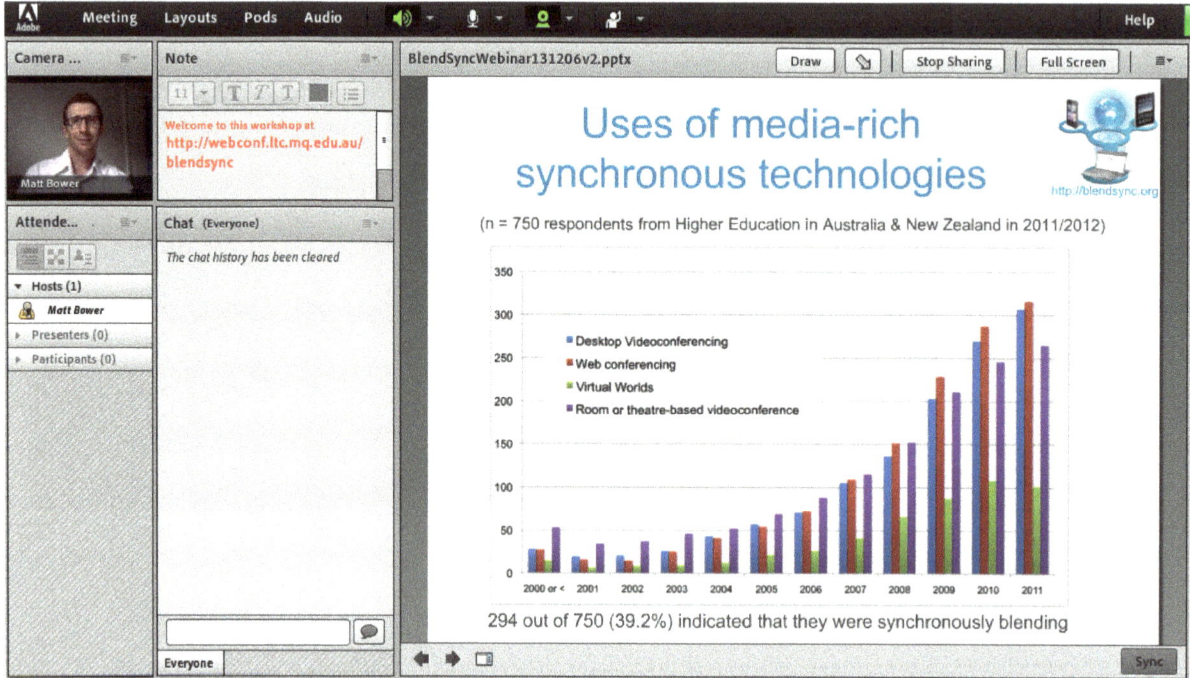

Figure 2: Screenshot of the Adobe Connect web conferencing environment

There is growing evidence of cohesive strategies to develop web conferencing approaches within and across institutions. The use of web conferencing systems is a response to the general need to engage students with rich and/or synchronous online learning settings (Spanier, 2011). Proponents of web conferencing argue for broad and strategic adoption within universities that maximises potential benefits to the institution and avails students and staff with lasting open access (de Groot, et al., 2011). While there is an emerging body of research in this area, and notwithstanding the increased uptake and use of web conferencing tools, there remains a need for a deeper understanding of how to make effective pedagogical use of these technologies (Munkvold, Khazanchi, & Zigurs, 2011).

Virtual worlds

Virtual worlds are online representations of physical environments in which users, represented by avatars, can move around and interact with other objects and users, usually in three dimensions. Virtual worlds such as *Second Life* (see Figure 3), *Open Sim* and *AvayaLive Engage* permit rich actions and interactions, including the ability for users to exchange messages and objects with other users, see one another's avatars interacting with the environment, and 'experience' the world through touch, voice communication and engagement in quests (Messinger, Stroulia, & Lyons, 2008). Hew and Cheung (Hew & Cheung, 2010) note the three defining features of virtual worlds reported in the literature and add a fourth. The first three are "the illusion of 3-D space, avatars that serve as visual representations of users and an interactive chat tool for users to communicate with one another" (Dickey, 2005, cited in Hew & Cheung, 2010, p. 34). The fourth feature they add is the ability of a user to 'act' on the world by using object properties in the virtual world, which enables, by implication, learning by doing rather than by listening or reading (Hew & Cheung, 2010). Virtual worlds allow for free navigation from a first-person perspective, and also offer opportunities to represent the world in natural semantics rather than through abstractions and symbols. This means that virtual worlds can be created for students so they can experience micro or macro environments (e.g. biological systems and cells) that would otherwise not be possible (Mikropoulos & Natsis, 2011). Dede (2009) contends that one of the advantages of virtual worlds is that the digital replication of real-world experience creates immersive presence that can give rise to learning through situated experiences and multiple perspectives, thus leading to greater transfer of learning to other contexts.

Figure 3: Screenshot of a scene in the Second Life virtual world (image sourced from www.flickr.com/photos/nmc-campus/5100944310/)

Virtual worlds afford learning tasks that can lead to enhanced spatial knowledge representation and increased intrinsic motivation and engagement as well as learning that is experiential, contextualised and collaborative (Dalgarno & Lee, 2010). Lim (2009) has proposed a 'Six Learnings' framework that highlights the breadth of potential learning designs that can be instantiated in virtual worlds, including exploration, collaboration, role-play, building, championing and expressing. The ability to provide different levels of structure and scaffolding for tasks enacted in virtual worlds gives teachers a degree of pedagogical control (Jacobson, Kim, Miao, Shen, & Chavez, 2010). While there are issues associated with the integration of virtual worlds in a Higher Education setting, including a range of technical, cultural, interactional, economic, scheduling, standards, scaffolding persistence, social and identity-related issues (Warburton, 2009), studies have found that the majority of virtual world educators believe using virtual worlds positively impacts on their students' learning (Dalgarno, Lee, Carlson, Gregory, & Tynan, 2011b).

Blended Synchronous Learning Design

The ways in which blended synchronous learning tools are utilised in educational contexts is driven in large part by the learning designs that underpin their usage. The term 'learning design' has been defined in a number of ways by educational researchers (Dobozy, 2013). A recent symposium of international learning design experts conceptualised learning design as the descriptive frameworks, learning and teaching concepts, and educator practices surrounding the creation of learning tasks that are increasingly technologically based (Dalziel, et al., 2012). In essence, for any given learning outcome/s a learning design describes or characterises the resources to be used, the role of students and teachers in learning interactions, and any assistance that is required to support these interactions.

At a broad level Biggs (1989) provides a 3Ps model for conceptualising learning that incorporates three levels:

- presage factors – contextual elements influencing design;
- process factors – elements that influence how designs are enacted and interaction is supported; and
- product factors – outcomes resulting from the implementation of lessons.

The Presage Process Product model (Biggs, 1989) has been used as a framework for conceptualising the design of online learning communities (Brook & Oliver, 2003) and how online educational resources influence outcomes in blended learning environments (Kember, McNaught, Chong, Lam, & Cheng, 2010). Because it provides a generally accepted and flexible approach to describing lesson design, enactment and outcomes, it has been used to structure the reporting of the case studies to follow.

Other broad principles such as Biggs and Tang's (2011) 'constructive alignment' (alignment between intended learning outcomes, learning activities, and assessment), and principles of collaborative and cooperative learning (see Barkley, Cross, & Major, 2004; Slavin, 1995) provide an important baseline for learning activities incorporating blended synchronous learning tools. Constructive alignment is important because many well-intentioned educational initiatives are unsuccessful due to lack of alignment between the intended learning outcomes, the designed activities, and the assessment tasks that students are required to complete. Collaborative and cooperative learning are fundamental to blended synchronous learning design if students are to be actively engaged in the learning experience rather than passive recipients of information.

At a more detailed level, a number of national and international projects have developed frameworks to support thinking about and describing learning design. Three such frameworks are briefly presented here, in order to illustrate the wide range of approaches to conceptualising, describing, undertaking, and sharing learning designs. Interested readers are encouraged to review the literature and websites associated with each of these projects.

The AUTC Learning Design Project

The AUTC Learning Design Project (Harper, Oliver, Hedberg, & Wills, 2003) was commissioned in 2000 by the Australian Universities Teaching Committee (AUTC) to explore the use of Information and Communication Technologies to facilitate flexible learning opportunities for students. The project identified learning designs that had been demonstrated to contribute to high quality learning experiences and determined which learning designs could be redeveloped into more generic forms (Harper, et al., 2003). A key aspect of the project was to develop learning design resources for educators and document learning design exemplars (e.g. simulation, problem-based, project based, role play and collaborative learning designs). These exemplars have proved highly useful to practitioners and readers are encouraged to review these from the project website (see <learningdesigns.uow.edu.au>).

The project described learning designs in terms of the (i) resources, (ii) tasks and (iii) supports that were required to implement them. A 'jigsaw' learning design (whereby teams of students research different topics and then teams share the findings with other groups) is shown in Figure 4 below. The learning designs reported in this project include descriptions of the implementation context (setting, outcomes, assessment and ICT contribution) and designers' reflections (pedagogical notes, history and evaluation).

The Pedagogical Patterns Project

The homepage of the Pedagogical Patterns Project (2006) describes pedagogical patterns as trying to *"capture expert knowledge of the practice of teaching and learning. The intent is to capture the essence of the practice in a compact form that can be easily communicated to those who need the knowledge."* The Pedagogical Patterns Project (2006) and the E-LEN Project (2007) each have an extensive repository of general pedagogical patterns. There have also been pedagogical patterns proposed in the field of computer science (Bergin, 2002) as well as work in the field of e-learning (Retalis, Georgiakakis, & Dimitriadis, 2006).

The way in which pedagogical patterns are described is critically important if practitioners are to effectively find and successfully apply the knowledge that is being passed on (Haberman, 2006). Pedagogical pattern specifications describe the educational context, the forces contributing to the learning need such as the problem at hand, and the solution (Haberman, 2006; Pedagogical Patterns Project, 2006). Proponents emphasise that in order to increase transferability, the consequences of applying the pattern should be explained, the limitations and advantages discussed, and specific examples provided (Derntl & Botturi, 2006; Haberman, 2006, p. 89).

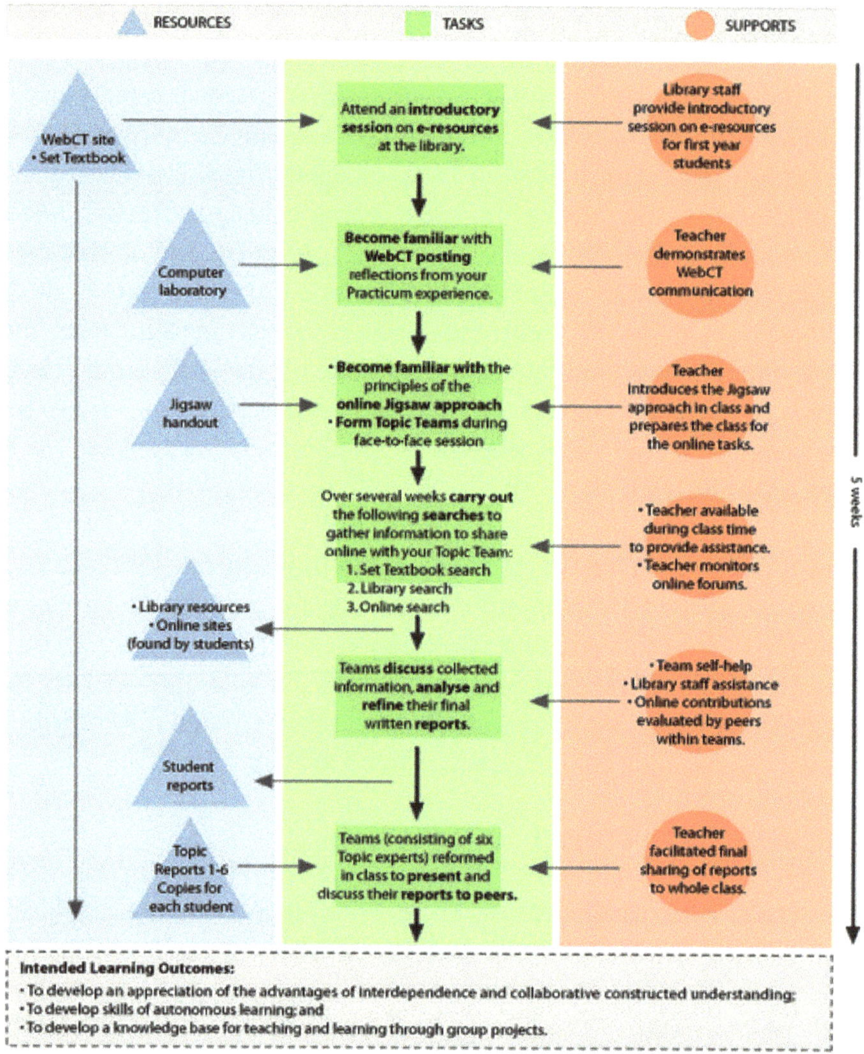

Figure 4: Representation of a 'Jigsaw' learning design using the AUTC Learning Design project representation

The Learning Design Support Environment

The Learning Design Support Environment (Laurillard, Masterman, Magoulas, Boyle, & Manton, 2011) is an interactive tool and set of resources to scaffold teachers' technology enhanced learning design thinking (Laurillard, et al., 2011). Using the main design tool (called the 'Learning Designer') educators can select from a range of teaching and learning activities and schedule them along a timeline. Activities have default levels of cognitive activity (acquisition, inquiry, discussion, practice and production) and social nature (personalised, social, one-size-fits-all), which can be adjusted by the user. The design interface is shown in Figure 5 below.

Once learning modules and sessions have been drafted the Learning Designer can provide an overarching analysis of the learning experience in terms of the different proportions of cognitive activities and the social structure (see Figure 6). The system is also integrated with an intelligent database feature that enables it to offer context sensitive scaffolding for the design process. This demonstrates how learning design descriptive frameworks can interweave with learning design concepts to assist learning design practice.

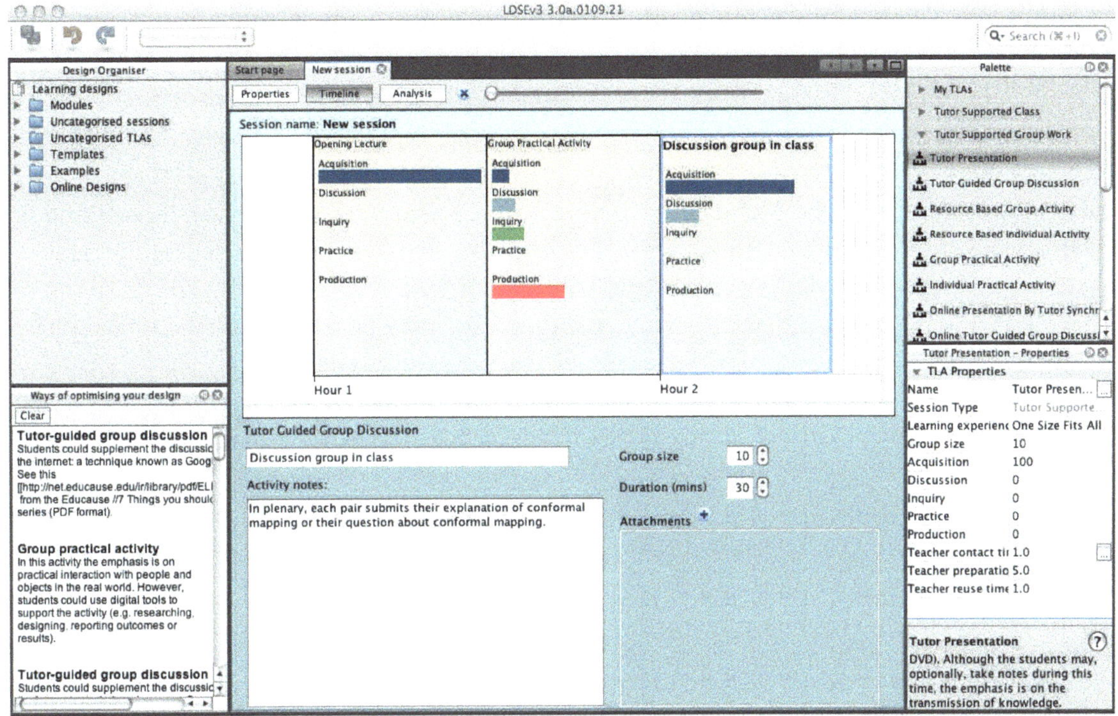

Figure 5: The design view of the Learning Designer (image sourced from <sites.google.com/a/lkl.ac.uk/ldse/downloads>

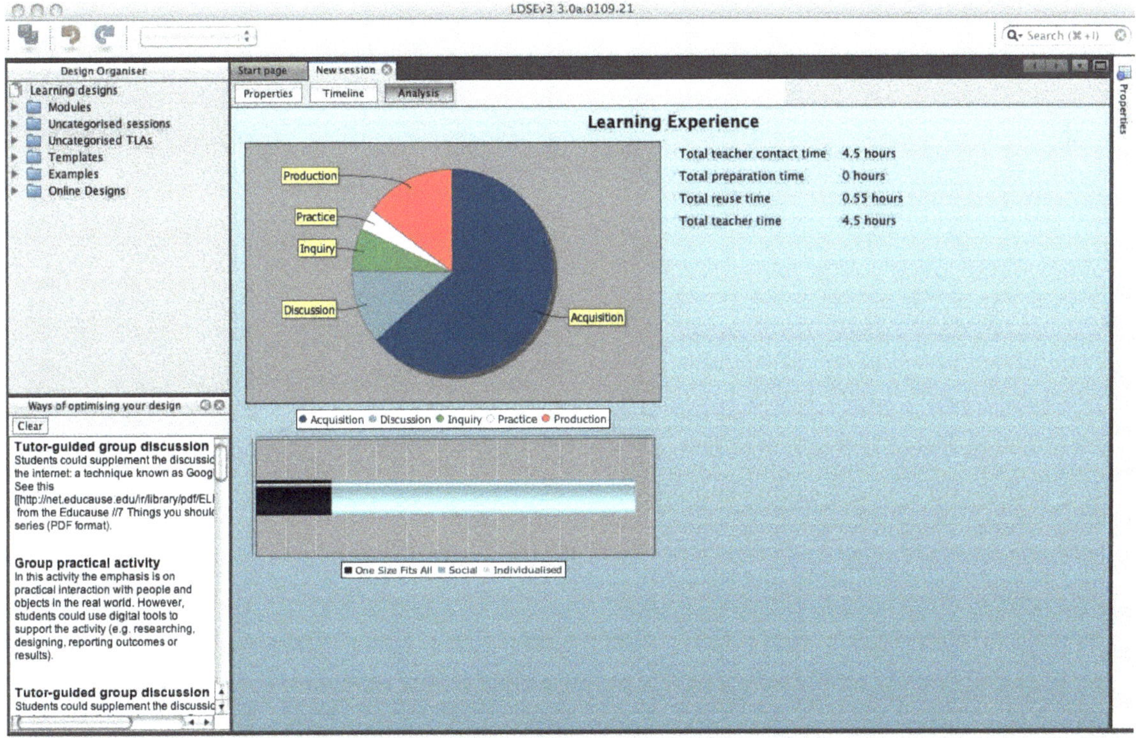

Figure 6: The analysis view of the Learning Designer (image sourced from <sites.google.com/a/lkl.ac.uk/ldse/downloads>)

The AUTC Learning Design Project, the Pedagogical Patterns Project, and the Learning Design Support Environment are but three of many learning design description and support frameworks (for a comprehensive mapping of such projects see Figure 1 of the Larnaca Declaration, Dalziel, et al., 2012). They serve to illustrate the range of approaches and emphases that can be adopted for the purposes of describing learning designs. The current project team drew from each of learning design projects described above as well as other literature, in both creating the Rich-Media Technology Capabilities Framework developed as part of this project and in refining and describing the blended synchronous learning case studies.

Chapter 3: The Blended Synchronous Learning Scoping Study

An initial component of the Blended Synchronous Learning Project was a benchmarking review of how the Australian and New Zealand tertiary sectors had previously and were currently using blended synchronous learning. A questionnaire was developed for this purpose which contained three substantive sections: a section on general demographic and teaching questions, a section about rich-media synchronous tool usage, and a section on whether/how media-rich real-time collaboration tools were being used to synchronously unite face-to-face and remote students (the Blended Synchronous Learning Scoping Study survey instrument is provided in Appendix A). Participants were also asked to provide their perceptions of the best reasons to use video conferencing, web conferencing and virtual worlds. Only a subset of the findings will be reported in this Handbook due to space limitations, but interested readers should consult the project website at <blendsync.org> for a full list of publications which contain further results (for example, Bower, et al., 2012).

The survey was advertised via national and international educational technology mailing lists (e.g. ascilite, HERDSA, ODLAA, DEANZ, ACODE, EDUCAUSE, ITForum) and through personal contact of members of the project team. Of the 1748 survey responses received, 750 were complete responses from employees of Australian and New Zealand Universities and were sufficiently complete to use in the analysis. Slightly more females than males responded (females: 54.2%; males: 45.8%), and the mean age of respondents was approximately 48 years old. Responses were received from 38 of the 39 Australian universities and all 8 of the New Zealand universities.

Figure 7 shows the years in which respondents had used desktop-video conferencing, room-based video conferencing, web conferencing and virtual worlds in their teaching since the year 2000. The graph shown in Figure 7 clearly indicates that the usage of rich-media real-time collaboration tools in the classroom has increased significantly since 2000, but more interesting is the relative use of each type of tool. Room-based video conferencing was the dominant technology for rich-media real-time communication in 2000, and maintained this position at least until 2003. From 2004 to 2008 there was, broadly speaking, comparable use of room-based video conferencing, web conferencing and desktop conferencing. From 2009 to 2010, web conferencing and desktop video conferencing tools were used by more respondents than room-based video conferencing, and the usage of these tools approximately doubled between 2008 and 2010. Moreover, while all four technologies have seen progressive growth in their user base, virtual worlds do not enjoy the penetration of the other three technologies, and even show a slight decrease in usage from 2010 to 2011. This may in part be explained by the existence of a number of barriers to usage and institutional support issues associated with virtual worlds (Dalgarno, et al., 2011b) as compared to web conferencing in particular, which tends to be institutionally supported.

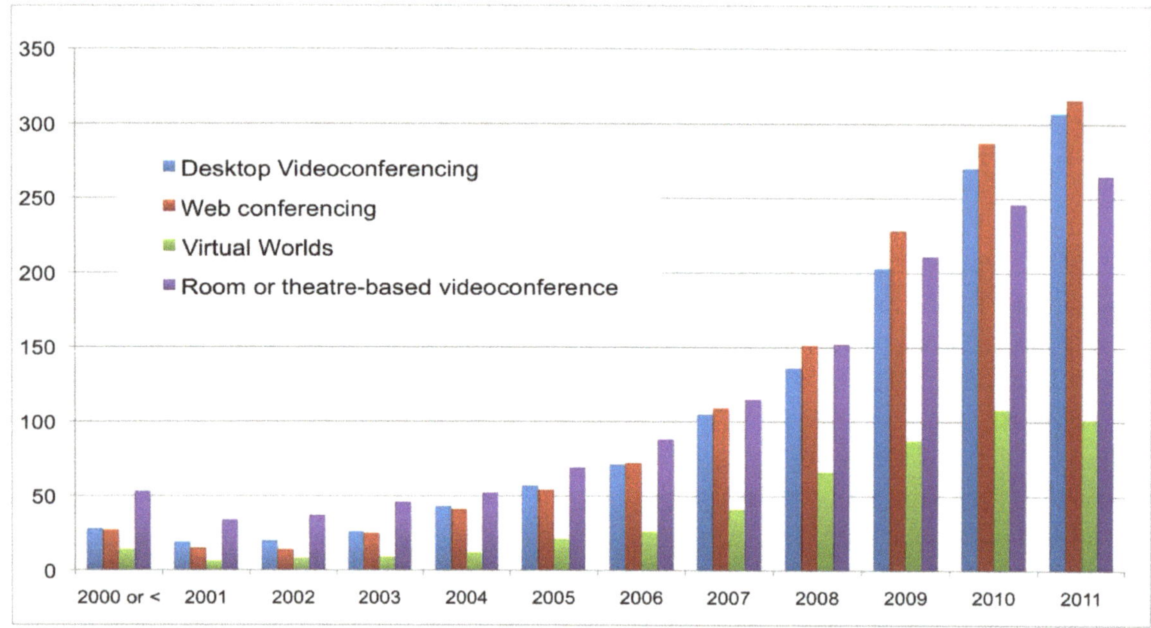

Figure 7: Use of rich-media real-time collaboration tools by year

Figure 8 shows the percentage of respondents in the sample who used specific web conferencing products. It can be seen that four tools in the web conferencing category enjoyed especially healthy patronage: *Elluminate* (30.9%), *Blackboard Collaborate* (30.6%), *Wimba* (20.8%) and *Adobe Connect* (20.5%). It is noteworthy that *Elluminate* was acquired by Blackboard, Inc. in 2010 and was rebadged as *Blackboard Collaborate*. It is therefore likely that some respondents would have used *Elluminate* but not *Blackboard Collaborate*, some would have switched from *Elluminate* to *Blackboard Collaborate*, and others would have adopted *Blackboard Collaborate* without having previously used *Elluminate*. A consequence of this is that collectively, the proportion of people using either *Elluminate* or *Blackboard Collaborate* may well be substantially larger than 30%. Additionally, *Wimba* has been taken over by Blackboard, and although at the time of the survey it continued to be supported as a separate product (Wimba Inc., 2010), its long term future appears uncertain.

Figure 9 displays the percentage of respondents using each of the products in the desktop video conferencing category. Clearly *Skype* is the most popular tool, with 59.1% of respondents indicating they had used this tool in their teaching, which is double the number of users of the most popular web conferencing tool. *Windows Live Messenger* (16.0%), *Google Voice and Video Chat* (12.5%) and *Yahoo! Messenger* (9.8%) enjoyed moderate use. With the recent emergence of the popular *Google Plus* collaborative platform it is likely that these percentages will have changed considerably since the survey was implemented.

The proportion of respondents using different virtual world platforms is depicted in Figure 10. It shows that use of virtual worlds is low compared to the other rich-media real-time collaboration tools. *Second Life* is the only tool with a significant user base, and even then it represents only 14.9% of the sample. Interest in *OpenSim* has grown in recent years, and a number of third-party grid providers have emerged (Dalgarno, Lee, Carlson, Gregory, & Tynan, 2011a). Commentary from the Australian Virtual Worlds Working Group supports this claim, and it may be anticipated that people will increasingly choose these alternate platforms to *Second Life* in the coming years.

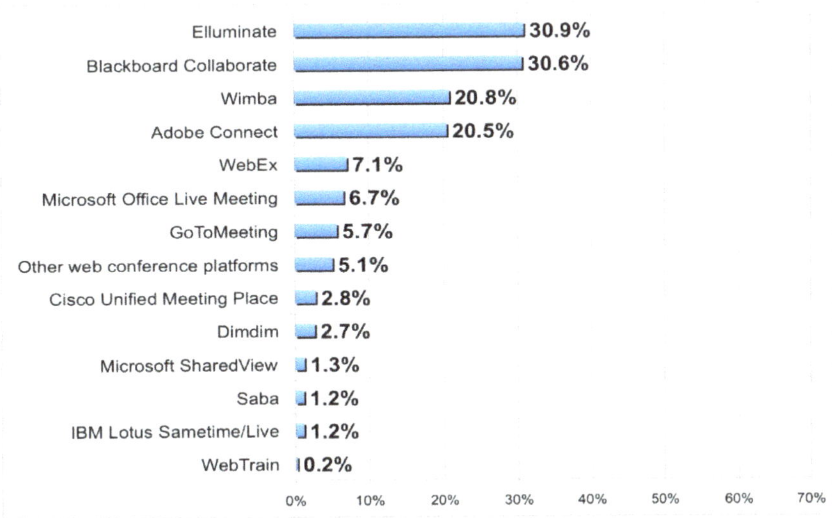

Figure 8: Percentage of respondents using a range of web conferencing tools

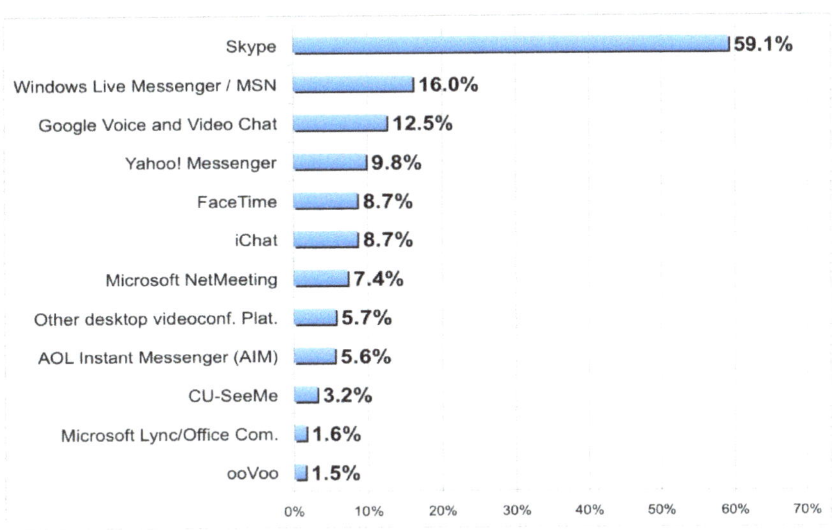

Figure 9: Percentage of respondents using a range of desktop video conferencing tools

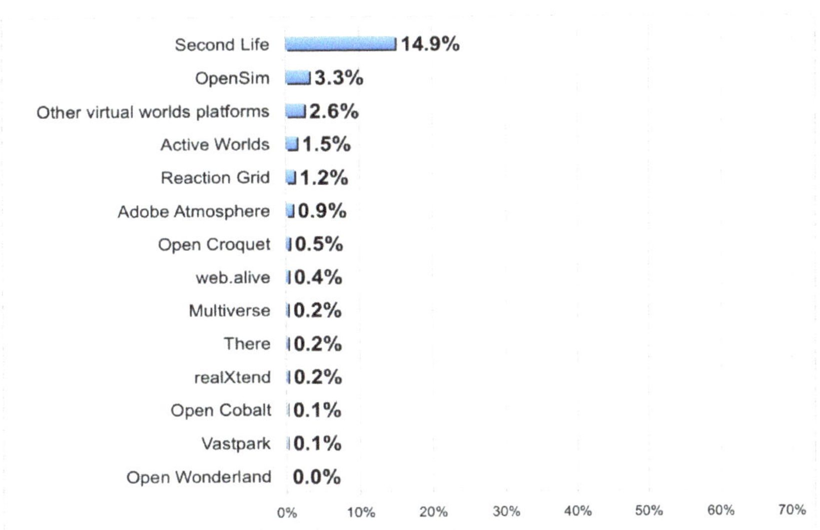

Figure 10: Percentage of respondents using a range of virtual world platform

The reflections of respondents with a broad range of experience teaching with rich-media real-time collaboration tools were analysed to examine the perceived best uses of video conferencing, web conferencing and virtual worlds. Responses indicated that desktop video conferencing is generally most suitable for small-group and often informal sessions where audio and video are the modes of communication required. According to respondents, web conferencing has the potential to cater to a larger audience and enables more advanced modes of sharing (presentation slides, voting, drawing on a shared whiteboard, and use of breakout rooms for small-group discussion), but needs greater levels of facilitator skill and preparation. Virtual worlds were essentially seen by respondents as useful simulation environments, which are able to overcome real-world logistics and to facilitate a more situated or contextualised and immersive learning experience. Desktop video conferencing was seen as easier to use than web conferencing, which in turn was seen as having a lower technical overhead than virtual worlds.

Finally, it is interesting to note that of the 750 respondents to the survey, 294 (39.2%) indicated that they had used rich-media real-time collaboration tools to simultaneously involve face-to-face and remotely located students in learning and teaching activities. While it is possible that some of these respondents had misinterpreted the question as relating to purely online synchronous learning and teaching, the result appears to indicate that blended synchronous learning is a prevalent phenomenon in the contemporary tertiary education context.

Chapter 4: Rich-Media Synchronous Learning Technology Capabilities Framework

This chapter presents a Rich-Media Synchronous Learning Technology Capabilities Framework to support learning design in rich-media synchronous learning environments. A proposed outcome of the Blended Synchronous Learning Project was to develop a technology capabilities framework that provided:

- *a map of how the three general technologies being considered – video conferencing, web conferencing, 3D virtual worlds – can be used with particular types of collaborative learning tasks and activities; and*
- *a matrix of the capabilities and limitations of specific collaborative technologies (e.g. Wimba Classroom, Adobe Connect, Skype) on particular dimensions (e.g. types of communication channels, kinds of interactions supported, degree of synchronicity, visibility of participants).*

We have integrated these two deliverables in the Rich-Media Synchronous Learning Technology Capabilities Framework. The Framework is intended to help teachers or practitioners think through how they negotiate the relationship between designing learning tasks for students and the appropriate selection of rich-media tools to support these designs. The broad framework outlined in Figure 11 shows how the Rich-Media Synchronous Learning Technology Capabilities Framework can support learning design processes by helping educators decide how their learning and teaching activities can be instantiated using specific technologies. Note that in order to cater to a broad readership, this Handbook refers to the design of learning activities, though it is noted that some academics distinguish between learning tasks which can be designed and learning activities as the enactments of those designs (for instance, see Goodyear & Retalis, 2010).

The top half of Figure 11 shows how teachers move from articulating students' envisaged learning outcomes, to the designing of learning activities that underpin these outcomes manifested as technology-based activities. The bottom half of Figure 11 shows how different types of rich-media synchronous tools have various capabilities that can differentially support these learning activities, and how this is realised by specific rich-media products (i.e. *Skype*, etc). The Framework is based on the idea that once a pedagogical design is established, the choice of technology should be based on how the different affordances of the available technologies can best support this pedagogical design. For the purposes of this document, we use the term 'affordances' to simply describe the properties or features of a technology that determines how it can be used.

It is important to note at the outset that the framework proposed is intended neither as a prescription nor an algorithm. Rather, it is intended as a reference for teachers and practitioners to support their decision-making processes associated with aligning the tasks they design for students with the range of rich-media tools available to them so as to more effectively support students to achieve the desired learning outcomes.

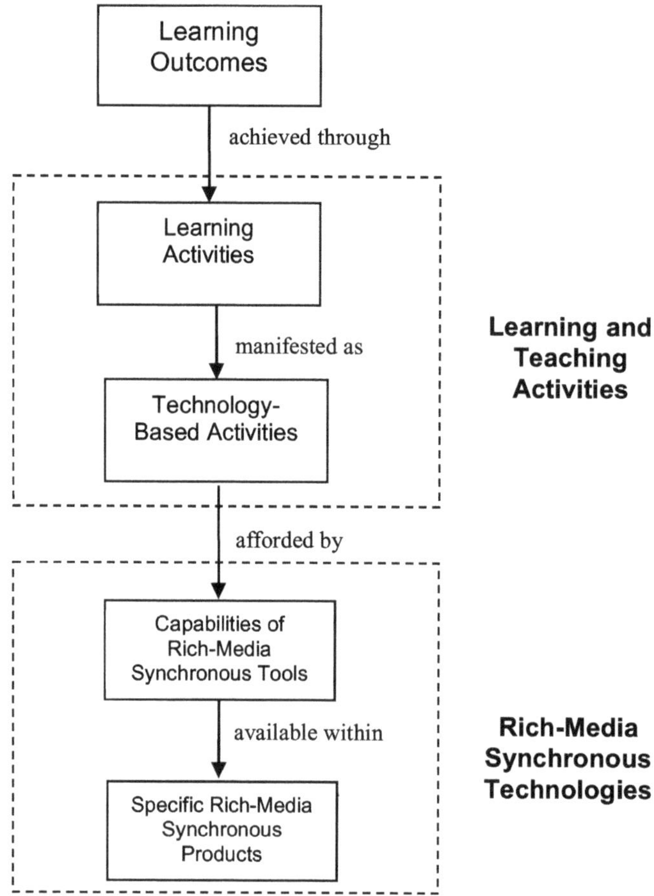

Figure 11: Overview of the Rich-Media Synchronous Learning Technology Capabilities Framework

The next sections explain the different components of the Framework.

Learning Outcomes and Learning Activities

Taking a set of desired learning outcomes and deciding upon the optimal range of learning activities that will support the achievement of these outcomes is fundamental to the art of teaching and is broadly captured by the idea of teachers designing for learning, or learning designs. Discipline knowledge and teaching experience make a vital contribution to designing learning activities, and many of the broad aspects associated with learning design have been covered in Chapter 2. Given that the intended learning outcomes will very much depend on the concepts, skills and abilities that educators intend students to develop, and because a range of alternative learning activities can lead to the accomplishment of a single learning outcome, it is not possible to provide specific guidelines about their relationship here. Excellent sources of advice and support in this area include Biggs and Tang's (2011) "Teaching for Quality Learning at University", and general texts on learning design such as Laurillard's (2012) "Teaching as a Design Science" and Conole's (2012) "Designing for Learning in an Open World".

Learning Activities and Technology-based Activities

There are a number of ways in which learning activities may be specified. A teacher might express their learning activities in terms of the general way in which an individual lesson or teaching event is organised. For example, a lecture might be followed by a whole-of-class discussion or within a tutorial a student paper might be followed by a guided group discussion. Educators also express their learning activities as more formalised pedagogical patterns. For example, a teacher might implement a simulation-based activity to their class based on the rubric of 'predict, observe, explain', they might introduce a student role play, or a debate, or they might structure a discussion activity using the idea of 'think-pair-share'. Ways of expressing these have been covered in Chapter 2.

In learning environments that are both distributed and based on collaborative learning designs and activities – the primary focus of this project – it is critical to consider how these activities can be supported by different technologies. In making judgments in this area it is often useful to think through how the types of teaching and learning activities specified above – lectures, tutorials, discussions, student presentations, paired and group activities, debates, peer based document sharing – can be *supported by* technology or can *manifest themselves in* a technology mediated context. That is, whether the learning occurs in face-to-face or online settings, different teaching and learning activities can be stimulated by, predicated on or conducted through different communication modalities: text, audio, video, 2D and 3D animation, images and diagrams. In some cases the intention is for the technology to provide a means of representing discipline specific knowledge, for instance through visualisation. In other cases the technology is intended to provide a platform for sharing between participants through discursive or collaborative interactions. In other cases the technology is intended to foster community by promoting a sense of co-presence between participants. In some cases the intention of the technology may be to accomplish all three of these elements at once. Thus a fundamental decision that educators need to make is the appropriate type of technologies that can be used to support knowledge representation, sharing and co-presence for the intended teaching and learning activities.

Table 1 provides an overview of different learning and teaching activities and matches them with potential affordances of three different classes of rich-media synchronous technologies (desktop video conferencing, web conferencing and virtual worlds). It important to note that there are often many possible ways in which a given task can be supported and represented using technology, and there is no rule for deciding which technology is best for a particular task. While experienced educational designers and educators may have some rules of thumb that they use, the ideal mode of representation – visual, text, audio – will typically depend on a complex relationship between the intended learning outcomes, the learning activities and the content involved. It is often the case that the desired mode of representation needs to be considered as part of a broader consideration of the tool requirements for the learning activities.

The first column in Table 1 indicates the mode of representation (visual, text, audio) for those teaching and learning activities which are mode dependent. For other activities the first column shows a descriptor of the key characteristics of the student learning experience for learning and teaching activities in this category.

Table 1: Modes of communication and learning & teaching activities afforded by different types of rich-media synchronous technologies (✓=yes, ×=no, ~=conditionally)

Mode of Communication	Desired Learning & Teaching Activity	Features of rich-media tools affording the specified learning activities		
		Desktop Video Conferencing	**Web conferencing**	**Virtual Worlds**
Visual	***Present slides***	~ (possible in some systems by screen broadcasting)	✓ Slide presentation tool	~ (possible in some systems but may require converting slides to images)
Visual	***Co-create slides***	× (work-around in some systems using screen broadcast & audio)	✓ Screen sharing	× (work-around in some systems using screen broadcast & audio)
Visual	***Present image / diagram / handwriting***	~ (possible in some systems using whiteboard plug-in, or file share or screen broadcast)	✓ Whiteboard	~ (possible in some systems by feeding in a whiteboard plug-in, or by file share or screen broadcast)
Visual	***Co-create image / diagram / handwriting***	~ (some systems enable the use of a whiteboard plug-in)	✓ Whiteboard	× (work-around in some systems by feeding in whiteboard plug-in but requires external system)
Visual	***Present computing process***	~ (possible in some systems using screen broadcast)	✓ Screen broadcast	~ (possible in some systems using screen broadcast)
Visual	***Co-perform computing process***	× (work-around in some systems by one person screen broadcasting and others using text/audio)	✓ Screen sharing	× (work-around in some systems by one person screen broadcasting and others using text/audio)
Visual	***Present live process (e.g. sign***	✓ Webcam	✓ Webcam	~ (possible in some systems)
Text	***Deliver text monologue***	✓ Text chat	✓ Text chat	✓ Text chat
Text	***Hold text conversation***	✓ Text chat (all participants)	✓ Text chat (all participants)	✓ Text chat (all participants)
Text	***Create typed text (including live edit)***	× (work-around in some systems by one person screen broadcasting document if facility available)	✓ Notes tool (most systems, or work-around by one person screen broadcasting document if facility available)	~ (possible in some systems, or work-around by screen broadcasting or feeding in an notepad plug-in)
Text	***Co-create typed text***	× (work-around in some systems by one person screen broadcasting document and others using text/audio)	✓ Notes tool (most systems) or potentially whiteboard	~ (possible in some systems, or work-around by screen broadcast or feeding in an notepad plug-in with others using text/audio)
Audio	***Deliver an audio presentation (broadcast)***	✓ Microphone	✓ Microphone	✓ Microphone (most systems)

Mode of Communication	Desired Learning & Teaching Activity	Features of rich-media tools affording the specified learning activities		
		Desktop Video Conferencing	**Web conferencing**	**Virtual Worlds**
	Audio discussion	✓ Microphone (all participants)	✓ Microphone (all participants)	✓ Microphone (all participants, most systems)
File share	***Disseminate file***	✓ File share	✓ File share	~ (some systems)
File share	***Many-to-many file sharing***	✓ File share (all participants)	✓ File share (all participants)	✓ File share (all participants)
Spatial	***Present a 3D virtual space***	✗ (work-around in some systems by screen broadcast of 3D environment)	✗ (work-around in some systems by screen broadcast of 3D environment)	✓ Native in 3D environment
Spatial	***Move around a 3D space***	✗ (work-around in some systems by screen broadcast of 3D environment)	✗ (work-around in some systems by screen broadcast of 3D environment)	✓ Native in 3D environment
Spatial	***Collaborate in a 3D space***	✗ (work-around in some systems by screen broadcast of 3D environment)	✗ (work-around in some systems by screen broadcast of 3D environment)	✓ Native in 3D environment
Spatial	***Create a 3D space***	✗ (work-around in some systems by screen broadcast of 3D environment)	✗ (work-around in some systems by screen broadcast of 3D environment)	✓ Native in 3D environment
Presence	***Represent Identity***	✓ Name / photo / webcam	✓ Name / photo / webcam	✓ Avatar
Presence	***Display Status***	~ (not native but can indicate by text or video gesture)	✓ Status tool	~ (not native but can indicate by text or avatar gesture)
Presence	***Indicate preference***	✓ Not native tool but can use text, audio or webcam	✓ Voting tool, or can use text, audio or webcam	✓ Not native tool but use text, audio or avatar movements
Group-work	***Group work***	✗ (not native but can organise people into separate group meetings)	✓ Breakout rooms	✓ Participants move into separate locations

It is important to note the descriptions of specific tool features in Table 1 are necessarily generic, as specific products within each type of rich-media synchronous technology may have slightly different feature sets. Moreover, recording functionality has not been included as an item in the table because it does not relate to the types of learning activities that are possible. Many products have native recording functionality, though desktop recording software can be used to record sessions in cases where a tool does not enable recording.

Types of Tools to Specific Products

A teacher or educational designer may have made a decision to use a particular type of rich-media synchronous technology (e.g. desktop video conferencing, web conferencing or virtual worlds), but she or he may then need to select a specific technology product, as different products can show variations in their functionality and features. There is generally a range of choices in each rich-media technology type, and the results of the Blended Synchronous Learning Scoping Study (Bower, et al., 2012) provide an indication of the relative popularity of each. While in practical terms, product selection will often depend on tool availability, face-to-face support, familiarity, and ease of use, Table 2 summarises the features of some popular rich-media synchronous technologies, which may be useful for practitioners who are interested in selecting specific products. It is worth noting that the features and functionality of learning technology products are frequently updated and as a result, summary tables such as these often quickly become outdated.

Closing Remarks

Providing advice and support for learning design processes without being prescriptive or formulaic is a challenging process. The Rich-Media Synchronous Learning Technology Capabilities Framework presented above aims to assist with decision making during the learning design process by outlining how the learning design and requirements of tasks created by teachers can be supported by the affordances of rich-media synchronous technologies. The Framework may be used to scaffold the entire learning design process, or a particular component of the Framework may be selected to support one aspect of decision-making. The Framework can be used for general online learning and teaching where all participants are in different locations (i.e. not blended synchronous learning where some participants are co-located with the teacher).

Attempting to create blended synchronous learning designs using rich-media synchronous technologies involves an extra layer of complication. The designer not only needs to think about how the technology should be used to facilitate the learning process for remote participants, but also how face-to-face students will perceive the experience *and* how to organise and support interaction between remote and face-to-face participants.

The fundamental principles embedded in the Rich-Media Synchronous Learning Technology Capabilities Framework also inform the blended synchronous learning design process. As remote students are by definition involved in blended synchronous learning, educators need to devise learning tasks that support learning outcomes, decide how technology can be used to implement those tasks and also select specific tools which can be used to accommodate learning activities and interactions of face-to-face and remote participants. Thus, a fundamental challenge when designing blended synchronous learning tasks is to create lessons that simultaneously cater for face-to-face participants (either through the technology or without having the technology obstruct their experience) and how the technology can effectively enable interaction between and among remote and face-to-face students.

There is only an emerging literature base examining the challenge of using technology to unite remote and face-to-face students in the same, synchronous learning experiences. The case studies presented in the chapters that follow provide significant insight into how this challenge was broached in seven classes across Australia.

Table 2: Modes of communication and learning activities afforded by specific rich-media synchronous products (✓=yes, ×=no, ~=conditionally)

	Activity	Specific Tool Affordances					
		Desktop Video Conferencing		Web conferencing		Virtual Worlds	
		Skype	Google Plus	Adobe Connect	Blackboard Collaborate	Second Life	Open Sim
Visual	*Present slides*	~ (possible using screen broadcast, to more than one person is premium feature)	~ (possible using screen broadcast, up to nine people in a Hangout)	✓ Slide presentation tool	✓ Slide presentation tool	✓ (requires some work to convert slides to images prior to display)	× (not native feature)
	Co-create slides	× (work-around using screen broadcast and audio/text)	× (work-around using screen broadcast and audio/text)	✓ Screen sharing	✓ Screen sharing	× (work-around by feeding in screen broadcast and using audio or text, but often time lag)	× (work-around by feeding in screen broadcast and using text, but often time lag)
	Present image / diagram / handwriting	~ (possible using screen broadcast, file share, or third party whiteboard plug-in)	✓ Whiteboard	✓ Whiteboard	✓ Whiteboard	~ (possible using file-share or by feeding in whiteboard from external system)	× (can be made possible but requires scripting and an external system)
	Co-create image / diagram / handwriting	× (work-around using screen broadcast and audio/text, or third party plug-in)	✓ Whiteboard	✓ Whiteboard	✓ Whiteboard	× (work-around by feeding a whiteboard from external system)	× (can be made possible but requires scripting and an external system)
	Present computing process	✓ Screen broadcast	✓ Screen broadcast	✓ Screen broadcast	✓ Screen broadcast	× (work-around by feeding in screen stream)	× (not available)
	Co-perform computing process	× (work-around by one person broadcasting screen and others providing text/audio instructions)	× (work-around by one person broadcasting screen and others providing text/audio instructions)	✓ Screen sharing	✓ Screen sharing	× (work-around by feeding in screen stream and others providing text/audio instructions)	× (not available)
	Present live process (e.g. sign language)	✓ Webcam	✓ Webcam	✓ Webcam	✓ Webcam	× (work-around by feeding in video stream or by avatar simulating)	× (work-around by avatar simulating)

	Activity	Specific Tool Affordances					
		Desktop Video Conferencing		Web conferencing		Virtual Worlds	
		Skype	**Google Plus**	**Adobe Connect**	**Blackboard Collaborate**	**Second Life**	**Open Sim**
Text	***Deliver text monologue***	✓ Text chat	✓ Text chat	✓ Text chat	✓ Text chat	✓ Text chat	✓ Text chat
	Hold text conversation	✓ Text chat (all)	✓ Text chat (all)	✓ Text chat (all)	✓ Text chat (all)	✓ Text chat (all)	✓ Text chat (all)
	Create a typed text (including live edit)	✗ (work-around by one person screen broadcasting a document)	✗ (work-around by one person screen broadcasting a document)	✓ Notes tool	✗ (work-around by one person screen broadcasting a document)	✗ (work-around by feeding a notepad from external system)	✗ (can be made possible but requires scripting and an external system)
	Co-create a typed text	✗ (work-around by one person screen broadcasting a document and others using text/audio)	✗ (work-around by one person screen broadcasting a document and others using text/audio)	✓ Notes tool	✗ (work-around by one person screen broadcasting a document and others using text/audio)	✗ (work-around by feeding a notepad from external system)	✗ (can be made possible but requires scripting and an external system)
Audio	***Deliver an audio presentation (broadcast)***	✓ Microphone	✓ Microphone	✓ Microphone	✓ Microphone	✓ Microphone	✗ (not native)
	Audio discussion	✓ Microphone (all)	✓ Microphone (all)	✓ Microphone (all)	✓ Microphone (all)	✓ Microphone (all)	✗ (not native)
Fileshare	***Disseminate file***	✓ File share	✓ File share	✓ File share	✓ File share	✓ File share	✗ (not native)
	Many-to-many file sharing	✓ File share (all)	✓ File share (all)	✓ File share (all)	✓ File share (all)	✓ File share (all)	✗ (not native)
Spatial	***Present a 3D virtual space***	✗ (work-around using screen broadcast of virtual world)	✗ (work-around using screen broadcast of virtual world)	✗ (work-around using screen broadcast of virtual world)	✗ (work-around using screen broadcast of virtual world)	✓ Native 3D	✓ Native 3D
	Move around a 3D space	✗ (work-around using screen broadcast of virtual world)	✗ (work-around using screen broadcast of virtual world)	✗ (work-around using screen broadcast of virtual world)	✗ (work-around using screen broadcast of virtual world)	✓ Native 3D	✓ Native 3D
	Collaborate in a 3D space	✗ (work-around using screen broadcast of virtual world)	✗ (work-around using screen broadcast of virtual world)	✗ (work-around using screen broadcast of virtual world)	✗ (work-around using screen broadcast of virtual world)	✓ Native 3D	✓ Native 3D
	Create a 3D space	✗ (work-around using screen broadcast of virtual world)	✗ (work-around using screen broadcast of virtual world)	✗ (work-around using screen broadcast of virtual world)	✗ (work-around using screen broadcast of virtual world)	✓ Native 3D	✓ Native 3D
Presenc	***Represent Identity***	✓ Name / photo / webcam	✓ Name / photo / webcam	✓ Name / photo / webcam	✓ Name / photo / webcam	✓ Avatar	✓ Avatar

	Activity	Specific Tool Affordances					
		Desktop Video Conferencing		**Web conferencing**		**Virtual Worlds**	
		Skype	**Google Plus**	**Adobe Connect**	**Blackboard Collaborate**	**Second Life**	**Open Sim**
	Display Status	~ (not native but can indicate through text or video gesture)	~ (not native but can indicate through text or video gesture)	✓ Status tool	✓ Status tool	~ (not native but can indicate through text or video gesture)	~ (not native but can indicate through text or video gesture)
	Indicate preference	✓ Not native tool but can be done by text, audio or webcam	✓ Not native tool but can be done by text, audio or webcam	✓ Voting tool, or can be done by text, audio or webcam	✓ Voting tool, or can be done by text, audio or webcam	✓ Not native tool but can be done by text, audio or avatar movements	✓ Not native tool but can be done by text or avatar movements
Group work	***Group work***	✗ (not native but can organise separate meetings)	✗ (not native but can organise separate meetings)	✓ Breakout rooms	✓ Breakout rooms	✓ Participants move into separate locations	✓ Participants move into separate locations

Chapter 5: Overview of Case Study Reports

Organisation of the Case Study Chapters

The following chapters provide detailed description and analysis of the seven cases of blended synchronous learning that were implemented as part of this project. In order to assist with the description of and comparison across the cases, a common format has been established for the reporting of cases. The first part of each case study report describes the blended synchronous learning design that was adopted in the case. The elements of the learning design descriptions along with the rationale for including each element are outlined in Table 3.

Table 3: Elements of the Blended Synchronous Learning Design descriptions

Learning Design Descriptive Element	**Rationale for inclusion**
Brief overview	Provide an overall picture of the case to anchor more detailed reasoning
Institutional context (institution, teachers, project team members involved, discipline, subject, level of study)	Provides specific information about the case that foreground observations and may influence results
Intended learning outcome(s)	Establishes the learning outcomes that were intended to be supported by the learning design
Description of the learning activity/tasks (learning design as intended)	Explains the tasks that were designed to achieve the learning outcomes
Technology and environment setup/configuration	Explains how the technology was designed to facilitate blended synchronous learning
Resources	Explains the resources that were used to assist learning and teaching processes
Support for staff	Details ways in which staff were supported in order to manage the blended synchronous learning design and implementation processes
Support for students	Explains how students were supported before, during and after the lessons
Assessment	Establishes how the learning design may have been related to student assessment tasks
Project team's input into the learning design	Explains the extent to which the project team worked with teachers to refine the design prior to lesson observation.

There are clear commonalities between the Learning Design Frameworks presented in Chapter 2 and the descriptive approach presented in Table 3. While including critical pedagogical dimensions, the descriptive method presented in Table 3 also places particular emphasis on the technology and environment setup and configuration, as these tended to be quite complex for blended synchronous learning environments. The blended synchronous learning design descriptions also emphasise the influence of context on the design and implementation process, not only by including an 'Institutional Context' section, but also through descriptions of the support required for staff and students, and the input of the project team. The technology and environment setup/configuration, resources, support for staff and students, assessment and project team's input into the learning design have all been included in a 'Presage Factors' section as elements that contributed to implementation of the lesson before the event.

The second part of each case study chapter focuses on the lesson as enacted; describing the lesson as it actually transpired. In essence this relates to the 'process' of implementing the learning design and it is from this section that many of the process factors for Blended Synchronous Learning Designs have been derived.

The third part of each chapter reports on perceptions, analysis and interpretation of the lesson, including student perceptions, teacher perceptions, and a discussion section that incorporates project team observations. A summary of findings is provided at the end of each chapter to distil the key points of learning from each case study.

Case Study Methodology

Case study partners were selected from 1,748 responses to the questionnaire that was used in the Blended Sync Scoping Study (see Chapter 2; Bower et al., 2012). Criteria for selection of case study partners included:

- whether they were synchronously uniting face-to-face and remote students using rich-media technologies;
- the extent to which the case involved high-quality pedagogical practices; and
- the maturity of the design in terms of number of implementations.

Cases were also selected so as to represent a range of technologies and discipline areas. Discussions were held with potential case study partners to determine appropriateness for inclusion in the project and willingness to participate. This resulted in the selection of seven case study partners. Prior to case study observations, the project team worked with case study partners to reflect upon and in some cases refine the pedagogical and technological aspects of the blended synchronous learning designs. However, it is important to note that the extent to which designs were adjusted was always at the discretion of the case study partners.

This project adopted a collective case study methodology, using standard case study data collection and analysis approaches as outlined by Yin (2009). Several sources of data were relied upon for each case study, including:

- a pre-observation teacher-documented overview of the case, as it had been implemented in the past;
- pre-observation teacher interviews in order to determine the rationale for the learning design of the case, as well as teachers' insights into the blended synchronous learning approach;
- video and screen recordings of the blended synchronous learning lessons;
- researcher observations of the lessons (both in class and in the online environment);
- post-observation student survey responses;
- post-observation student focus group interviews; and
- post-observation teacher interviews.

The summary of each of the designs was primarily derived from the pre-observation teacher-documented overviews, but also the researcher observations of the lessons as well as the video and screen recordings of the blended synchronous learning lessons. Similarly, the lesson as enacted was based upon researcher observations and video and screen recordings. Student perceptions were determined by synthesising the student questionnaire and focus group interview responses. The student questionnaire was answered anonymously and included 30 items relating to students ability to interact and share resources, as well as their general perceptions of the lesson and their sense of co-presence (the post-lesson student survey instrument is provided in Appendix B). The semi-structured focus groups provided students with the opportunity to discuss general strategies used in the lesson and to elaborate on their questionnaire responses. Teacher perceptions were distilled from the pre- and post-observation teacher interviews.

Multiple sources of data were analysed and cross-checked by the team in order to establish that appropriate data were being collected within the study. For example, the student questionnaire, student focus group transcripts, and teacher interviews were all compared to confirm there was consistency between the concepts of interest and the constructs being addressed in responses by participants. Multiple sources of data were used to triangulate results within cases, and repeated observation of primary outcomes noted across the multiple cases. This triangulation also involved having multiple project team members reviewing and interpreting data, which in turn contributed to the validity and reliability of findings. The project team established a well-structured project database containing multiple sources of data (all case study interview transcripts, transcripts of the lessons, video footage of lessons and all student survey data), which was used to establish a 'chain of evidence' from the claims made in the investigation back to their evidential sources. The reporting of findings relies heavily on primary data (for instance, student and teacher quotes, survey responses from all students, photos and video footage from lessons). These rich, thick descriptions have been used in part to avoid researcher bias from influencing reporting and also to allow readers to assess the extent to which results may be transferable to their own institutions and educational contexts.

Chapter 6: Case Study 1 – Web Conferencing to Develop Investment Understanding

Brief Overview

In this case a small team of academics from the Department of Applied Finance and Actuarial Studies at Macquarie University attempted a collaborative evaluation activity using the Adobe Connect web conferencing system. After the teacher briefly introduced the task, remote and face-to-face students were randomly grouped into two breakout rooms where they had to evaluate the written responses of two past students to an examination question. The students negotiated marks using text chat, and summarised findings about examination technique in a notes pod. Remote and face-to face students were randomly grouped together, which meant that people in the face-to-face classroom did not necessarily have the opportunity to talk with one another. However, using the web conferencing system in this way levelled the playing field for remote and face-to-face participants. A lack of student understanding of how to operate the technology temporarily interfered with their ability to undertake the exercise. A teaching aid provided substantial operational assistance to ensure that remote students were receiving all teacher communications and able to contribute to discussions. The teacher (with the assistance of the teaching aid) was then able to share groups' findings and discuss them with the class. The blended synchronous learning design did enable remote and face-to-face students to successfully complete the collaborative evaluation activity together.

Institutional Context

Institution: Macquarie University

Teaching team: James McCulloch (Lecturer), Tim Kyng (Subject coordinator), David Pitt (Subject examiner), Hong Xie (Teaching assistant)

Project team members involved: Matt Bower, Jacqueline Kenney

Discipline: Actuarial Studies, Department of Applied Finance and Actuarial Studies

Subject/unit: Institute of Actuaries of Australia Course 5A: Investment Management and Finance

Level of study: Postgraduate Professional Part III Institute of Actuaries of Australia subject

Intended learning outcome(s):

- The student can critically evaluate key elements of examination technique as they relate to investment management and finance.

Description of the Learning Activity/Tasks (Learning Design as Intended)

1. The first phase of this lesson involves the teacher delivering a brief (5-10 minute) introduction to the activity on examination technique. This includes the teacher explaining the reason for the importance of the activity, the resources to be used (two student solutions to a past examination question), and instructions regarding how to collaboratively write evaluations in breakout rooms.
2. Students in two breakout rooms then use the text chat to negotiate appropriate marks for each of the seven examination question parts, for each of the two students. They document their agreed marks in separate notes areas allocated to each of the two past students, and also summarise the key points of examination technique garnered from the activity in a third text area. Approximately 30 minutes are allocated to this phase of the lesson.
3. The third phase involves the teacher reviewing the responses from the two groups, inviting questions and facilitating an open discussion (approximately 15 minutes).

Presage Factors

Technology and environment setup/configuration

The tutorial room utilised a typical computer laboratory layout with a screen at the front of the room, a lectern in the front corner opposing the entrance, and three rows of desks perpendicular to the front wall of the room (see Figure 12). The teacher presented from the lectern computer at the front of the room. An external microphone was attached to the lectern computer to capture all teacher audio (and some student audio).

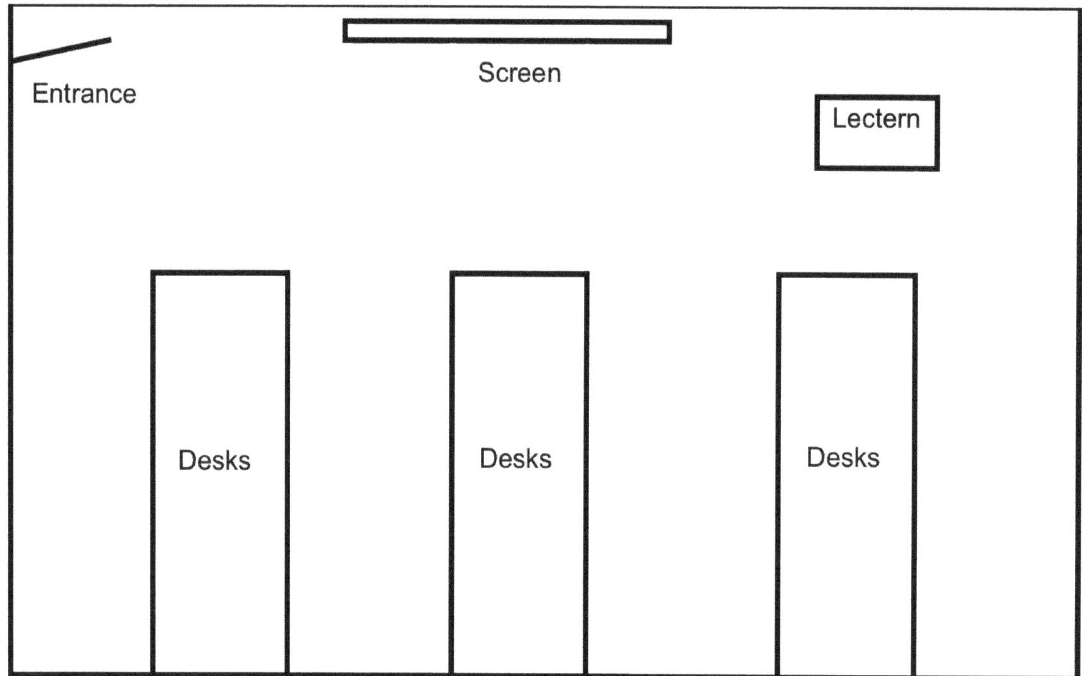

Figure 12: Case Study 1 room layout

Students in the face-to-face room could participate in the activity via desktop machines available in the computer lab (see Figure 13). Remote students participated from their own computers.

Figure 13: Case Study 1 face-to-face room layout

A data projector in the face-to-face classroom displayed the web conferencing interface onto a screen at the front of the room. The Adobe Connect web conferencing system was used to facilitate all interactions between remote and face-to-face participants. The web conferencing interface was designed so as to show all of the information channels that students required for the task (see Figure 14).

The web conferencing interface included:

- the document containing the student exam papers in the main sharing area of the window;
- an attendee list in the top-left corner;
- a text chat area on the left-hand side below the attendee list;
- a file share pod placed in the bottom right corner below the main sharing area so that students could download the student solutions document to their computer if they wanted; and
- three small collaborative note-taking areas provided below the main sharing area (between the text chat and the file sharing pods). The first two notes areas were for student groups to record the marks that they negotiated for each student (skeleton text outlining the different numbered parts to the question was placed in each note taking area so that students did not have to type this). The third note-taking area was for students to record their reflections about what they learnt about examination technique.

Once the teacher had introduced the activity, the students were randomly divided into two breakout rooms using the random grouping function of the web conferencing system. The interface layout of the breakout rooms was identical to the main web conferencing room.

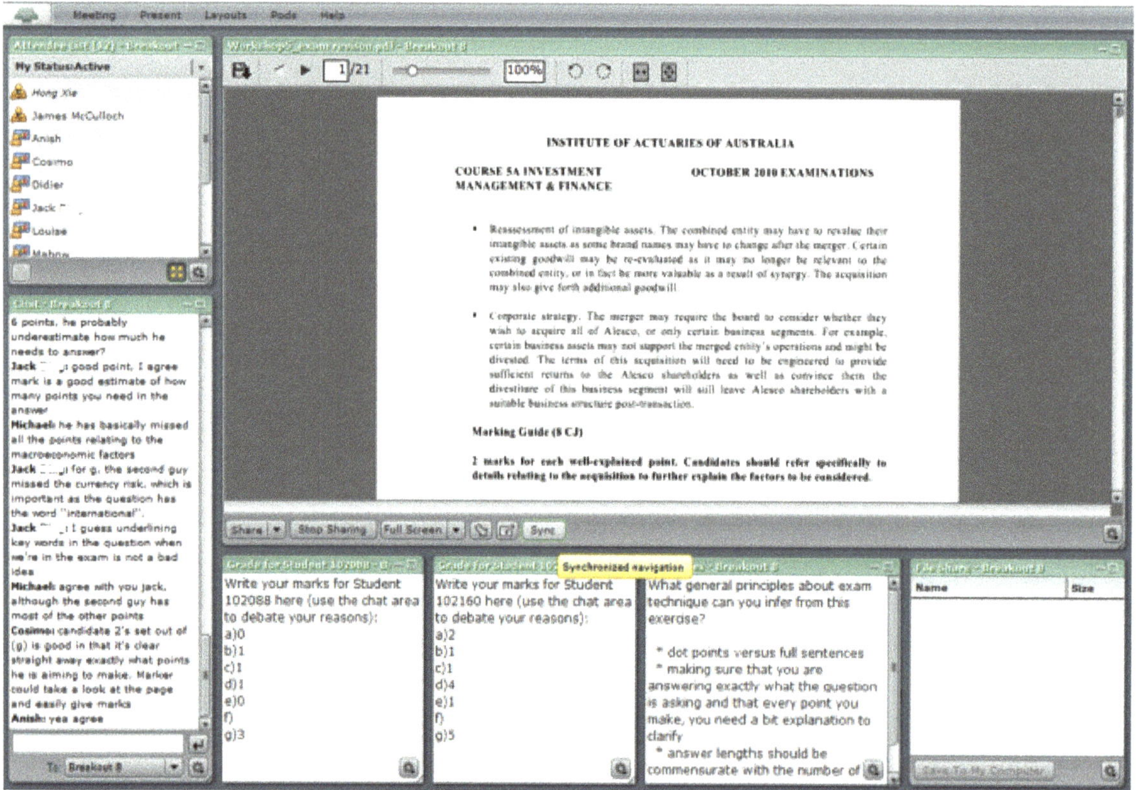

Figure 14: Case Study 1 remote student view

Resources

- Two student solutions to a past paper examination question available via sharing area of the web conferencing environment.
- The same two solution files available as a downloadable file from the Learning Management System.

Support for staff

The teacher was provided with technical support throughout the lesson from a colleague from the Applied Finance and Actuarial Studies Department. This colleague facilitated all of the management of the web conferencing system, including construction of the interface layout for the group work activities, allocation of students to groups during the lesson, switching students between groups, and managing and monitoring the audio broadcast by the lecture. This colleague also monitored remote student text chat contributions and relayed important information to the teacher.

Support for students

The colleague providing technical support along with a third colleague offered assistance to students when they started undertaking their group work. In particular, they explained how to increase the size of the view to make the documents legible. They also explained how to turn off synchronised scrolling so that a student adjusting their position in the document being reviewed did not affect the view of other students. The teacher also offered verbal instructions to the whole class about this, after consultation with his colleagues.

Assessment

This task was not assessable in itself, but did support students to prepare for their major examination.

Project team's input into the learning design

The project team worked closely with the case study partners to develop the learning design into a more collaborative experience for students. Previous lessons throughout the semester had only involved the teacher presenting materials to the whole class, and occasional class discussion. During class discussions face-to-face students would make verbal contributions and remote students would use text chat.

The project team suggested ways that group work could be used to promote greater student contribution, and how the notes areas could be deployed in order to provide students with a solution space. The project team conducted a trial of the lesson prior to implementation, to test systems and ensure that the case study partners were able to use the technology as required for the task.

Class Size and Location/Distribution of Participants

Altogether 18 students participated in this activity, from a total of 31 students in the unit. Of these 11 students were in the room and 7 were located off campus. Some of the off-campus students were participating from overseas (for instance, China).

The Lesson as Enacted

Initially the teacher spent approximately five minutes describing the task to students. He explained that students were supposed to collaboratively decide upon the marks to award two previous examination responses, and provided brief reference to the technology they were supposed to use to coordinate their responses. The students were then placed into breakout rooms by the teaching assistant, who was logged into a second computer so that he could help to coordinate student activity and monitor the audio quality. The teacher repeated aspects of the instructions as a way of encouraging them to commence the task.

Students began working on the task quite quickly, and all students appeared to be engaged with the task. Initially several students expressed difficulty in using the web conferencing system (this was the first time that they had used the technology to collaborate in this way). Students had not been given any explanation about how to use the new tools, for instance the scrolling or zooming features of the document sharing tool. Because students had been granted 'presenter' permissions in their breakout rooms, some of them inadvertently scrolled the page down before turning the synchronised scrolling feature off. These sorts of problems meant that teachers devoted a considerable proportion of time in the first ten minutes of the activity to responding to student technical questions. After this initial disruption experienced in this period, students' technological questions abated and students settled into the activity.

Over the course of the next 30 minutes the groups of students in the breakout room discussed their reasons for the marks they would allocate to the different parts of the two past examination papers. As well as negotiating the marks that the group would award, a substantial amount of student time was necessarily devoted to reading the examination questions and reflecting on the quality of the past student responses. Students also briefly summarised what had been learnt about examination technique in a separate notes area. During this period the activity in the room was almost entirely student-centred, with very little teacher input required. High levels of interaction between students co-located in the main classroom, between remote students and co-located students, and between remote students were noticed by the research team. The teacher would occasionally provide a suggestion relating to the technology or words of encouragement.

The teaching assistant notified students that there were only a few minutes remaining, and students finalised their mark allocations. Students also worked to finish their summaries of good examination technique in the separate notes area that had been provided.

The teaching assistant then placed all students into the first breakout room, and the teacher discussed the marks that the group awarded in comparison with the marks that were actually awarded by the examiners. Discussion points included the reasons for the examiner's mark allocations, the subjectivity and interpretation that can exist when assigning marks, and the need to make sure that responses focused upon the question being addressed. The teaching assistant then placed all students in the second breakout room, and the teacher briefly reviewed these mark allocations with reference to the examiner's evaluation and that of the other group.

Face-to-face students asked questions about examination technique during this review phase. Whenever students asked a question the teacher attempted to summarise and repeat the question so that the off-campus students could hear it (the microphone in the classroom did not capture face-to-face student audio). The entire episode took approximately 1 hour and 6 minutes, including approximately 5 minutes of discussion that related to the upcoming examination and not the task at hand. Apart from the screen resizing issue, the only other technological issue from the teachers' perspective was that there was approximately two minutes of audio that was not broadcasted to students because the microphone switch in the web conferencing breakout room was not turned on.

Student Perceptions

The proportions of students who completed the questionnaire face-to-face and remotely were 67% (n=8) and 33% (n=4) respectively. Students were asked a range of questions about their experiences with the activities they were presented with in class. Table 1 reports on the degree to which students agreed or disagreed with eight items.

Table 4: Summary of Case Study 1 student responses to key evaluation questions

Item	Face-to-face (n=8)			Remote (n=4)		
	Agree	Neutral	Disagree	Agree	Neutral	Disagree
I was able to communicate verbally in an effective manner with people in the face-to-face class	75.0	25.0	0.0	66.7	33.3	0.0
I was able to communicate verbally in an effective manner with people who participated remotely	42.9	28.6	28.6	50.0	50.0	0.0
In this lesson I was able to effectively share visual artefacts with others (e.g. images, photos, etc.)	42.9	42.9	14.3	66.7	0.0	33.3
In this lesson I was able to jointly create, edit, and share material with others in an effective manner	28.6	57.1	14.3	66.7	33.3	0.0
In this lesson I was able to effectively indicate my status to others (e.g. wanting attention, etc.)	42.9	42.9	14.3	100.0	0.0	0.0
In this lesson I felt like I was present with people who were participating remotely	75.0	25.0	0.0	50.0	50.0	0.0
In this lesson I felt like I was present with people who were in the same room as the teacher	85.7	14.3	0.0	66.7	0.0	33.3
The collaborative technology provided clear and accurate representation of information and people	62.5	25.0	12.5	100.0	0.0	0.0

There was a broadly positive response to all items with a clear majority of both face-to-face and remote students agreeing with the statements. For most items there were also a small number of students who disagreed with the statements. Local students tended to have a more neutral response to items about sharing and creating materials with others, as well as indicating their status to others. Remote students were unanimous about the ability of the system to clearly represent information and indicate their status.

All except for one student felt that the lesson was generally “good”, though four students felt that the technology could have performed better (for instance commenting that it was “clunky”). Students could see the potential of the approach for “getting online participants involved”. One student encapsulated these two aspects of the student perspective with the comment “the concept is great, technology was a bit lagged”. The remote students were more positive about the experience, for instance “both the lecture in the main room and discussions in the breakout room are excellent ... the sound was so clear too”.

Verbal communication for remote students was constrained by the use of text chat to collaborate because “typing speed restricted the rate of communication”. Another verbal contribution disparity that students in the face-to-face class pointed out was the fact that they may be seated next to someone in their group, but talking face-to-face meant disconnecting with the thread of the group conversation.

I could easily chat to my peers next to me but by the time we were done discussing among ourselves, the people online might be talking about something different or have moved on already. Also, as we're sitting in front of computers, we couldn't come together as a group to discuss, you could only really talk to the people directly next to you.

As well, students noticed the differences between talking in a face-to-face group and communicating via text chat:

The discussion is more disjointed in the sense that multiple people are putting forward their points and so you need to put your own opinion forward and respond to the multiple other opinions being put forth at the same time.

In response to questions about sharing and creating visual artefacts, most students indicated that this was not really attempted. Some students related this to the sharing of the examination responses, and pointed out how permissions and lack of familiarity with operation of the web conferencing system interfered with their ability to collaborate:

When I was in the breakout room, everyone has been promoted as a presenter. It was a bit annoyed when some students always moved PDF slides or changed the slides to full screen.

One student felt that this problem would easily be overcome if the activity was repeated again:

Seems this is our first time experience, we all took some time to understand the system before we finally realise how to use it. It shouldn't be a big problem if we are second- or third-time user.

In terms of presence, once students were in their group work room there was a degree of egalitarianism between remote and face-to-face students, with one student observing that you "can't really identify who is remote and who is not". One person indicated that typing instead of talking reduced the sense of co-presence, but that this was an inevitability of collaborating in this way.

Students identified that there were advantages of having remote and face-to-face students participating in the one lesson in terms of having a greater variety of viewpoints contributing to the discussion.

Very good experience with both internal and external students together in a same classroom. People can see remote students' idea through the messages they left in the chat pod and their feedback.

However several students noted how technological issues interrupted the flow of the lesson. In the post-class discussion some students felt that the blended learning approach was more valuable for remote students, potentially at the expense of face-to-face students. One student pointed out that changing the grouping strategy could have improved the overall experience:

It would be far more efficient to perhaps group people in the class together and then let the online participants use this software.

Two students suggested that the lesson could be improved by enabling the audio feature for remote students. Four students also emphasised the importance of the teacher repeating the questions from in the room.

In addition to these questions students were also asked whether they would like the approach used in the current class to be used in other subjects they studied. A total of 58.3% of students agreed with this, while only one student (8.3%) indicated they would not like this to be the case. Reasons for using the approach in other classes included that it "encourage group discussion and participation", and enabled students to "revisit the lecture to cover off points they may have missed".

Finally, students were asked whether they learnt "less", "the same", or "more" than if the lesson had run in a normal face-to-face mode. A total of 58.3% of students reported they would have learnt the same, 25.0% reported they learnt less, and 16.7% reported they learnt more. Two of the three people who felt that they learnt less were remote students, pointing out that the approach "took longer to get across the points". The two people who felt that they learnt more were both face-to-face students, indicating that the more collaborative approach and the ability to include off-campus students were advantages.

Teacher Perceptions

There was a degree of teacher apprehension about shifting from previous delivery approaches to teaching (where tutorials would consist of the teacher broadcasting tutorial answers) to an approach where students were collaborating with one another. But the teachers also felt that engaging these sorts of approaches was an inevitability: "this is coming, once everyone has got 100 mbs per second into their household, having you know 12 students up on a screen and being able to click and point and really talk to them, while they are sitting there in the study, that's going to happen".

The teachers' reflections of the lesson focused on the technology, its functionality, its ease of use, and their overall perceptions of it. When asked about how they measured the success of the lesson, it emerged that enthusiasm and contribution were seen as indicators of quality learning and teaching, which caused the teachers to re-evaluate their perceptions of what transpired to take into account the heightened levels of student activity. As well as acknowledging that the experience of the remote students was far superior, they also reflected that the experience of the face-to-face students had the potential to be better using these approaches. For instance, students who might experience 'stage fear' may be more willing to make comments, and ask questions in an online space.

The main teacher indicated that having a good teaching assistant meant that he was able to teach fairly much as he normally would. However he did mention that he felt more detached from the remote students because he was not able to see their body language.

Based on pre- and post- interviews it was apparent that teachers were aware of a range of strategies for enhancing the blended synchronous learning experience in their classes. Presage factors included putting lesson resources on the LMS before the class so students had a copy to browse during the lesson, and starting the web conferencing session 10 minutes early to help students test their audio. During the lesson teachers recommended always typing a question asking whether students can hear, asking questions to promote discussion, explicitly asking distance students whether or not they have any questions (because it can take time for them to write in which case the lesson might have already moved on), and asking students to use the prefix "Q" to distinguish text chat questions (requiring responses) from comments. They felt all of these micro strategies and protocols supported more efficient lesson implementation.

Discussion

For this lesson the lead teacher provided the main directions to students, and the assistant teacher performed all of the technology management functions such as placing students into breakout rooms, alerting the teacher about recent student contributions to the text chat, making announcements in breakout rooms, and so on. While the lead teacher needed to be aware of the task and its design, the support of the teaching assistant meant that the lead teacher could more or less teach as they normally would and did not need to manage the technology in any significant way. This reduced the cognitive load that would have otherwise been imposed by having to manage the face-to-face students, the remote students, and the technology all at the same time. For instance, having a teaching assistant monitor the text chat stream in the web conferencing system meant that the teacher could be alerted to remote student comments as soon as they occurred without having to monitor this independently. Because the teaching assistant was logged into the web conferencing system he could also checking that the audio was streaming correctly.

Creating a space for students to contribute (both in the web conferencing environment and within the lesson) increased the level of student engagement, and some students reported on the positive contribution this made to the lesson.

At times the teacher's repetition of face-to-face student comments and questions did not entirely capture the intended meaning, so it was possible that remote students could not fully understand what was happening in classroom. A room-based microphone capture system would have been useful to resolve this problem. The design of the web conferencing layout may have been improved by enlarging the text chat pod in which students held their conversations. Providing students with instructions on how to use the required web conferencing system before they commenced the activity could have averted some of the initial technological difficulties that they experienced.

Randomly grouping students was an attempt to transcend physical boundaries between remote and face-to-face students, however because the mediating technology did not provide the same level of communicative efficiency as speaking with an adjacent person, face-to-face students felt this constrained their ability to communicate. This highlights how grouping is an important blended synchronous learning issue, and students in the same room may best be grouped together for a first round of activities, with group responses across locations/groups then shared between the whole class.

Introducing audio for all students would have potentially enhanced collaboration, but also would have introduced a range of technical issues (such as microphone and speaker operation) that could have interfered with the lesson implementation. Another, more advanced activity was proposed, involving students typing and writing mathematical responses on collaborative whiteboard pods, but this idea was discarded because it would have required a range of new technological competencies on the part of students.

Summary of Findings

Student and teacher feedback was generally positive about the enactment of this blended synchronous learning design, though there were some students who were not in favour of the approach. Key findings include:

Learning design/pedagogy issues

- Considerable presage and design rethinking was required to setup the learning environment in a way that was conducive to collaborative learning (design of collaborative tasks, tool selection and placement, and provision of resources).
- Having remote and face-to-face participants holding discussions through the web conferencing system levelled the playing field for remote students, and may have encouraged face-to-face students who are normally reluctant to engage in conversations.
- Students made significantly greater contributions to the lesson than under the previous 'delivery' approaches to teaching.
- Allocating all students in the class into random groups meant that students sitting next to one another in the face-to-face classroom weren't necessarily able to collaborate in face-to-face mode because they needed to include their remote team members in the conversation.

Technology issues

- The fact that students lacked the technological understanding of how to operate the document-sharing and viewing capabilities temporarily interfered with their engagement with the task, though concerted student support from the teachers was able to rectify the situation.
- Using a microphone that could capture the audio from the face-to-face classroom would have meant that the teacher did not need to repeat comments so that remote students could hear.
- Using text chat rather than audio constrained the ability of people to make rapid contributions during the collaborative activity and may have decreased their sense of co-presence (however requiring students to use audio for this already novel approach may have increased the risk of extra technology issues occurring during the lesson).

Setup and logistic issues

- There was substantial value in having a teaching aid to support the main teacher attend to technical aspects of the lesson and help manage remote student activity.
- Having the teaching assistant logged in on a second computer meant that he could check the quality of the audio stream.

Chapter 7: Case Study 2 – Room-based Video Conferencing to Develop Understanding of Healthcare Quality Improvement Approaches

Brief overview

This lesson used Access Grid room-based video conferencing to bring together students on three university campuses. The lesson, in the discipline of health informatics, involved a combination of a lecture and a small group activity with a report back to the whole group. As well as the lecturer and tutor present at one site, there was also a tutor present at one of the other two sites. The Access Grid setup involved the use of multiple screens showing students at each site and the teachers, as well as an additional area for showing presentation slides. During the report back phase of the lesson, students made use of an interactive whiteboard to share diagrams with students on the other sites. The lesson proceeded smoothly with students on all sites able to participate effectively. Although student questionnaire and focus group responses were generally positive, some students nevertheless indicated a preference for face-to-face classes. Some issues that students identified included an inability to hear the questions asked by students on remote sites, and difficulty in making out the details of the material shared through the interactive whiteboard. The effectiveness of the strategies used by the lecturer to involve students on other campuses was highlighted in student feedback, and the role of the remote tutor in encouraging input from remote students emerged as an important element of the lesson.
Institutional Context

Institution: University of Western Sydney (UWS)

Teaching team: Joanne Curry (subject coordinator/lecturer), Heidi Bearing (co-lecturer/tutor)

Project team members involved: Matt Bower, Jacqueline Kenney

Discipline: Health Informatics, School of Computing, Engineering & Mathematics

Subject/unit: Introduction to Health Informatics

Level of study: Second year (undergraduate); Bachelor degree and Graduate certificate

Intended learning outcome(s):

- The student can assess the advantages and disadvantages of the different techniques used to conduct patient journey modelling. This aligns with the broader unit objective of giving students exposure to and experience with various healthcare service redesign methods.

Description of the Learning Activity/Tasks (Learning Design as Intended)

1. The teacher delivers a 50-minute lecture on patient modelling and healthcare transformation to all three campuses. As part of the lecture, students are introduced to three contemporary frameworks for patient journey modelling.
2. Students located at each campus split up into groups of four. Each group assumed the role of a team of business analysts working for a consulting firm contracted to analyse the diabetes patient journey at the local hospital. Each group is required to critique the three patient journey modelling frameworks covered in the lecture in terms of their suitability for this purpose.
3. The groups at each campus present their findings in terms of advantages and disadvantages to the entire cohort via networked interactive whiteboards for discussion, debate and extension. (One group per campus is selected by the lecturer to present on behalf of all groups at that campus, with the remaining groups given the opportunity to contribute additional points.)
4. A final review/debrief is led by the lecturer to provide opportunities for reflection and links to a related mid-semester assessment task.

Presage Factors

Technology and environment setup/configuration

Access Grid was setup in the classrooms of the three UWS campuses involved in the study (Parramatta, Campbelltown and Penrith). Access Grid is a networked room-based hardware and software system that enables high-bandwidth audio and video data to be shared between remote locations (for detailed information about this technology see http://www.accessgrid.org).

The main tutorial room was configured with three rows of desks, a small lectern at the end of the first row of desks near the entrance, an interactive whiteboard on the side wall near the lectern, an Access Grid control desk in the back corner opposing the entrance, and a large Access Grid screen at the front of the room Figure 15.

The Access Grid screen spanned several meters in width and was able to display multiple sources of information. These included:

- a close-up video feed of the lecturer;
- a side-of-room perspective of the lecturer that included the interactive whiteboard and lectern;
- a back-of-room perspective of the lecturer that included the presentation slides in the background;
- a close-up view of students at the Parramatta campus;

a wide-angle lens view of the whole Parramatta classroom (three long rows of desks, seating 10 students per row);

- a close-up view of the students at Campbelltown that included the interactive whiteboard and tutor;
- a side-of-room view of the Campbelltown class;
- a back-of-room view of the Campbelltown class that included both the projector screen and the interactive whiteboard;
- a whole-of-room view of the Campbelltown class from a front-of-room perspective;
- a front-of-room view of the class in Penrith; and
- a view of the interactive whiteboard at Penrith from a side/front camera angle.

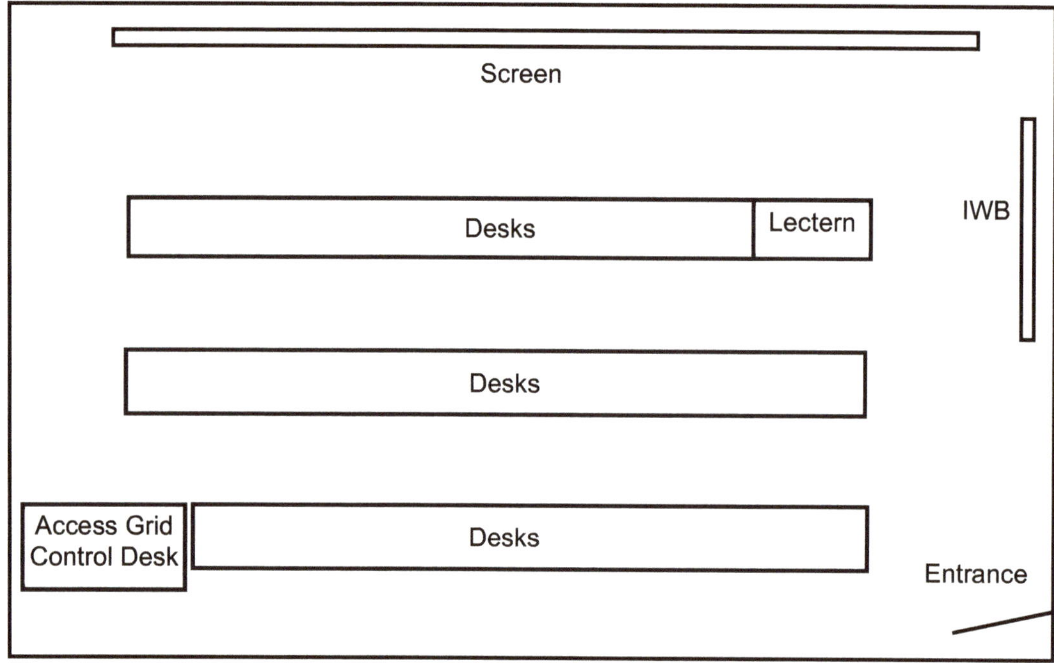

Figure 15: Case Study 2 room layout

Audio was captured using microphones that were placed around the room at each campus. The cameras were mounted on the walls and ceiling and microphones picked up sound from the front of the room.

The interactive whiteboard was located on the side wall of the room so it could be accessed by both the teacher and students. Bridgit interactive whiteboard software was used to enable students at all three campuses to write on the interactive whiteboards in each room and for students at other campuses to see what they were writing (for more information about Bridgit see http://www.smarttech.com/bridgited). A view of the main Parramatta Campus classroom is shown in Figure 16. A remote student view is shown in Figure 17.

Figure 16: Case Study 2 face-to-face room setup

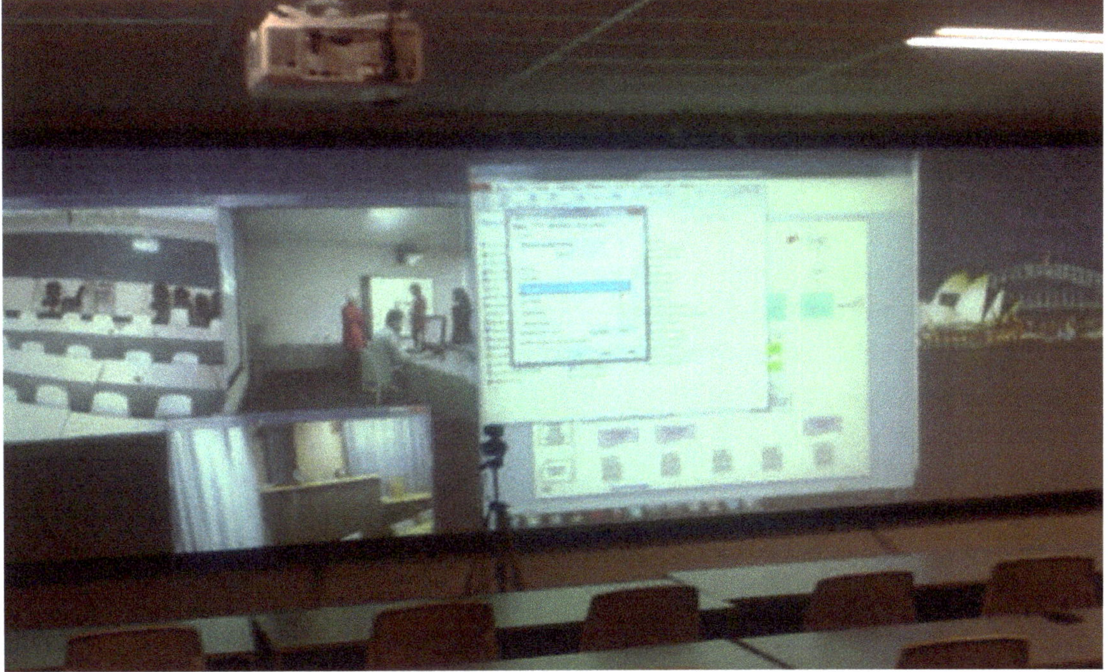

Figure 17: Case Study 2 face-to-face room setup

Resources

- PowerPoint slides used as visual aids in the lecture;
- An article and various web-based readings on patient journey-modelling processes and frameworks, made available via the University's Blackboard-based Learning Management System; and
- Written instructions to students for the small-group activity.

Support for staff

The lecturer's School at UWS, the School of Computing and Mathematics, has its own dedicated team of technical support staff in addition to the University-wide Information Technology Services department. School-based technical support staff were present in the relevant classrooms at each campus to set up the technical equipment and activate the respective video conferencing links at the start of the session. They arrived approximately 15 minutes prior to the start of the session as the lecturer was pre-loading the PowerPoint slides to the system, and in the case of the Parramatta and Campbelltown campuses, remained on hand 10 minutes into the session to ensure that the technology was running smoothly. Thereafter, they could be contacted via telephone should any problems or the need for additional support arise. At the Penrith campus, where there was no teaching staff member present, a technical support officer stayed in the room for the entire duration of the session. The lecturer at the main campus provided prompts and support to the students at Penrith. There was a tutor at the Campbelltown class, along with a technical support officer.

Being an academic within the Computing discipline and a frequent user of Access Grid and video conferencing technology in her teaching, the lecturer did not need formal technical training in preparation for the activity. However, she did obtain informal, one-on-one training from a member of the School's technical support team on how to use some of the features of the interactive whiteboard, since she had not previously used it in her classes.

Support for students

Students were not required to operate the videoconferencing equipment themselves, thus minimal additional technical support was necessary beyond that which was already provided to staff (as described in the previous section). The students were guided and assisted in the use of the interactive whiteboard as required during the activity by the teaching staff. For example, they were instructed on how to bring up a new page on the interactive whiteboard display when they had filled the viewable area of the display with responses/notes.

In terms of pedagogical support, the teaching staff monitored the students' progress during the small-group activity, with the lecturer overseeing the groups at the Parramatta campus (where she was physically located, and which contained the largest number of students), while the tutor (based at Campbelltown) took responsibility for the groups at the remaining two campuses. They visited and 'checked in' with each group to ensure its members were on task, to respond to queries, and to generally assist with resolving difficulties encountered. Rather than directly giving students answers to the task, the lecturer and tutor supplied scaffolding in the form of leading questions as well as by referring students to relevant aspects of the supporting resources (e.g. suggesting that they revisit a particular slide or look at a certain part of the readings).

Assessment

The blended synchronous learning activities were not formally assessed, however they did enable the teacher to formatively gauge the extent to which the class had acquired an understanding of key concepts. The tasks also assisted students to prepare for an upcoming assignment in which they had to apply one of the three patient journey-modelling frameworks to a case study. In particular, it was hoped that through the activities, the students would gain a better appreciation of the relative strengths of and rationale for using the particular framework they were required to employ in the assignment.

Project team's input into the learning design

The lecturer had previously delivered the lesson in cross-campus mode a number of times before. Working with the project team, she enhanced her learning design in an effort to promote greater levels of interaction between students who were located remotely from one another, in addition to that between those who were co-located. On the recommendation of the project team, she introduced a component in which students from each campus were explicitly directed to share the outputs of their face-to-face deliberations with the wider cohort spanning the three campuses. She identified the utility of networked interactive whiteboards for facilitating this sharing, and subsequently sought training on the technology, employing it for the first time during the lesson.

Class Size and Location/Distribution of Participants

Of the 41 students who participated in the activity, 24 students were located at the Parramatta campus, 12 at the Campbelltown campus, and 5 at the Penrith campus. For the purpose of the small-group activity, there were 6 groups at Parramatta, 3 at Campbelltown, and 1 at Penrith.

The Lesson as Enacted

During the first 50 minutes of the lesson the lecturer at the Parramatta campus delivered a lecture punctuated by questions for students. In some cases students were asked to respond to questions by raising their hands (e.g. "how many of you have started your assignment?") and in other places students provided short (single word or single phrase) answers. In the first part of the lecture only students on the lecturer's campus answered questions. During the second half of the lecture some questions were specifically directed at students on the remote campuses. In the first instance where questions were directed at students on the Campbelltown campus no response was received despite prompting from the lecturer. At this point the face-to-face tutor intervened and re-asked the question and following this the students responded. From this point on the face-to-face tutor frequently assisted in facilitating responses from students on this campus when questions were asked by the lecturer. Students on the Penrith campus, where there was no tutor present, answered questions when they were specifically directed to their campus by the lecturer but did not tend to answer questions directed at the group as a whole. However, on occasion the students did spontaneously respond to teacher prompts or by offering uninvited input. The tutor pointed out during the lesson that students at the Campbelltown campus could not hear questions or responses from students at the Parramatta campus and asked the lecturer to repeat them.

During the lecture the video displays showing views of the remote campuses were fixed, that is, they did not change angle or zoom as a result of people talking on a particular campus and they were not controlled by the teaching or technical staff. Some minor technical problems occurred and these were quickly addressed (e.g. a lapel microphone was found to be not working and instead a desktop microphone was used).

Following the lecture there was a 10 minute break followed by a 60 minute tutorial activity in which students worked in 10 groups of a maximum of 4 students. The task required students to adopt the role of a business analyst with a consultancy company and report on an analysis of the journey experienced by diabetes patients at hospital using three different patient care models. The groups were required to compare and contrast the advantages and disadvantages of each model. Students were grouped within their campus and worked on the problems with team members at their campus. The teachers circulated amongst student groups to provide them with assistance and keep them on task.

In the final section of the lesson the lecturer selected a group from each campus to report back to the whole cohort of students. Using the networked interactive whiteboard system (Bridgit) a representative from each group was able to write down their findings so that it was visible on the screens at all three campuses. The lecturer facilitated discussion and monitored the activity across all three campuses. Although there was a degree of interactive whiteboard latency it was possible for students to share their written appraisals of the three models with both their on-site and remotely located peers.

After the lesson students completed the online survey and participated in focus groups.

Student Perceptions

Student reflections on the lesson were gathered through a questionnaire completed by 10 students present on the lecturer's campus and 18 students present on remote campuses, and through an in class focus group at the conclusion of the lesson. The in-class focus group took place in the main campus and included all students via video link, as it was conducted in the same fashion as the class itself.

Table 5 reports on the degree to which students in their post-lesson survey responses agreed or disagreed with eight items relating to specific aspects of their experience.

In general, responses indicated that the lesson was viewed positively by the majority of students. Students were most positive about the technology allowing learning to occur, the technology providing a clear and accurate representation of people and information, and their ability to jointly create, edit and share material, and communicate with people in remote contexts. For most items there were some students who disagreed with the statements, but this was invariably a minority of respondents, and in most cases less than 10% of recorded responses. There was also a reasonable degree of consistency between remote and face-to-face responses, which accords with the similar technology setup provided by the University in the three classrooms.

Table 5: Summary of Case Study 2 student responses to key evaluation questions

Item	Face-to-face (n=11)			Remote (n=17)		
	Agree	Neutral	Disagree	Agree	Neutral	Disagree
I was able to communicate verbally in an effective manner with people in the face-to-face class	90.9	0.0	9.1	76.5	17.6	5.9
I was able to communicate verbally in an effective manner with people who participated remotely	90.9	9.1	0.0	64.7	29.4	5.9
In this lesson I was able to effectively share visual artefacts with others (e.g. images, photos, etc.)	72.7	27.3	0.0	70.6	17.6	11.8
In this lesson I was able to jointly create, edit, and share material with others in an effective manner	100.0	0.0	0.0	76.5	23.5	0.0
In this lesson I was able to effectively indicate my status to others (e.g. wanting attention, etc.)	90.9	9.1	0.0	70.6	23.5	5.9
In this lesson I felt like I was present with people who were participating remotely	72.7	9.1	18.2	70.6	23.5	5.9
In this lesson I felt like I was present with people who were in the same room as the teacher	80.0	20.0	0.0	58.8	29.4	11.8
The collaborative technology provided clear and accurate representation of information and people	100.0	0.0	0.0	88.2	5.9	5.9

Students who were co-located with the lecturer generally indicated that they were able to communicate effectively in the environment, as summarised by one student:

> *I had no problem communicating with the lecturer and remote students. The communication is clear to everyone and is much better than shouting across a lecture theatre.*

There were a minority of students who pointed out that the performance of the technology inhibited communications, for instance that "soft microphones restricted verbal communications and being able to hear at times" and that the "[teacher] needed to repeat herself and students a lot". In total ten students raised the issue of audio communication restrictions due to the microphone capture and broadcast quality.

In total 100% of co-located respondents and 77% of remote respondents indicated that they were able to jointly create, edit and share material with other students. The following positive questionnaire response is consistent with this:

> *I was quite impressed with the technology used in the class. The interactive and electronic whiteboard was very helpful between classes as it acts as a chalkboard instead of having to talk all the time.*

The students who disagreed or were neutral about the statement regarding their ability to share visual artefacts (29% of face-to-face students and 29% of remote students) explained their responses using comments such as it was "a bit difficult to understand the writing on the smart board [interactive whiteboard]". While sixteen survey respondents pointed out how the interactive supported learning, four students indicated that latency and quality inhibited learning.

A total of 100% of co-located students and 88% of remote students felt that the technology provided a clear and accurate representation of people and information. As one remote student put it:

> *The microphones and cameras always being on makes it easier to respond with simple gestures or noises to indicate status.*

No students raised any items that restricted their ability to indicate their status.
There was a mixed sense of co-presence expressed by respondents. Many felt co-present and saw that the role technology played in creating this sense of co-presence. The following comment by a remote student exemplifies a positive sentiment expressed by students.

> *Having a normal intuitive means of communication made it seem like they were not remote at all.*

On the other hand another remote student did feel distant:

> *It is obvious that we are experiencing real-time communication, but there is always going to be a sense of distance when communicating through a screen.*

Students voiced positive comments about the degree of interactivity in the lesson and in particular the strategies used by the lecturer for involving students on all campuses:

> *This lesson was highly educating, the teacher communicated with the other students throughout the campuses.*
>
> *Good to get other people's opinions from different campuses.*

Other students commented on the fact that the technology increased their engagement with the lesson, for example:

> *I think, I kind of feel more engaged by it, because we are using technology ... technology providing us with the entertainment.*
>
> *I think the technology engages the younger generations because it is associated with gaming, entertainment and social networks.*

Students expressed the importance of having a remote tutor/teacher present in the classroom, for example:

> *more interactive if I had the teacher in the same room as me, allow me to pay more attention then always dosing off [remote student indicating distance from teacher]*
> *I think we are more inclined to respond when there is a teacher in front of us.*

Some students indicated that the high fidelity broadcast nature of the technology may have led to a reluctance to communicate in some circumstances:

> *Sometimes [remote] students did not actively participate across campus because they were not face-to-face.*
>
> *Having the lecturer in the room is an advantage if you want to talk more one and one as oppose[d] to having your voice heard over 3 campuses.*

In summative responses students felt that the best aspects of the lesson were the engaging nature of the lecturer, the good uses of technology (particularly the interactive whiteboard), and the interactivity in the lesson ("more interaction, and more shared thoughts"). Many did not make any suggestions for improvements, but those that did primarily focused on the microphone and interactive whiteboard performance. Recommendations for teachers trying to teach in this mode included:

> *Try and include all campus's at a regular interval.* (face-to-face student)
>
> *Have a good connection, and make sure no latency.* (face-to-face student)
>
> *They should definitely try it as it provides a great learning experience.* (remote student)
>
> *Interaction is extremely important. Keeping the students across all campuses engaged* (face-to-face student)

A total of 91% of face-to-face students and 65% of remote students agreed that they would like the approach used in the current class to be used in other subjects they studied while 18% indicated they would not like this to be the case. Those who were in favour thought it enabled greater interactivity, sharing of more views, and access to the best teaching. Reasons for not being in favour included a personal preference for face-to-face teaching and the fact that the approach may not have been suitable for other contexts (for instance, the mathematics discipline).

A total of 39% of students (six face-to-face and four remote students) felt they learnt more using this approach than a traditional teaching approach. Students explained this in terms of the engagement promoted by the teacher. Only one student (a remote student) felt they learnt less, expressing the preference for a standard lecture approach.

Teacher Perceptions

In pre-observation interviews the teacher explained that the rationale for the approach was essentially a resourcing issue, and the available Access Grid system provided a solution:

> *Basically we just taught on one campus, but as the student numbers grew, there was demand across the three different campuses and so – because there was a resourcing issue, we couldn't spread our resources across the three campuses so we needed a medium to really have one delivery that could be seen by multiple campuses.*

Teacher reflections upon the lesson were very positive. She highlighted the fact that the technology worked well and that students seemed to enjoy the interactive exercises and particularly interacting with students on other campuses. In discussing why the lesson went well, the importance of technical support was again highlighted, as was the need to stay aware of the students on each campus and whether they are engaged and on task. The teacher felt that the authentic activity (business analysts required to make a recommendation to their boss about patient management approach) heightened student engagement. The use of the interactive whiteboard was also seen as an important element of the activity because it allowed for sharing of student work across campuses and this appeared to engage and motivate students.

The teacher provided a number of general recommendations for other teachers considering the use of Access Grid or video conferencing technologies for cross campus teaching. Firstly, the teacher felt that it was important to be more animated than when teaching students on a single campus:

> *you've got to be more animated to make it successful.... if you're not cognisant of that, so if you don't reflect on how the students are reacting to you, and if you don't reflect on your results and your assessment outcomes, then you're not going to be recognising that changes in style are required... [that's why] I think you have to put on a show when using this technique, far more than when I teach face-to-face.*

Teacher direction was seen as crucial to regularly encourage participation across multiple sites:

> *you really have to prompt quite strongly to get the campuses that you are not physically attending to get a response... I might say, 'Penrith, this question is for you' or 'Campbelltown, now it is your turn'*

The teacher also felt that flexibility was another essential attribute when teaching in blended synchronous learning mode, explaining the nature of this flexibility and required composure as follows:

> *When you have technical problems, you can't lose your lolly; instead, you have to think: How long will it be down? What is the cost–benefit of waiting?*

Appropriate technical support was also identified as a critical requirement for success.

> *You have to have great technical support. This is not something that an average lecturer could really set up, I don't believe, for large numbers of students; I think you need dedicated technical support. Not only to set it up but to have available each week to make sure it starts properly and initiates all 3 campuses.*

One issue that the teacher highlighted was the inability to video record Access Grid sessions (audio is recorded through a hand-held audio recording device). This was considered desirable by the lecturer but is not possible using the technology setup available in the Access Grid rooms, even though it is available in other lecture theatres within the University through standard lecture recording facilities. This meant that the students who missed the lesson only had access to the presentation slides and audio recordings.

The teacher also identified workload as an issue, noting that there was no recognition for academics who take on blended synchronous learning as part of their workload:

> *The introduction of blended learning must be given adequate time in academic workload. You just can't do this quickly. It wouldn't work to be told that in two weeks*

you will start to deliver blended synchronous classes. It has to be planned, software bought, training given and then ongoing support on how to do that, both from a technology and L&T perspective.

Discussion

This was an interesting case study and somewhat different to other case studies because rather than some students participating from their own homes or workplaces, all students participated from a university campus. That is, the face-to-face students participated at Parramatta campus where the lecturer for the session was located, while the remote students participated from either Campbelltown or Penrith campus. Having all students located on a University campus with technology support staff available increased the likelihood that technology problems could be seamlessly resolved during the lesson. This is noteworthy because remote students in other case studies are responsible for managing the technologies at their end and technology problems that do occur for these students can have an impact on their own experience and also the experience of other students if the teacher has to help them troubleshoot remotely.

Given the on-campus location of all students, and given also that for one group of remote students there was actually a tutor present in the room with them, one might expect the experience of the remote students to be closer to the experience of the face-to-face students than might be expected for some of the other cases. Consistent with this, comments from a number of students and questionnaire responses indicate that for many students the experiences are very similar. Importantly, however, there was still a sizable minority of students who indicated that they would learn more if physically present with the lecturer. An important additional consideration in interpreting this data is the fact that this was the first lecture in the subject delivered from Parramatta campus, with previous lectures all delivered from Campbelltown and consequently Campbelltown students may have been experiencing remote participation (at least in this subject) for the first time.

One of the key aspects of the student experience that was different to what it would have been if all students had been co-located was student-to-student communication. Responses in the questionnaire suggest that it was difficult or impossible for questions or comments from students on another campus to be heard, which meant that they had to be repeated by the lecturer (and this was not always done). This appeared to have a negative impact on students' perceived ability to communicate with remote students and is probably a key factor in responses suggesting that students would have learnt more if all students had been co-located.

The group activity was carried out in such a way that students were grouped only with students on their own campus. Communication with students on other campuses as part of the activity only occurred at the conclusion of the group work, where a report back to students on the other campuses was carried out by representatives of some groups. The report back process seemed to work well, although there were some problems experienced by some students with the clarity or legibility of material on the interactive whiteboard used to present information across campuses. The fact that groups were made up of co-located students was not reported as being a problem by either the lecturer or the students. It may be that in some contexts there is an advantage to being able to group students across locations (which would not have been feasible using Access Grid due to the single communication channel between campuses), but this was not a requirement of this particular learning design.

It is worth highlighting that the lecturer was experienced in teaching across campuses using these technologies and seemed to be quite skilled in facilitating engagement by students at each location. Student comments suggest that their overall experience of the lesson was positive, including both the content, teaching style and strategies for involving students across campuses. This is important because of the well-known tendency for student responses to an individual questionnaire item to be effected by their overall experience. It may be that if the overall lesson experience had not been quite as positive students may not have been as positive in their responses to questions about the degree to which the technology allowed certain specific communication and collaboration tasks to be performed successfully. Certainly, however, the responses suggest that a positive learning experience for this type of activity is possible when the technology works and when appropriate facilitation strategies are in place.

The impact of having a tutor present on a remote campus in this type of teaching needs more exploration. It appeared that the tutor was successful in eliciting responses from students on her campus in situations where the remote lecturer had not been able to elicit responses. However, it is not clear whether if the tutor had not been present the students may have actually responded to the questions from the remote lecturer more readily. That is, it may be that the students on the Campbelltown campus saw the tutor (who was normally the lecturer for the subject) as "their" teacher and did not easily form a student-teacher relationship with the remote lecturer, at least initially in the lecture. It would be interesting to explore the different way in which students at the Penrith campus (where there was not a tutor present), responded to direct questions from the remote lecturer and whether their experience was different to Campbelltown students.

Summary of Findings

The following is a summary of the key issues and take-home messages emerging from this case, broken up into broad themes.

Learning design/pedagogy issues

- The use of an interactive whiteboard provided an extra level of sharing to the room-based video conferencing approach by enabling students to co-construct written notes that could be seen across campuses.
- The lecturer felt a need for lecture presentations to be more animated when delivered via video conferencing to help maintain the interest and engagement of students on all campuses.
- Awareness of the level of engagement of remote students and explicit questioning of students on each campus seemed to be an important teaching strategy in this mode.

- The lecturer's interactive lecturing style was well received by students and this appeared to have a positive effect on students' evaluation of the lesson and approach.
- Having students conduct group work with peers in the same location and then report back to students at other campuses suited the Access Grid setup.
- Having a tutor present at remote campuses may improve engagement and participation of remote students.
- The relevant task (business consultancy evaluation) appeared to heighten student motivation.

Technology issues

- There were variations in the sense of presence that students experienced using this high bandwidth technology, with many feeling that there was little difference between being on the main campus versus the remote campus, but with some remote students indicating that they would prefer to be on the lecturer's campus.
- Audibility of student comments was an issue; the inability of remote students to hear comments from face-to-face students meant that student comments needed to be repeated by the lecturer.
- Use of an interactive whiteboard for sharing the output from small group work was effective and was positively received by students, although difficulty reading the screen and latency were mentioned as issues by some students.
- The quality of the video appeared sufficient for students to communicate through gestures such as raising their hand.

Setup and logistic issues

- In order for teaching staff to use Access Grid, institutions need to have first made a considerable investment in the substantial hardware and software systems.
- There is a need for on-hand technical support when using Access Grid video conferencing due to the complexity and range of different technologies that are integrated together.

Chapter 8: Case Study 3 – Web Conferencing to Support Microscopic Tissue Analysis

Brief overview

This lesson used Adobe Connect to bring together on-campus students in a computer laboratory and distance education students participating from off-campus locations to perform an interactive review of medical science (histology) material for an upcoming exam. During the first part of the lesson, the teacher, wearing a microphone to allow her speech to be audible to remote students through Connect, presented a series of multiple-choice and short-answer questions. Students (on campus and remote) answered the questions using the Adobe Connect student-response tools. Summaries of student responses were presented graphically, and the teacher explained why each answer was correct or incorrect. Students asked clarifying questions either verbally (on-campus students) or using the text chat tool in Connect (remote students). During the second part of the lesson, students were grouped in pairs and asked to complete tissue image identification and labelling tasks in breakout rooms within Connect. Group members reported back on the task and the teacher supplied feedback and clarification. During the first of those tasks, on-campus students were grouped with on-campus students and remote with remote, whereas during the second task on-campus students were grouped with remote students. Communication between on-campus students was noticeably smoother than that between remote students, with the absence of an audio channel apparently making it difficult to coordinate the labelling task for some groups. The whole-group aspects of the lesson (questions at the beginning and reports back at the end) proceeded smoothly, with the teacher able to effectively monitor the face-to-face classroom and web conferencing environment and respond to questions and comments from students in both modalities.

Institutional Context

Institution: Charles Sturt University (CSU)

Teaching team: Lucy Webster (Subject coordinator/lecturer)

Project team members involved: Barney Dalgarno, Jacqueline Kenney

Discipline: Medical Science, School of Biomedical Sciences

Subject/unit: BMS229 Histotechniques

Level of study: Second year (undergraduate)

Intended learning outcome(s):

- The student can apply an understanding of normal vertebrate tissue structure in the context of histology image analysis

Description of the Learning Activity/Tasks (Learning Design as Intended)

1. The first phase of this lesson (with duration approximately one hour) involves the teacher facilitating a question and answer session focusing on a review of material previously studied in the subject. Students respond to multiple choice and short answer questions using the Adobe Connect student response (Active Polling) features. Using this tool, the teacher shows a graphical summary of the proportion of responses to each option (for multiple choice questions) or a list of all responses (short answer questions), before explaining the answer to each question.
2. The second phase of this lesson (with duration approximately 30 minutes) involves an activity in which students identify and label the tissue structures evident within provided microscopic histologic images. Students work in pairs on this task with each pair allocated a different image to analyse, and with the teacher pairing on-campus students with on-campus students and remote students paired with remote students.
3. In the third phase of this lesson (duration about 30 minutes) a representative of each group reports back to the group as a whole. On campus students use the teacher's headset during the report back so that remote students can hear their audio. The teacher provides feedback and further explanation following each report back. For remote students without a microphone, the teacher displays the results of their work and provides feedback and further explanation for the benefit of the group as a whole.
4. In the final phase of this lesson (duration approximately 20 minutes) a second tissue image identification and labelling task is carried out, this time with remote and on-campus students paired together. Instead of a full report back from each group, in this part of the activity, the teacher quickly goes through each group's images and provides some brief feedback and pointers.

Presage Factors

Technology and environment setup/configuration

The lesson was carried out in a computer laboratory with desks in rows parallel to the front wall (see Figure 18). The teacher used computer at the end of the second row of desks, which was projected to a screen at the front of the room via a data projector. The teacher donned a microphone headset connected to her computer to allow remote students to hear her.

Nine of the on-campus students sat in front of a desktop computer, while three students participated using an iPad (provided to them). Students using the computers were not provided with microphones. The iPads were provided as part of a trial of the use of iPads supported by the CSU Divisions of Learning and Teaching Services.
A number of 'pod' layouts within Adobe Connect were created before the lesson, including

layouts for presenting slides, for quiz questions and for histology image analysis questions. Breakout rooms each containing different histology images for analysis were also created in advance. The face-to-face classroom view is shown in Figure 19 below. The remote student view is shown in Figure 20.

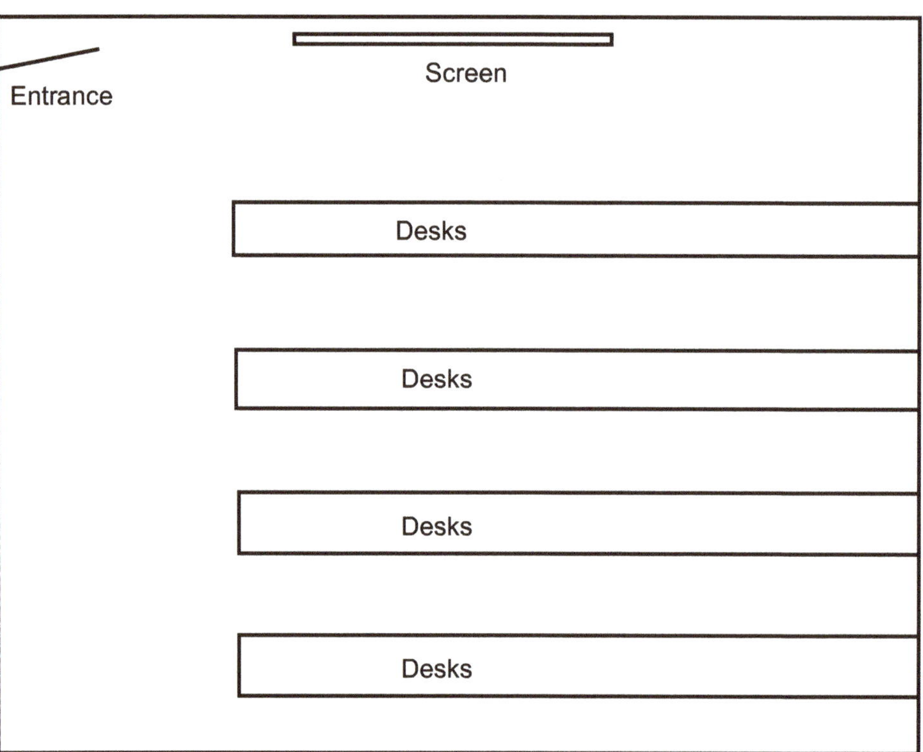

Figure 18: Case Study 3 room layout

Figure 19: Case Study 3 face-to-face room setup

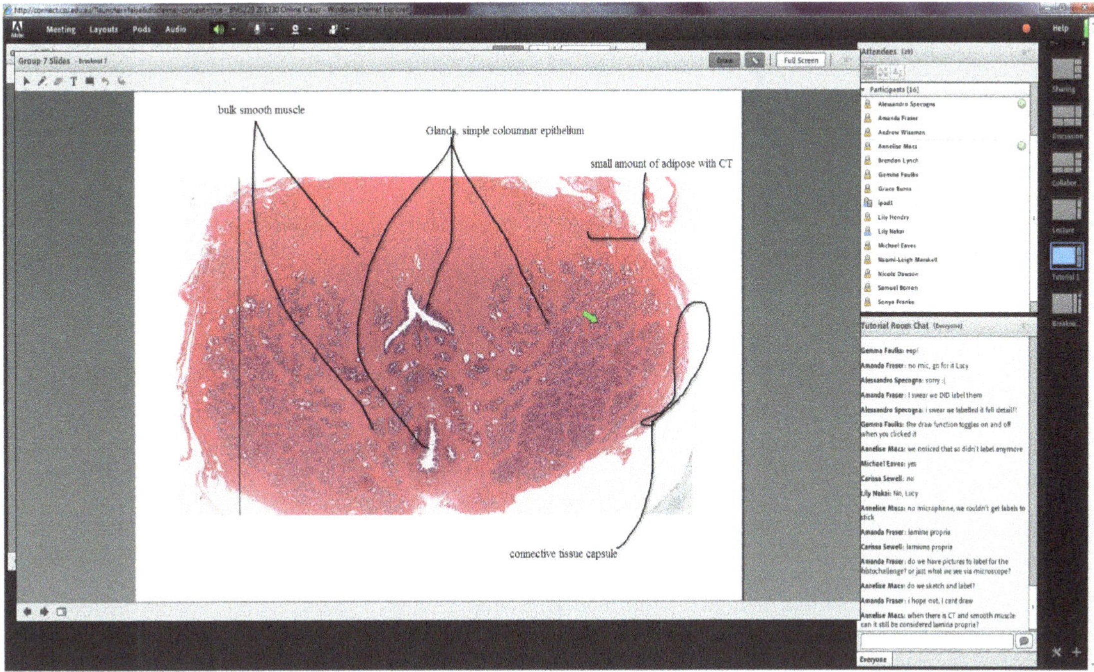

Figure 20: Case Study 3 remote student view

Resources

- Multiple choice and short answer questions were prepared in advance within Adobe Connect, some containing text only while some containing microscopic tissue images.
- Images for identification and labelling tasks were prepared in advance and placed in breakout rooms.

Support for staff

The teacher had been using web conferencing tools over the previous three years (previously Wimba) and consequently had developed her capacity to use Adobe connect without the need for any IT support. CSU provide telephone IT support to all staff, with a priority hotline available for technology issues emerging during on campus teaching. No IT support was needed during this particular session, however. The presentation and question/answer parts of the lesson were similar to other lessons the teacher had previously delivered, however this was the first time that she had facilitated group activities using breakout rooms.

Support for students

Students had been using Adobe Connect since the beginning of the teaching session (i.e. for a period of about 6 or 7 weeks), and so appeared to be quite familiar with the features of the software they needed to use during the lesson. Many of the students had also studied a previous subject taught by the teacher and so had experienced similar teaching strategies in this earlier subject. The teacher provided instruction to the students about the operation of the technology as needed during the session. The teacher also monitored the group activity and provided assistance of both a logistical and pedagogical nature during the activity.

Assessment

The two activities were closely aligned to the subject assessment, with the question and answer session aligned to a theory exam, and the group activity closely aligned to a practical examination activity. Student responses enabled the teacher to formatively assess the understanding of the class. However the tasks themselves were not assessable.

Project team's input into the learning design

The question and answer activity was similar to activities used regularly in the subject as part of lecture and tutorial sessions. No input from the project team was needed for this activity.

The group diagram labelling activity was designed in consultation with the project team. Similar activities had been undertaken in the past in other offerings of the subject on an individual basis, however this was the first time this had been undertaken in pairs using breakout rooms.

Class Size and Location/Distribution of Participants

Of the 23 students who participated in the activity, 12 were initially located in the computer laboratory on campus and the remaining 11 participated remotely. The number of remote participants varied during the session with some leaving before the end of the session and some arriving late. One student participated remotely for the first half of the lesson and then joined the class for the second half.

The Lesson as Enacted

All face-to-face and remote students logged into Adobe Connect at the beginning of the lesson. During the first 15 minutes of the lesson, the teacher introduced the research project, provided students with information about an upcoming examination and explained the activities to be undertaken during today's class. Prior to commencing, the teacher monitored Adobe Connect and welcomed remote participants, and confirmed that they could hear her audio. For this lesson none of the remote students had a microphone and so all communication by remote students was undertaken using text chat.

During the next 50 minutes, the teacher facilitated a question and answer session during which students responded to multiple choice and short answer questions using the Adobe Connect polling feature. Following each question, the teacher displayed a graphical summary of responses before explaining the answer to the question. Remote students were able to effectively ask questions using the Adobe Connect text chat stream. The teacher was able to effectively monitor the text chat stream while also responding to co-located students. The majority of interactions during this activity were between co-located students, between remote students and the teacher, and between co-located students and the teacher. There were no interactions between remote students or between remote and co-located students during this part of the lesson.

Following a 30 minute break, the teacher spent 15 minutes explaining the next activity which involved identification and labelling of the tissue structures evident within provided microscopic histologic images. The teacher then allocated students to pairs using the breakout rooms feature of Adobe Connect. This activity was designed to prepare students for an upcoming examination task, referred to as the 'Histochallenge' which involved similar tissue identification and labelling.

Students worked for 25 minutes in pairs on this task, with the teacher manually pairing on-campus students with on-campus students and remote students paired with remote students. Some on-campus students chose to move alongside their pair so that they could communicate orally, while others stayed where they were and communicated using Adobe Connect chat.

The group was brought back together and a representative of each group was asked to report back to the group as a whole on the analysis of their allocated images. On campus students wore the teacher's headset during the report back so that remote students could hear their audio. The teacher provided feedback and further explanation following each report back. Some on-campus students chose not to take the headset during the report back but instead asked the teacher to show their work and provide feedback without a report back. Remote students were not able to report back because none had a microphone. They were given the opportunity to report back using text chat but chose not to. Instead the teacher displayed the results of their work and provided feedback and further explanation for the benefit of the group as a whole. This report back session took approximately 25 minutes.

A second tissue image identification and labelling task was then commenced, this time with remote student paired with on-campus students. Group allocation for this activity took slightly longer (about 10 minutes) due to the difficulty of grouping face-to-face and remote students and due to some technical issues encountered by the teacher on her computer.

In total approximately 20 minutes was devoted to the activity, with some students only having 10 minutes to work on the task due to delays in grouping. There were some problems experienced by students communicating through Adobe Connect during the group activity, particularly in coordinating their work. Specifically, there were difficulties experienced by some students with their partner moving to other images while they were still entering labels and in some cases this resulted in lost work. These problems did not seem to occur during the earlier activity where students worked in pairs with the student next to them, which suggests that coordinating group activity is difficult without the use of audio and body language.

There was not sufficient time for a report back by students following this task but the teacher quickly went through each group's images and provided some brief feedback and pointers, devoting 5 minutes to this.

Other technical difficulties experienced during the lesson included the teacher's computer crashing (perhaps due to the number of windows that needed to be open during the synchronous session) and a glitch in the setup of the breakout room that meant that text chat wasn't possible for one group.

At the conclusion of the lesson students completed a questionnaire and then participated in a focus group session.

Student Perceptions

Student reflections on the lesson were gathered through a questionnaire completed by 10 students present on campus and 3 students participating remotely. The 12 on-campus students participated in a focus group interview following the lesson. All remote students participated in a focus group interview two weeks later when they were on campus for a residential school. The focus group interviews provided an opportunity for a general discussion about the strategies used in the lesson.

Table 6 reports on whether students agreed or disagreed with eight of the survey questions about their experiences with the class activities.

Table 6: Summary of Case Study 3 student responses to key evaluation questions

Item	Face-to-face (n=10)			Remote (n=3)		
	Agree	Neutral	Disagree	Agree	Neutral	Disagree
I was able to communicate verbally in an effective manner with people in the face-to-face class	100.0	0.0	0.0	100.0	0.0	0.0
I was able to communicate verbally in an effective manner with people who participated remotely	90.0	0.0	10.0	50.0	50.0	0.0
In this lesson I was able to effectively share visual artefacts with others (e.g. images, photos, etc.)	100.0	0.0	0.0	100.0	0.0	0.0
In this lesson I was able to jointly create, edit, and share material with others in an effective manner	100.0	0.0	0.0	100.0	0.0	0.0
In this lesson I was able to effectively indicate my status to others (e.g. wanting attention, etc.)	100.0	0.0	0.0	100.0	0.0	0.0
In this lesson I felt like I was present with people who were participating remotely	90.0	0.0	10.0	100.0	0.0	0.0
In this lesson I felt like I was present with people who were in the same room as the teacher	100.0	0.0	0.0	100.0	0.0	0.0
The collaborative technology provided clear and accurate representation of information and people	80.0	20.0	0.0	100.0	0.0	0.0

Both face-to-face and remote students responded positively to all items and in fact responses were almost uniformly positive, with the overwhelming majority of students agreeing with all statements. The exceptions to this were one face-to-face and one remote student expressing some misgivings about their ability to effectively verbally communicate with other students who were also participating remotely; one face-to-face student not agreeing that they felt present with students who were remote and two face-to-face students indicating they were neutral about the ability of the technology to provided clear representations of information and people.

Comments from face-to-face students about the lesson as a whole suggested that the technology-supported strategies were very effective in engaging students:

> *This lesson is so much more engaging than your average lecture or tutorial. I find personally I'm more attentive, and the active participation components help the information to sink in more easily.*
>
> *The many communication forums in this format allow for better learning in that we can voice our individual concerns over material being presented for better clarification than in a normal lecture setting. The matter is presented in a more engaging and creative way, and I find this helps me to focus on the subject for longer periods of time.*

Some remote student comments are also helpful in understanding students' generally positive perceptions, for instance the following comment highlighting way in which the technology was able to bridge the gap between face-to-face and remote students:

> *It was really good to be able to participate in the class in real time and partake in activities inside a tute session. Although there are occasional hiccups, it's far more engaging as a DE student to be able to 'attend' class.*

Student responses to the questions shown in Table 1 suggest in general that the technology allowed them to undertake the communication requirements of the lesson effectively. For example 100% of face-to-face and remote respondents indicated that they were able to communicate verbally with face-to-face students and 90% of face-to-face and 50% of remote respondents indicated that they were able to communicate verbally with remote students. Student questionnaire responses indicated that verbal communication was supported by the teacher repeating questions from face-to-face students for the benefit of remote students and by the availability of the text chat tool to allow questions to be posed without interrupting. For example face-to-face students commented that "I could write my questions into the text box without having to directly ask the teacher or stop the flow of the class" and "the text chat box was helpful for communicating with offsite students". One face-to-face student contrasted the way in which they could ask questions using this tool to the opportunities within their conventional lectures:

> *It's a better way to ask questions as well, you know you take one of our normal lectures and if you have a question, there's usually so many people in that lecture theatre that you kind of have to wait until you go home and post it on the forum, and you have to wait another 3 days from the lecture for someone to answer it. So it's better to be able to ask her face-to-face and to type it in the chat box and have her go okay well this is what's been asked here.*

The lack of a microphone restricted verbal communication to text chat for the three remote students. One remote student commented that "sometimes it is much easier to speak rather than having to type everything", while another commented:

> *I don't have a microphone, so was not able to communicate verbally. This type of interaction would work so much better if each student had a microphone.*

The following questionnaire response from a remote student suggests that although the web conferencing system technically allows verbal communication between face-to-face and remote students, it does not mean the facility will be utilised, with students potentially opting to listen and interact in non-verbal ways.

> *It helps me see where I should be with my studies mostly by listening to where others are at and hearing Lucy's comments. I don't think I want to speak to other people because I feel it would crowd the experience but I like to have the interaction with teacher and class mates.*

The choice of appropriate communication mode is also a matter of context, as highlighted by one face to-face student who commented "I feel a bit weird chatting to somebody who's in the same room as me".

The 100% positive responses to the questionnaire items asking about visual sharing of artefacts and joint creation, editing and sharing of material suggests that the technology was effective in supporting the collaborative diagram annotation and note composition tasks. Some comments suggested that the technology made this activity easier than it would have been in a face-to-face environment without technology, for example "I was able to work with another student to label a diagram - which in person is a much more laborious task". As another student commented:

> *having the ability to label, write notes, and flick through the slides to gain an understanding of the content was so much easier using the technology because it didn't matter what your handwriting is like, or how long you take to write your part, and being able to look at the same material at the same time and edit it together is awesome.*

Nevertheless some aspects of this process were found to be somewhat cumbersome for students working in groups consisting of face-to-face and remote students, with one student commenting that "it was easier to do this with the people sitting next to us rather than online with offsite students". One reason for this appeared to be difficulty in collaborating without the ability to communicate using spoken audio, as evidenced by the following comments:

> *Only problem was the communication, and changing of slides by other students while others were writing on them. Again, if everyone had a microphone, at least they could make sure people were finished before they changed the slide.*

> *It was easy to do it with students within the class but there was still a bit of a barrier with distant students as we have to type everything and when trying to identify certain structures on the photo it was hard because you could not physically point to it.*

Students also pointed out that collaborative notes composition was difficult because if more than one person typed in the notes area the cursor would move about.

Questionnaire responses indicate that students felt that the technology provided a clear and accurate representation of people and information, provided mechanisms to indicate their status, and to some extent made the students feel that they were co-present with co-located and remote students. One student commented that "everyone feels comfortable in the chat room and it feels like they are in the room with us" although another student suggested that "making individual profiles for every user so other students whether DE or internal can get to know a little bit more about their peers" would improve the representation of people.

Student comments indicated that they were aware of the way in which the Adobe Connect software allowed them to request attention by raising their hand, although other comments suggested that many students chose to just use the text chat area for doing this. One student commented that the teacher did not always immediately notice their request for attention, which could mean their comment was not considered.

The role of the teacher in helping students to feel co-present with students in other locations was highlighted in the following comments:

> *As Lucy always asks the remote students to say where they are from to give us internal students the opportunity to get to know them :).*

> *Their input in text chat was quite valuable, and Lucy is very good at including remote students in her teaching.*

One face-to-face student suggested that they may have felt more co-present with remote students if the remote students had microphones and had been able to communicate using spoken audio:

> *Like I mean it's fine how it is now, but if you wanted that little bit more interaction, … verbalising it is going to come across better than if you just type it.*

Remote students were asked in the focus group interview whether participating in a lecture remotely is similar to participating face-to-face. The following responses suggest that they find it similar but not identical:

> *It's not too different to being … it's you can still ask questions it's like being in the class really as long as Lucy is watching the screen.*

Remote students were also asked how the experience of attending a remote lecture or tutorial differed to listening to a recording of the session. The following comments illustrate that there is an advantage to attending live but that nevertheless listening to the recordings is valuable.

> *When it's a recording you sort of just go oh yeah I think that's this and then you don't think much of it but then when you actually have to make a decision and say A, B, C or D I find that sort of works a lot better.*

> *And even watching those recordings afterwards where you've got time where everyone's thinking you think about it yourself and then you see the answer come up anyway so even the recordings of the tutes are good.*

Students appeared to be somewhat split on the question of whether there were advantages to having remote and face-to-face students participating in the one lesson, with one commenting that “it gave a broader range of views and ideas” and another that “more students = more ideas and more questions, different experiences, different knowledge base”, while one internal student suggested that they didn’t think they benefited from the involvement of remote students but that “I'm sure it would have helped external students”.

Despite the overall positive perceptions of students there were some suggestions for improvements, including having a microphone that captured on-campus student comments, more explanation of how to use the technology to complete unfamiliar tasks, and having the ability to see external students. Some students noted instances where there were temporary delays in commencing tasks, for instance due to time taken to allocate students to groups or because of the way their access privileges were set up, but also pointed out that these were quickly resolved. Some remote students also suggested that they experienced difficult with the reliability of the technology, but acknowledged that this may have been due to their personal technology setup or firewall issues rather than the system.

Students also made comments that related to the design and pedagogy of the lesson. They unanimously valued the interactivity of the question and answer polling activities, with some students indicating that the ability to respond anonymously meant they felt less intimidated. Students also appreciated how the polling activities enabled the teacher to gauge student understanding and be adaptive in her teaching.

> *She likes to sort of see where we’re at, what we need to know, what we don’t know; it also gives us an idea of what we need to study for as well.*

Students suggested that the collaborative labelling and note taking activities were also highly valuable. Notwithstanding the difficulties coordinating activity between students in different locations (raised above), they appreciated how their peers could help them to fill gaps in their knowledge, for instance as one student commented:

> *to get the other person’s perspective on something ... we had the slides and you might not know something on the slide but that other person does and then they tell you and you obviously can pick it up which I found really good.*

Students also appreciated the way in which the teacher adeptly and positively responded to student misconceptions:

> *I like how she can – how you can write something on it and then she will be like, that’s not right, but this is how it is. Like “I’ll show you where” say like “That’s not a blood vessel, this is where it actually is” so like she can show you, she can actually show you where things are.*

Students were asked whether they would like the approach used in the current class to be used in other subjects they studied. A total of 92.3% of students agreed with this, while only 7.7% of students indicated they were neutral about it. Positive comments about the potential for use of these strategies in other subjects included “it would make my university study much more engaging and effective if this was how all subjects were run”, and “it allows for a more active learning environment”. However there were counter opinions with one student commenting that "all my other classes are quite large and it probably wouldn't work so well with that many students" and another that "I still prefer the pen and paper, and to have my lecture notes on paper". Students were also asked whether they learnt "less", "the same", or "more" than if the lesson had run in a normal face-to-face mode. No students reported they learnt less, 15.4% of students reported they would have learnt the same (one face-to-face, one remote), while 84.6% of students indicated they learnt more.

A remote student summarised the benefit of blended synchronous learning in terms of expedience:

> *It's certainly much better just having Lucy as the dedicated resource for X amount of time cause I'm so much more inclined to whack my hand up and go listen yeah I need help with this I've got no idea what you're talking about whatsoever as opposed to drafting a 10 page email going what's going on here, don't get this, ... don't understand this cause sometimes it's hard to articulate what you don't know.*

Though another student pointed out that there were some aspects of learning that were not possible if attending remotely:

> *The other thing that I pick up a lot on when I'm here together with the other students is there's different study techniques and everything like there's so much more like I actually really noticed how people are writing stuff out for themselves or just all those kind of organisational skills as well because I'll go down my way of doing stuff and then it's not always the best idea ... I'm actually getting a lot just from observing how other people kind of work their material too.*

Transcending these sentiments, some student comments suggest that this sort of flexible participation using synchronous technology is becoming quite common, comfortable, and tantamount to 'being there', for instance:

> *We all communicate using the chat room and we are able to have a conversation with each other. It's not a difficult task to comprehend because we do this everyday over social media. Everyone feels comfortable in the chat room and it feels like they are in the room with us.*

Teacher Perceptions

In the pre-observation interview the teacher discussed her initial motivation for adopting blended teaching strategies. She explained that in the bulk of her teaching there were students enrolled on campus and in distance education mode in the one subject, and so the adoption of blended synchronous strategies provided a way to allow the distance students to have access to the lectures, and the ability to record the sessions meant that such students could either attend synchronously online or listen to recordings in their own time.

> *So it was a way for me to actually easily capture my lectures live without having to edit them, filter them, do anything.*

She also explained that because of the interactive opportunities afforded by the web conferencing tools she then began timetabling her on campus classes into computer laboratories so that both distance and on-campus students attending could engage interactively during the lessons. She noted the added benefits for internal students as a result of this.

> *All of this was originally designed to benefit distance students. That was my original thinking. I've been amazed at the benefit it's had for internal students to be honest. Not only in the flexibility it offers them, I mean, if they can't attend during the day... even just the interaction for the internal student's, being able to actively answer questions, even type in a text chat box, for the shy internal student that might not have raised their hand in class, I think has been really good.*

The teacher also explained the way that her approaches had evolved over time, particularly the increased use of tasks requiring students to participate, and her ability to adapt teaching based on student responses:

> *A lot more activities for the student's to complete ... quizzes, labelling, pictures, being more spontaneous I think probably with asking a question, or the student's asking a question of me and actually being able to quickly adapt a question or an activity around what might have been asked.*

The teacher also highlighted critical considerations when teaching in blended synchronous learning mode. Being well prepared was seen as essential:

> *I would say preparation is key. Making sure that you do have everything you need preloaded, well organised before the class starts. Making sure the students are prepared before the class as well, not just from the technology perspective, but that's important, so at the start of a session making sure you clearly announce to the student's that this is what your computer will need, this is what you'll need to be able to access this.*

Remembering that distance students were part of the class was deemed crucial, as was being able to quickly choose between courses of action. If there were large numbers of students in the class, the teacher felt a second teacher would be invaluable:

> *I think if you had huge numbers, then you would certainly need 2 academics in the room. One managing the questions coming from the remote student's, and one actually managing the class,...it's a completely different style again to giving a lecture. You're still giving a lecture, but you've got a lot of stuff going on in the background, that you either choose to ignore, or that you respond to.*

In reflecting on how the lesson went, the teacher was very positive. When asked what worked well in the class, she first of all commented on the question and answer part of the lesson as follows:

> *What worked well? I think – the first thing about the design really relates to the fact that the internal students who were present in the room, and the off campus students were all logged in through Connect, which I actually think increases the engagement for the internal student's as well. Being able to actively participate in answering multiple choice questions or answering the short answer questions by typing in their responses as opposed to having student's just sitting in a lecture theatre, where they just look at the one screen together.*

In relation to the group activity she commented:

> *I think – I was quite surprised, I had never used the breakout rooms before. It did take some time to pre-load and prepare for that session but I actually think on the whole that session worked really well in terms of setting up the expectations for the student's on the type of activity and then putting them in those breakout rooms.*

When asked what she would do differently, the teacher highlighted aspects of the process of moving between the breakout room group activity and the whole group report back and the need to manage the windows in Adobe Connect. She also commented on the inability of the remote students to use audio as something that constrained the group activity and the report back. The inability to record the breakout room activity was also noted as a limitation. The recording of sessions was noted as being of value both to students involved in the lesson who may want to go back and listen/watch the recording as part of future study as well as students unable to be present at that particular time.

In terms of improving the overall approach, the teacher indicated that she would like to work towards having the remote student experience be as good as if remote students were in the room.

Discussion

This lesson proceeded very smoothly. There was evidence of high engagement during the first part of the lesson, with students keen to get the correct answer to questions and so referring to their notes and other computer-based resources during the question and answer session. The second set of activities also proceeded smoothly with students generally quite engaged with the collaborative labelling task. There were minimal delays associated with grouping and regrouping of students between activities primarily due to the advance preparation of the breakout rooms, although grouping of remote and face-to-face students seemed to take longer.

Communication between co-located students was noticeably smoother than communication between remote students, with the absence of an audio channel apparently making it difficult to coordinate the labelling task for some groups (e.g. some students labelled an image and then had their labels overridden by their partner etc.). The use of audio (perhaps with remote students asked to setup and use a microphone and with headsets provided to on-campus students) would be one solution to promoting more effective collaboration between remote and face-to-face students. Alternatively there may be ways to structure activities like this differently to make it easier to coordinate the work through text chat (e.g. by allocating one group member to do the labelling with the other contributing ideas through text chat, to avoid the students interfering with each others' work).

Overall the lesson was an excellent example of blended synchronous teaching, in that face-to-face and remote students both experienced an engaging learning experience. Interactivity and engagement seemed to be promoted by the combination of the technology, the tasks and the teacher. The polling activities encouraged students to participate in a low-risk environment, and the use of breakout rooms to perform diagram labelling tasks and collaborative writing tasks enabled students to be more productive.

The teacher saw blended synchronous learning as a way to increase participation of all students (both face-to-face and remote). The tasks enabled the teacher to be adaptive and responsive in her pedagogical approach. The teacher's constructive way of attending to misconceptions added to the positive perceptions of the lesson. The inclusive environment that the teacher established by responding to remote students and treating them as individuals also appeared to contribute to students' sense of co-presence.

The technology setup constrained the ability for the whole class to communicate, with no room-based microphone to capture comments from the face-to-face classroom, and remote students who did not utilise microphones to contribute to discussions. However, some remote students did not feel the need to use audio to contribute, and saw advantages in being able to participate via text chat.

Students appreciated that blended synchronous learning enabled a broader range of views and ideas to be shared. Remote students were perceived to derive greatest gains from the approach through active synchronous participation and access to teacher. The success of the lesson was evidenced through the number of students who wanted this approach to be adopted in other subjects (over 90%) and the number of students who felt they learnt more using this approach (85%). There were indications that these sort of synchronous approaches are becoming more socially acceptable, comfortable and mainstream.

Summary of Findings

The following is a summary of the key issues and take-home messages emerging from this case, broken up into broad themes.

Learning design/pedagogy issues

- The teacher was able to effectively monitor the web conferencing stream while also responding to face-to face-students, although she pointed out that this can be challenging for large cohorts.
- A number of students commented on the value of the interactive and collaborative tasks (multiple choice question and responses, collaborative diagram labelling, collaborative composition).
- The polling tool provided a mechanism where all students could anonymously respond to questions from the teacher and receive feedback on their responses.
- The breakout room in Adobe Connect provided mechanisms for collaborative problems solving and sharing of ideas, however this was challenging for students in different locations if they weren't able to coordinate their activities using audio communication.
- Pairing face-to-face students together and remote students together appeared to be more effective than grouping face-to-face students with remote students because it took less time to allocate groups and face-to-face students were able to collaborate more naturally.

- The design of the tasks requiring student responses enabled the teacher to adapt their teaching to meet the needs of students.
- The positive environment that the teacher established through her encouraging, personal and constructive approach appeared to contribute to students' sense of engagement and inclusion.

Technology issues

- The use of the web conferencing technology by face-to-face students facilitated different types of engagement than would normally be expected in a face-to-face classroom, as well as allowing remote students to participate.
- The text chat stream provided a separate stream for students to communicate with each other or the teacher during lecture/presentation components although remote students tended to use this stream more than face-to-face students who tended to prefer conventional audio communication in this small class context.
- The absence of a room-based microphone meant that remote students were not able to hear the comments of face-to-face students and thus the teacher needed to relay them.
- Of the technology problems that occurred, some related to the reliability of the system (computer crashes, text chat not working properly in a breakout room) and others related to coordination of activity between distributed learners (for instance identifying points of focus during diagram labelling activities and nominating writers during collaborative authoring tasks).

Setup and logistic issues

- A substantial amount of teacher preparation (setting up polls and breakout room activities in advance and being fluent in the use of these tools) meant that the lesson was able to flow smoothly.

Chapter 9: Case Study 4 – Web Conferencing For Participation in Statistics Tutorials

Brief overview

This design used the Blackboard Collaborate web conferencing system to enable remote students to participate in introductory statistics tutorials. The teacher logged into the Collaborate session via her tablet computer so that she could write on the slides in the web conferencing environment. The screen was projected at the front of the face-to-face classroom so that students who were physically present could see the visual material as well as the list of participants who were attending remotely. The teacher then presented a series of slides that led students through the logic of hypothesis testing, annotating the slides to model problem-solving processes. The demonstration included how to select the correct statistical test from a decision chart, how to lookup *p*-values from a table of critical values, and how to run statistical tests using a spreadsheet package. The teacher regularly asked both face-to-face as well as remote students whether or not they understood or had any questions. She then provided time for students to solve problems of their own. Face-to-face students worked individually, in pairs, or in larger groups, and remote students worked in breakout rooms using text chat. The teacher sporadically repeated spoken conversation from the face-to-face classroom into the lectern microphone so that students at home could acquire a sense of the on-campus discussion. Although the face-to-face students did not have direct interaction with the remote students, the blended synchronous learning design appeared to support both cohorts to achieve the intended learning outcomes.

Institutional Context

Institution: Southern Cross University (SCU)

Teaching team: Nicola Jayne (Subject coordinator/lecturer)

Project team members involved: Barney Dalgarno, Jacqueline Kenney

Discipline: Statistics, Southern Cross Business School

Subject/unit: MAT10251: Statistical Analysis

Level of study: First year (undergraduate)
Intended learning outcome(s):

- The student can formulate null and alternative hypotheses;
- The student can test hypotheses about a single population mean or proportion;
- The student can interpret the p-value of a hypothesis test; and
- The student can write a full conclusion as to the results of the test, including the decision or the action recommended using ordinary (non-statistical) language.

Description of the Learning Activity/Tasks (Learning Design as Intended)

1. The first part of the two-hour lesson is a summary (students having already attended or reviewed the online lecture on the topic) by the teacher on the topic of hypothesis testing and the steps involved in undertaking the required statistical procedures (approximately 30 minutes). During this the teacher presents slides, documents, and shares the screen to demonstrate statistical processes in Excel. Students are shown one worked example and are invited to ask questions throughout the presentation.
2. Working with other students in a group, online and on-campus students construct full statistical solutions for tutorial problems involving hypothesis tests. Two sets of exercises are used involving formulation of hypotheses and writing full conclusions:
   a) Exercise Set 1. A large raw data set is given and students are required to use Excel/PhStat2. Either a p-value or a critical value approach can be used, with students required to obtain and use Excel/PhStat2 output to answer the question. The data used was gathered from students in the first tutorial to encourage student engagement and ownership of the data and questions. The data included measures of hours of paid employment by students in the previous week. This exercise set helps students practise or develop the skills required in their project.
   b) Exercise Set 2. Based on a small and/or summarised dataset students are required to utilise a critical value approach to solving the statistical problem, including, stating the decision rule and calculating the value of the test statistic using the test statistic formula provided on the formula pages. This enables students to practise or develop the skills required in the final exam where Excel is not available.

   After each set of exercises, there is a class discussion involving both online and on-campus students on the solution of each tutorial problem. Each exercise set and subsequent discussion is intended to take approximately 40 minutes.
3. The final activity involves a teacher-led summary of key learning from the two activities and its synthesis within overall unit learning (5 minutes).

Presage Factors

Technology and environment setup/configuration

The physical classroom contained two blocks of seating in rows facing the two screens on the front wall of the room (see Figure 21). The teacher plugged in their own tablet PC to the lectern at the front of the room in order to be able to write notes on slides using a tablet PC pen. The teacher also logged into Blackboard Collaborate as a student through a separate laptop computer positioned in a seated area to the side of the lectern so that she could use a headset to engage in private communication with remote groups during breakout activities. This also enabled her to appreciate the remote students' perspective of the class.

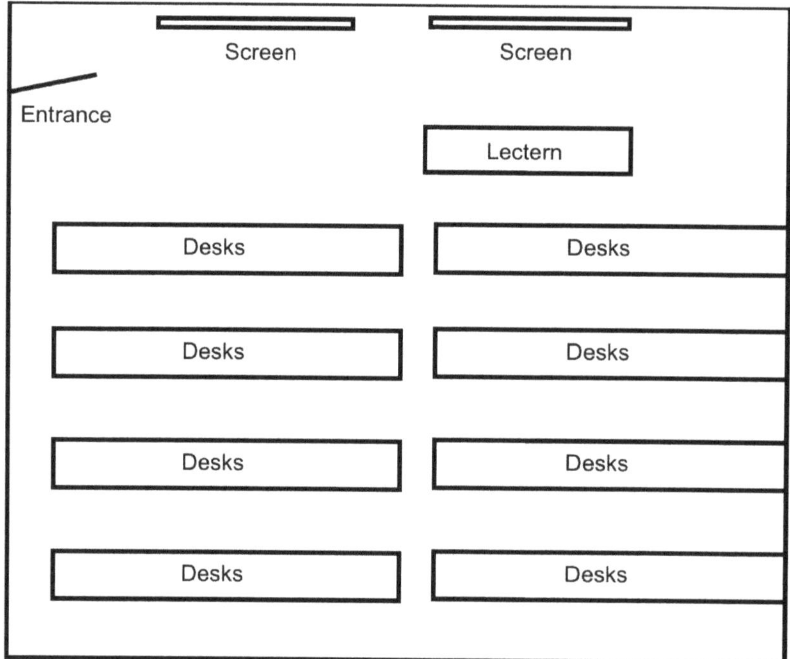

Figure 21: Case Study 4 room layout

Throughout the duration of the lesson the two large screens at the front of the room showed the web conferencing interface, which included the remote attendee names, the text chat panel, and the slides/screen-share panel. Students in the face-to-face classroom could see the typed contributions of remote students on the main screen yet did not log-in to Blackboard Collaborate to join the discussion with remote students or each other.

There were no audio or video feeds that enabled face-to-face students to interact directly with remote students other than via the teacher's microphone. This was to prevent audio feedback loops interrupting class interactions. Remote students could sometimes hear face-to-face student comments directly through the teacher's microphone feed, but where necessary when the teacher repeated them through the microphone. The speaker port of the teacher's machine was plugged into the lectern so remote student audio could be heard by the face-to-face students (this was not used in the observed lesson).

Face-to-face students did use their own computers to login to the Blackboard Learning Management System to download resources such as Excel data files for Exercise Set 1, but did not log in to Collaborate. The face-to-face classroom is shown in Figure 22 below. The remote student view is shown in Figure 23.

Resources

- PowerPoint slides that the teacher presented through BlackBoard Collaborate that were visible to face-to-face students on a projector and to remote students via an Internet connection to the virtual classroom.
- Six Blackboard Collaborate breakout rooms were designed prior to the class, containing problems for students to solve during the active learning section of the lesson (one for each of the three phases of the two exercise sets).

- A pre-prepared Microsoft Excel spreadsheet and a plug-in (PhStat) were used by the teacher to show t-test calculations (shared with remote students via Blackboard Collaborate screen sharing).

Figure 22: Case Study 4 face-to-face room setup

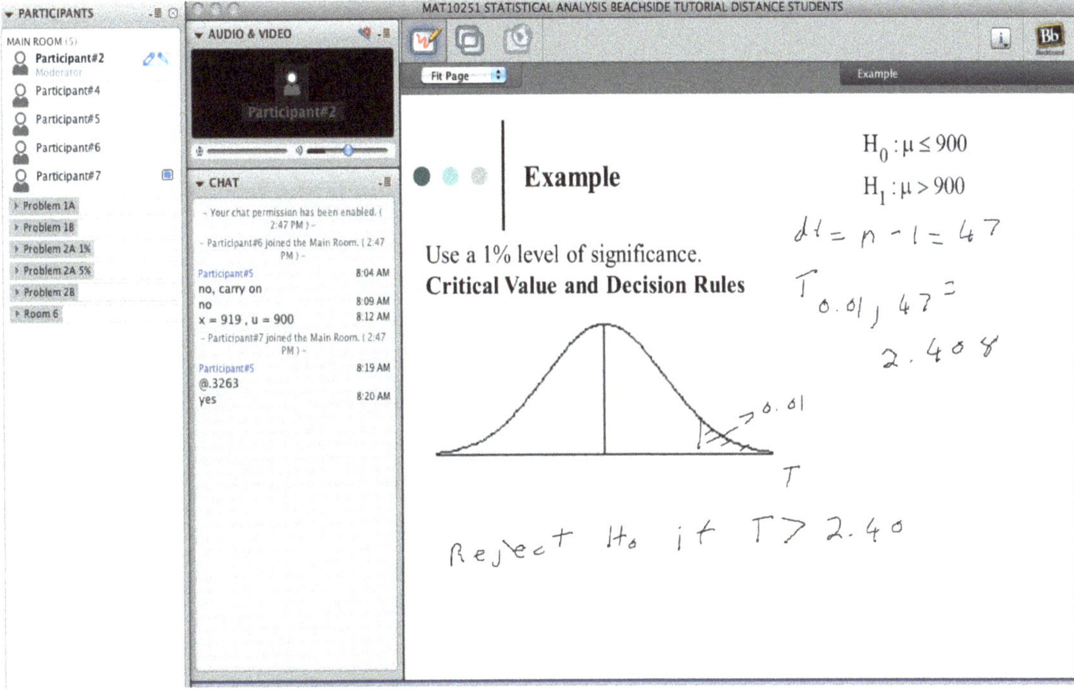

Figure 23: Case Study 4 remote student view

Support for staff

Teachers have access to a Blackboard support site that contains links to information on Blackboard Collaborate. Staff also have access to weekly training and support sessions for Blackboard Collaborate. Training sessions are also offered when there are major upgrades to Blackboard Collaborate. During live classes teachers may contact IT support at the Lismore campus for telephone support. The teacher had taught several iterations of the unit using web conferencing and so did not require access to any of this support.

Support for students

Students had already been exposed to the technology and teaching methods used in this class during earlier lecture and tutorial sessions, and the teacher assumes primary responsibility for garnering students with the necessary technical skills they will require to use BlackBoard Collaborate. Students may also have acquired technical and subject matter skills through the University's Peer Assisted Study Sessions (PASS) program. All students in Statistical Analysis are invited to attend PASS sessions, where a trained second or third year PASS leader holds weekly Blackboard Collaborate sessions to facilitate discussion of unit content.

Assessment

The tutorial session did not include any assessment task. However the session activities allowed students to practise the techniques of hypothesis testing for single means and proportions that directly aligned with the three assessment tasks undertaken throughout the semester (online test questions that could be in multiple choice or numeric calculations, part of the project assessment task, and the final examination).

Project team's input into the learning design

The project team discussed aspects of the lesson design with the teacher and the utility of two adjustments that would both serve to enhance student-to-student interaction. The first adjustment entailed a recommendation to design a statistical problem where students need to select between two different methods (T-test or Z-test). This was to encourage class discussion of the rationale for selecting the appropriate statistical method. The second adjustment that was discussed with the teacher would ensure that more than one group worked to solve each problem. This aimed to establish more common ground for discussion between students so that they could hold more nuanced discussion about the problem solving strategies they adopted.

Both of these recommendations were adopted by the teacher.

Class Size and Location/Distribution of Participants

There were 14 students who attended the first workshop, of which two were remote students. There were 31 students who attended a second workshop, however, none of these students were remote so observations and questionnaire and focus group data collected during this workshop were not included in the analysis.

The Lesson as Enacted

Students entered the classroom and chose their own seating. The teacher was already logged in to the Blackboard Collaborate web conferencing system and was prepared to commence.

The lesson began with an introduction and summary of the workshop agenda. Students were invited to ask any outstanding questions that had arisen from the lecture in the previous week on Hypothesis Testing and to answer the question, "what do you want to get out of this tutorial?" During the teacher's response to student questions the teacher welcomed the remote students and ran an audio check as she proceeded to give an overview of critical questions and processes to be covered in the tutorial activities and their relationship to the assessment task that was due the following week. As other remote and face-to-face students entered the classroom they were also welcomed to the class to acknowledge their arrival in the blended environment. The teacher also invited a remote student to post a 'smiley face' to indicate that they could hear. At the end of the introduction to the lesson the teacher asked the class and remote student if they had any further questions. The question directed to the remote student addressed them by name.

The teacher led the topic overview by running through a worked solution to an example problem. The solution to this problem consisted of a set of 'steps' for analysis that were presented on a PowerPoint slide. For each of the steps and based on that problem scenario students voluntarily identified key information. The teacher also directly prompted students at various points to drive discussion in additional areas. In the overview the teacher encouraged students to identify the relevant statistical test (population mean or population proportion) and other statistical elements that were essential to calculations, for instance nominating pieces of information such as the random variable, sample size, and sample mean. The teacher also made an effort to monitor the text chat and respond to remote students during her presentation.

Students volunteered answers, posed additional questions, and sought clarification as the activity continued with each step. They also began referring to formula tables and making calculations. At the request of students, the lecturer moved between earlier and later slides, calculation tables and wrote calculation details onto the slides via the tablet device. The lecturer used application sharing to show calculations for t-tests using a pre-prepared spreadsheet and an Excel add-in, PhStat. One remote student used text chat to indicate the audibility of the sound, typing "just", in response to being asked if they had heard an on-campus student comment. Accordingly, the lecturer repeated the material.

Once the solution to the example problem scenario had been discussed and the calculation procedures demonstrated, the face-to-face students divided themselves into to groups. The two remote students were assigned to a 'breakout room', which provided them with space to interact in writing and if they had audio capabilities on their computers would have allowed them to communicate using audio. As co-located students began to work in self-nominated groups on the first exercise the lecturer made use of the computer and headset to the side of the lectern to resolve an access problem to the breakout room that was being experienced by the remote students. One remote student changed computers to resolve the problem and another continued to experience problems accessing the slides potentially due to the use of an iPad. Neither remote student had time to solve the first problem prior to the timer being sounded to indicate the end of the allocated time for the activity. At this point the remote students were brought back into the main class area in Collaborate.

The lecturer ran through solutions to the first problem, showing pre-prepared slides on which she made calculation annotations using the tablet device. PDF viewer and Excel were used to present data that supported the verbal explanations of calculations and the procedures used to solve aspects of the set problem. The two remote students used text chat to discuss questions and answers together and the students interacted with the teacher and each other in discussing developed solutions.

The students were directed to complete the second activity in the same groups as the previous activity. The teacher, again, used the laptop and audio headset to settle the remote students into the breakout rooms and ensure that there were no access issues with the work areas, resources, and tool functions. The teacher moved from group to group in the physical classroom to answer questions and to provide support during the second activity before reviewing the answers in a similar fashion to the first activity.

The lesson was concluded with a teacher review of the procedures undertaken and the relevance of the steps given in the lesson to developing statistical solutions and accurately reporting of outcomes. At the end of the lesson students were asked to reflect on what they had learned and to review the solutions again once the solutions were loaded onto the Learning Management System.

Student Perceptions

Remote and face-to-face students completed the questionnaire and focus groups at the conclusion of the two observed lessons. The results from the first class are reported on as this class included both face-to-face and remotely located students, whereas, as stated previously, the second observed class had no remote students in attendance.

In the blended class there were a total of 13 survey respondent (n=13) with a higher number of face-to-face respondents (n=11, 84.6%) than remote respondents (n=2, 15.4%). Only one face-to-face student chose not to answer the survey. Table 1 reports on the extent to which students agreed or disagreed with each statement relative to their experience of the observed lesson.

The data included a small sample size overall and for remote and co-located student groups. There was little consensus about the experience of the lesson across the two groups. However there was some consensus within the group of face-to-face students and within the group of remote students in their responses to certain items. Specifically, face-to-face students unanimously agreed about their ability to effectively verbally communicate to co-located peers, as well as the clarity and accuracy of the web conferencing tool in representing information and people. The two remote students concurred on their neutrality towards the effectiveness of verbal communications with remote participants and creating, editing, and sharing materials, as well as the ineffectiveness of artefact sharing.

Table 7: Summary of Case Study 4 student responses to key evaluation questions

Item	Face-to-face (n=11)			Remote (n=2)		
	Agree	Neutral	Disagree	Agree	Neutral	Disagree
I was able to communicate verbally in an effective manner with people in the face-to-face class	100.0	0.0	0.0	0.0	50.0	50.0
I was able to communicate verbally in an effective manner with people who participated remotely	36.4	18.2	45.5	0.0	100.0	0.0
In this lesson I was able to effectively share visual artefacts with others (e.g. images, photos, etc.)	33.3	22.2	44.4	0.0	0.0	100.0
In this lesson I was able to jointly create, edit, and share material with others in an effective manner	50.0	30.0	20.0	0.0	100.0	0.0
In this lesson I was able to effectively indicate my status to others (e.g. wanting attention, etc.)	80.0	20.0	0.0	50.0	0.0	50.0
In this lesson I felt like I was present with people who were participating remotely	40.0	10.0	50.0	0.0	50.0	50.0
In this lesson I felt like I was present with people who were in the same room as the teacher	88.9	11.1	0.0	50.0	0.0	50.0
The collaborative technology provided clear and accurate representation of information and people	100.0	0.0	0.0	50.0	50.0	0.0

The lack of consensus in response categories on items across the remote and face-to-face groups may be indicative of the intended purposes of the lesson design itself. The design employed web conferencing to achieve specific aims, such as teacher instruction, collaborative activity, student-to-class participation, and student directed questions and answers. Conversely, the lesson did not include specific phases where face-to-face students needed to log in to the web conferencing system and collaborate with remote students. Rather, the blended learning setting was designed with teacher-facilitated student interaction as the goal, as opposed to cultivating direct student-student interactions between those attending in person and remotely. This potentially explains "disagree" responses to some items.

Correspondingly, survey data reflects strong agreement on peer interaction among and between face-to-face participants and neutral to negative perceptions regarding effective communications with remote participants (items one and two above) and, equally, agreement relating to the sharing of artefacts and the creating, editing, and sharing of materials as an embedded component of the lesson design only for remote students. Here, co-located students did not make use of laptops and other devices to enable direct sharing of artefacts with other students and they did not participate in breakout room activities necessitating the use of creating, editing, and sharing materials (items three and four).

In reviewing the results for remote students it is noted that problems were experienced during this class with access to the breakout activities. As the survey questions sought feedback solely on the lesson observed in isolation of other lessons in the unit where the same activity may have been used without technical problems, all survey items except six and seven appear to have been negatively affected. Item five, the ability to indicate status, shows one agree and one disagree response. The latter may have arisen from the one remote student who had difficulty communicating with the teacher and eventually attempted access using a different computer.

The fact that face-to-face students and remote students did not communicate directly with one another meant they had a limited sense of co-presence with one another:

> *I only notice the online students when the teacher is communicating with them* (face-to-face student)
>
> *the microphone in the room was not picking up the on-campus students' voices very well which did contribute to a sense of not quite participating with the on-campus students* (remote student)

Yet the collaborative group work within the physical classroom meant that face-to-face students could experience a strong sense of co-presence with their co-located peers:

> *I felt present as everyone in the class has the same purpose of being here, do exercises and understand them in a workable and calm environment* (face-to-face student)

And remote students could derive a sense of co-presence with and through the teacher:

> *Teacher kept her concentration on my messages and responded, also made me aware of others in the room* (remote student)

Several students commented positively on the competence of this teacher in facilitating the blended class using technology. Understanding how to use the web conferencing tool in a seamless manner that did not interrupt student activity and facilitating between face-to-face and remote students were key to a positive student experience, as one student says:

> *She has a lot of things going on during the class and she knows what she's doing. So then no time is wasted and you can help people online and they ask questions and she repeats the question for us, and the question's answer for us, and sometimes it is useful for us and for them*

This skill meant that both remote and face-to-face students were able to have a positive learning experience, even though they did not have an extensive sense of co-presence with one another:

> *Letting the external students participate is a good idea, and I felt learning was not hindered in any way* (face-to-face student)
>
> *Yes, I was able to go through the exercises at home in much the same fashion as I did when attending the on-campus tutorial later* (remote student)

The value of the active learning approaches that the teacher adopted were also recognised by students:

> *My other classes don't allow the amount of learning that this class does. We mainly listen to the teacher talk where as we are applying our knowledge in this class.* (face-to-face student)

However some face-to-face students expressed the view that the blended synchronous learning mode may have reduced the amount of teacher time they received:

> *If the teacher wasn't attending to the online students we would have more opportunities to engage with them about the tutorial problems*
>
> *I only find it annoying if the teacher has to repeat questions asked by the face-to-face students so the online students can hear*

However students did see some advantages of blended synchronous learning mode, in terms of accessibility and the variety of perspectives that could be shared:

> *its good if you need to miss a class or cant get to the uni because you can attend online* (face-to-face student)
>
> *They asked a lot of questions others in class may not ask* (face-to-face student)

One student pointed out that the extent of interactions may have been constrained by the nature of the discipline:

> *this is math based, so it's not like you're going to express your ideas, it's either you're right or wrong, it's just the number is the answer kind of thing. Whereas in other classes you could have a general... discussion*

Several face-to-face students commented on the benefits of having remote student participation opportunities for equality of access, external study modes, and flexible study with young children in the home:

> *The lessons are great I'm an internal student and was unable to attend a tutorial one day as my kids were sick so I did it online whilst I was minding my kids in the comfort of my home.*

In terms of advice for people teaching in blended synchronous learning mode, students suggested that teachers should continually check that everyone is up to the same point, balance attention between remote and face-to-face students, try as far as possible to make it feel like one classroom, use a microphone that can pick up face-to-face student comments, and have a competent understanding of the technology before teaching with it.

Teacher Perceptions

The teacher had adopted a blended synchronous learning approach since 2008-2009 for both lectures and tutorials in order to transcend the problems of static, asynchronous delivery. The approach was also seen to suit the technological nature of the processes that students were being taught.

The initial problem was that students did not feel confident just following the written instructions on using Excel that were in the textbook and study guide. There was a proportion of students who possibly because of their learning style, they needed to be shown. And also the advantage of the [web conferencing system] meant that they could follow on using the machine that they were doing their assignment project on, so they could actually follow during the session

The teacher considered that the design of the lesson from the student perspective is vital to developing quality learning outcomes. The classes are designed with consideration for the knowledge, skills and techniques students will acquire as well as the way in which students will experience the lesson:

thinking very carefully about what you want the student's to experience, or get out of this tutorial ... this sort of unit, which is really developing techniques, developing skills, being well prepared, ... leads to better outcomes

Lesson planning and delivery were seen to require an awareness of the different needs of face-to-face and remote students during blended class sessions. For example, "giving the online students just one or two cues about what's happening in the class because despite being able to hear what is going on in the classroom they are not able to see". More generally, the teacher noted the need for preparation time to develop activities for use in blended learning:

Really what I'm trying to do here is increase the active learning of students ... you've got to be more prepared, more organised ... students are given these tutorial exercises to work through them and we'll discuss it. This way I'm choosing selected tutorial questions to bring out the main points

The teacher observed that the use of the breakout rooms is somewhat reliant on student experience with using web conferencing tools, such as audio features. Where this experience is lacking, as it was during the observed lesson, additional support was required:

online breakout room didn't work, because the 2 students who were there didn't seem to have mikes and didn't seem to have – they were getting things organised, they were 2 students who hadn't attended online previously

The lower than expected number of students who attended the lesson remotely was seen to compromise the quality of the remote group work experience. Interestingly, while the teacher felt that there were technical problems with the breakout rooms, remote student survey respondents indicated that there were no technical problems during the lesson. The teacher indicated three strategies for teaching in a blended setting: spending time with students as they work in groups on activities in both the physical and remote classrooms, repeating questions to ensure distance students could hear class contributions and, in general, making efforts to incorporate the distance students in the class:

trying to incorporate the distance student's within the face-to-face classroom, just being aware of both groups of students. ... having things set up I think is the heart of it, as long as the technology works it I think it happens fairly seamlessly, and managing multiple breakout rooms. ... And when students are working in groups, being aware of those online as well as those within the classroom, and having to sort of make sure I spend time with those, within the breakout room, as well as the ones within the class, walking around answering questions.

The teacher reported that the lesson design might be improved to increase interaction. Current interaction levels tended to be driven by the lecturer because there is no audio support to facilitate direct communication between face-to-face and remote students. The teacher indicated that this could be solved at an institutional level:

even though we're in a brand new building, the fact that I've actually got to bring a mike and things to make it feasible, it would be nice, even though the room has the mike out, it doesn't have the mike [in], so I had to bring that mike.

The teacher felt that increased student-student interaction across the two groups would allow the negotiation and resolution of how answers are achieved without teacher support:

I haven't mixed those [face-to-face and remote] groups, and when they're presenting solutions, discussion solutions between remote and on-campus students ... then it can be fairly free but it's more, I sort of orchestrate that, in so much as, I ask questions of say the online student's, what results did you get, then do other student's agree or the other way around. So that's sort of a controlled interaction between the groups, but there is ... interaction ... and some discussion.

The teacher's perception of the interactions in the class indicated that the technology in some instances interferes with learning insofar as interactions in the blended setting required the repetition of ideas during moderation to allow both groups of students to hear what the other group had to say. The teacher also noted that facilitation was more challenging where the class had very large groups of students or a single student participation in completing activities online. The challenge of size was posed as it impacted the extent of facilitation required, and therefore, an increased demand on teacher time.

The teacher also noted the importance of being adaptive depending on the context and cohort, for instance that her third class was quite boisterous which meant she did not need to encourage discussion in the same way as her other two classes.

Discussion

The methods the teacher used elicited interaction among face-to-face students and among remote students in a blended setting through activity-related participation. The methods included a high-level of organisation and preparation for activities and the facilitation of discussion centred on core unit concepts that enabled both face-to-face and remote students to feel as though they were learning from the class with little emphasis on the technology in the process.

Remote students were able to participate in the lesson by posing questions and providing answers within the class discussion, as well as interact with each other via text chat in breakout rooms. Text responses from remote students were visible on the front screen, and the teacher would directly relay these points raised and answer text-based questions within her discussion. Remote students were able to respond to teacher prompting more easily than face-to-face students during the guided demonstration because they could just type text chat (as opposed to putting up their hand and interrupting the flow of the teacher narrative).

The way in which the web conferencing system was used enhanced the learning of both face-to-face and remote students. Using a tablet PC with Collaborate enabled the teacher to 'write' notes onto the slides to show working during problem solving that supplemented pre-prepared material. As well, the activities could be completed by remote students in real-time with the class and involved the same level of teacher interaction with the remote groups as those in the class. The one exception to this was the need to resolve a technical problem with a remote student. The use of application sharing during the session contributed to student learning by 'showing' how and when supplementary materials were to be used during learning tasks. Finally, the recording of the tutorial session allowed students to re-visit the workshop as they prepared critical assessment tasks requiring the application of similar statistical techniques.

Both remote and face-to-face students indicated that they had a satisfying learning experience, even though the two cohorts did not directly interact. Student and teacher feedback indicated that interaction during the tutorial might be facilitated by the use of face-to-face student use of Collaborate to enable text chat and also direct audio discussion. As raised by the teacher an improved built-in microphone system could allow direct audio discussion between face-to-face and remote students.

The available tools could potentially allow face-to-face students and remote students to engage in blended groups during class activities in breakout groups. However, the change would require the use of headsets by individual face-to-face students during the class if discussion as well as text interactions were sought during group interactions. The teacher proposed that such a solution might be best attempted using text chat to avoid the use of a 'sound problem' arising from surround noise in the classroom arising from the use of multiple headsets and disruptive audio feedback.

The learning design appeared to successfully achieve the desired class objectives. There was no obvious variation from the planned lesson, aside from addressing the emergent student questions and small technology queries that arose. The observed class and both teacher and student feedback and survey results provide ample support to claim that the lesson design for this blended learning class offer a high-level of flexibility in terms of meeting diverse student needs (structure), accommodating variably located students class-to-class (organisation), and face-to-face and remote student and student-teacher interaction opportunities (engagement and learning support). The teacher exhibited great skill in using the technology to present slides, provide live working, share applications, demonstrate discipline specific technological processes in Excel, and simultaneously cater to both remote and face-to-face students.

Summary of Findings

The following is a summary of the key issues and take-home messages emerging from this case, broken up into broad themes.

Learning design/pedagogy issues

- The learning design using web conferencing tools was developed to ensure that both remote and face-to-face students were able to contribute to the class spontaneously with questions, in response to set group activities, and during class discussion.
- The learning design accommodated the needs of remote and face-to-face students to enable full participation in class and group activities even though the remote and face-to-face students did not directly interact with one another.
- The visual modalities of communication through slide annotations and screen-sharing enabled clear representation of the concepts and processes.
- The fluency of the teacher with operating the technology and catering to remote students meant that face-to-face students generally did not perceive that synchronously blending remote students into the class interfered with the quality of learning in the lesson.
- The adaptability of the teacher and the active learning approaches that she used contributed to the positive student experience.

Technology issues

- No technology issues were experienced by face-to-face students because the teacher was performing all of the in-class technology operation.
- One remote student experienced difficulty operating the breakout rooms but the problem was quickly remedied with teacher assistance.
- The use of the tablet PC pen to write notes directly onto slides was highly successful in drawing attention to the points being made by the teacher as these enlivened existing teaching materials within the context of class participation.
- An audio-conferencing system in the classroom would have enabled the two cohorts of students to communicate directly with one another without the teacher needing to bring her own equipment and relay comments in class.

Setup and logistic issues

- Logging into a second computer enabled the teacher to privately liaise with the remote students and appreciate their view of the lesson.

Chapter 10: Case Study 5 – Virtual Worlds to Facilitate Chinese Language Learning

Brief Overview

In this lesson students participate in a tightly constructed virtual world role-play activity in Second Life. The activity is based on themes that appear in their main textbook and aimed at developing their Mandarin language communicative capabilities. Students could either choose to participate in on-campus computer laboratories or from external locations. At the time of the tutorial students logged in to the virtual world and were allocated into groups of two by the teacher, who was both in the physical classroom and in-world. The objective of the lesson was for students to make a bowl of soup dumplings in the kitchen of the virtual world restaurant. This required them to utilize a range of previously learned vocabulary, phrases and sentence patters to ask the non-player character (NPC) hostess of the restaurant about what ingredients they needed, where they could buy the ingredients, and how to get there. They then had to follow those directions and go to a traditional farmers' market and buy the ingredients from another NPC selling fruit, vegetables and meat. Finally they had to take the ingredients back to the kitchen of the restaurant and cook them on one of the stoves. Remote students were paired with face-to-face students. Students could communicate with each other via voice and text and with the NPCs via Chinese character text chat. Communication between students occurred mainly in English. Because the task and environment were so extensively designed the teacher did not need to provide much in-class instruction, and instead helped individuals in the on-campus computer lab. While initially communication between some pairs was slow to take off, through subsequent close collaboration most pairs were able to obtain the information they needed through conversing with the NPCs and navigate the environment to complete the various stages of the set task and finally make the bowl of soup dumplings.

Institutional Context

Institution: Monash University

Teaching team: Scott Grant (Subject coordinator/lecturer), Zhihua Yao and Zhiqun Chen (Tutors)

Project team members involved: Mark Lee, Barney Dalgarno, Jacqueline Kenney
Discipline: Arts

Subject/unit: Chinese Introductory 1

Level of study: First year (undergraduate)

Intended learning outcome(s):

- The student can write the correct Mandarin language in order to ask about ingredients in a traditional dish and for directions to a market where they purchase the ingredients.

- The student can follow basic directions and cooking instructions in Mandarin so as to make a bowl of soup dumplings.
- The student can collaborate in pairs in order to achieve the intended learning outcomes.

Description of the Learning Activity/Tasks (Learning Design as Intended)

1. In the first five to ten minutes of the lesson the teacher introduces the task to face-to-face students in the room, and also by speaking into an audio-headset for remote students in the virtual world. The task has also been outlined on the Learning Management System associated with the unit.
2. The teacher allocates students to pairs in the virtual world, with remote students being paired with face-to-face students in the computer laboratory (approximately 5-10 minutes).
3. The teacher lets students proceed with the task in their pairs, circulating amongst the physical classroom to offer face-to-face student support, as well as circulating within the virtual world to monitor remote student progress (90 minutes). The task that the students need to complete in this time is as follows:
   a) find out from the Non Player Character (NPC) waitress in restaurant (Jingjing) what two (2) ingredients are needed to make (**做**) Chinese dumplings, through instant messaging using Chinese characters;
   b) find out from waitress in restaurant (Jingjing) where to purchase the ingredients needed to make Chinese dumplings and how to get there;
   c) go and purchase the ingredients needed to make Chinese dumplings (talking to the NPC man selling the ingredients by using instant messaging with Chinese characters); and
   d) return to the restaurant kitchen and follow the instructions to make Chinese dumplings with the ingredients.

Presage Factors

Technology and environment setup/configuration

Chinese Island is a virtual world environment constructed in Second Life that is used in four units at Monash University, including the unit under investigation (Chinese Introductory 1). Mainland Chinese architecture and features are incorporated in order to provide an environment where students can practice and develop their Chinese language skills. The teacher had designed 'scripted' virtual robots (Non-Player Characters) in the virtual world with which students could interact. Where students gave linguistically correct requests the NPC responded by giving the information the student required to complete a set task. If students provided incorrect requests the NPC indicating that the request was not understood and required adjustment prior to instructions and information being provided.

The face-to-face classroom was set up with four small clusters of hexagonal computer tables in pods that seated six students each (see Figure 24). There were a number of computers on the rear and sides of the room on a single bench however, these were not occupied during the classes. The teacher's work area at the front left-side of the classroom had the teacher's laptop and also had a desktop computer that was projected onto the screen for students to see displayed material (desk area, top left of Figure 24).

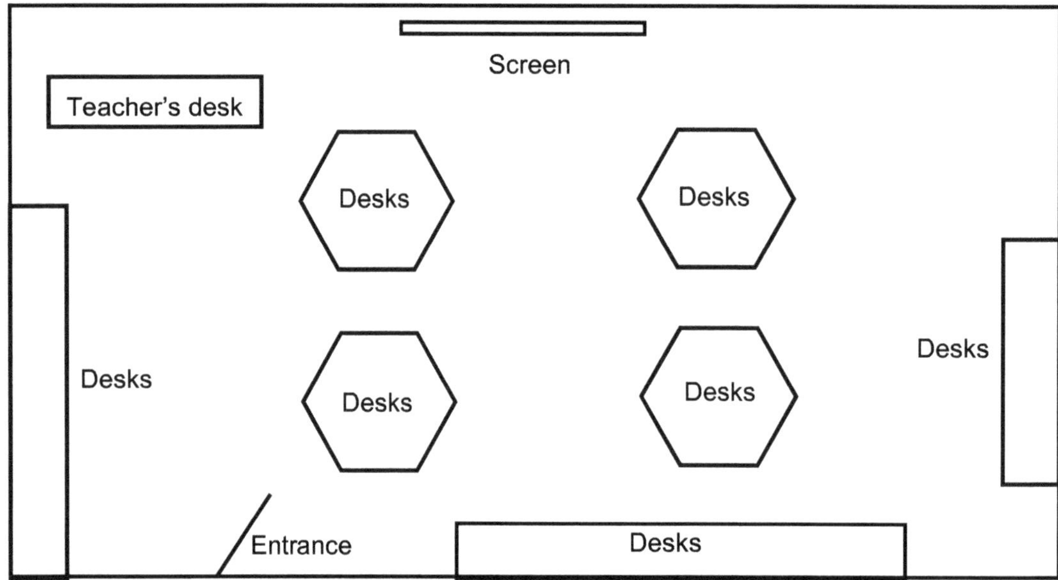

Figure 24: Case Study 5 room layout

Students in the face-to-face classroom and also the remote classroom used avatars, headsets and microphones to communicate with their partner to complete the task as well as text chat. Students had previously designed their own avatars to represent themselves in world. The face-to-face classroom is shown in Figure 25. A student view of the virtual world is shown in Figure 26.

Resources

- The Chinese Island virtual world containing two programmed Non-Player characters – a restaurant host who provided directions to the market and the ingredients that needed to be bought, and a market vendor from whom students bought the ingredients.
- Pre-prepared instructions available in the Learning Management System that included:
  - the lesson plan, lesson objectives, task details and an SLURL link for the lesson;
  - a brief explanation of how cultural content of the lesson is relevant to students' studies; and
  - a video that introduces the cultural topic in more detail including a brief historical overview.

Figure 25: Case Study 5 face-to-face room setup

Figure 26: Case Study 5 view of virtual world

- Learning support resources were also available in the Learning Management System, including:
  - links and references to the textbook to aid students during the in-world phase of the lesson; and
  - a list of new words that occur in the conversations with the non-player characters (NPCs) with some direct and some indirect explanations.
- Students drew upon self-selected external tools, such as Google Translate.
- A brief quiz on the content covered in the lesson was available for use after the class in order for students to self-test knowledge that was intended to be learned during the lesson.
- To design the environment the teacher drew on a number of technical resources, including, Artificial Intelligence Markup Language (AIML), libOpenMetaverse for running NPCs, the Linden Scripting Language used in Second Life, resources relating to the Second Life 3D online Multiuser Virtual Environment (MUVE), and Chinese Character input software.

Support for staff

Technical work to set up, run and support Chinese Island was undertaken by the teacher. The teacher conceived and developed the virtual learning environment over several years. Initially, to allow the use of Second Life in the School of Literature, Languages, Culture and Linguistics, an application for funding to buy 30 graphics cards was successfully made. Subsequent to this the computers were replaced with computers that have inbuilt graphics capabilities. The teacher has also sought and obtained funding to create virtual infrastructure in Chinese Island, such as roads and buildings, develop scripts to produce visual displays in Chinese Island; and, program the dialogue of NPC for student interactions. There was no training available from Monash University for the use of Second Life and Chinese Island and all support and training for students and staff is provided by the lecturer. The University provides Moodle training for staff.

Support for students

For this lesson students were provided with a link to an introductory video and an explanation of the historical relevance of cultural elements so that they could relate the lesson to prior learning. Ongoing feedback was provided to students in world through their conversations with NPCs and additional activity support was available from visual displays of information (banners) and interactive elements (artefacts) in Chinese Island.
Remote students located in the second on-campus location and at home as well as the face-to-face students located in the main classroom received assistance from the teacher. Students could individually or in pairs invite support from the teacher on an as-needs basis. Students in the face-to-face classroom drew on teacher support for themselves and their partner as required. This included during their efforts to communicate in Chinese in written and oral forms, individual interactions with in-world characters in written Chinese, and peer-to-peer discussion inside and outside the virtual world to negotiate both language learning and virtual world actions. When face-to-face students engaged teacher assistance this information was relayed to their partner via audio and text chat. Such support helped to

refine student selections of Chinese language.

Assessment

Attendance in this lesson contributes to the overall requirements for this class. There was no summative assessment associated with this activity. Formative assessment was provided through the use of a set of multiple-choice questions to test expected student learning during the tutorial activity, with the knowledge formally assessed during later summative assessment tasks. For example, items from Chinese Island lessons are included in mid-semester and end-of-semester examinations.

Project team's input into the learning design

Input from the research project team led to direct pairing between face-to-face and remote students during activities. Where in past lessons face-to-face and remote students worked together to complete activities, the current design placed students in a pair based on their physical location. The suggested pairing arrangement was designed to promote interaction between face-to-face and remote students.

Class Size and Location/Distribution of Participants

The two observed classes had a total of 21 students attending, one remote student located off campus, eight students located in a remote on-campus classroom, and 12 students attending from the classroom. The first class had a total of eight students attending, four students attended face-to-face and four attended remotely from a separate location on campus. The second class had a total of 13 students: eight students in the face-to-face classroom, four students attending remotely from a separate location on campus, and one student attending remotely from off-campus.

The Lesson as Enacted

At the commencement of the lesson students logged into the Learning Management System and Second Life and began following the task instructions on the Learning Management System. Immediately students began interacting with peers while they were being allocated into pairs and as they initiated audio and text channels of communication. Several minutes were required at the beginning of the lesson to allocate students to groups and for them to orient themselves towards understanding and starting the task. From the commencement of the lesson to its end, the teacher facilitated the task rather than directed activities and continued to circulate the room to provide support to students on a needs basis.

The designed activity in Chinese Island required students to multi-task between following instructions in the Learning Management System, engaging with their partner, and referring to support materials that were online and textbooks. Students in the face-to-face classroom showed each other screens with avatar designs and coached each other on how to navigate in the Second Life environment, such as giving tips on how to jump, run, and move faster or slower. As students familiarised themselves with the task, the required support materials and so forth, conversations with peers through audio and text (remote) and verbal and text (co-located) continued.

As the students commenced the first stage of tasks, locating the waitress 'Jingjing' (a NPC), and enquiring about ingredients and where to purchase them, the pair interactions continued using text and audio, as did the interactions within the classroom setting. Students trialled the use of questions and statements with Jingjing and discussed which word choices might be most appropriate. Doing this involved referring to the textbook, practising uses of vocabulary verbally and in writing, and for some students, using Google Translator at various points. Text options for vocabulary were copied and pasted into the text box to share the information with pairs and sometimes with other students in the class (both remote and face-to-face).

The teacher was initially concerned that some students delegated tasks within their pair rather than completing each task individually, but ultimately this was seen as a valuable catalyst for extra interaction and collaboration. Students made their way through the Chinese Island locations from the meeting point outside the restaurant, to the restaurant, and to the market to buy ingredients. Where students were slower to complete their task, or when they became 'lost' in the virtual environment en route to a new location, the pair student could remain in contact using text and audio communication to provide direction and support. On occasion the pair student would move their avatar to the previous location to act as a virtual guide to the other student and lead them to the new location.

Some minor technical failures occurred. For example, a pair of students had an instance of audio failure. Students were able to continue working together using text chat until they reset the audio feature and it functioned as intended. Another student was logged out by the Second Life system during the session. The student was able to log back in to the system and immediately continue working. Occasional poor performance of the audio channel constrained some discussions, which led to text chat being used.

A number of students sought teacher help during the stages of interacting with the waitress to obtain information about the ingredients because they could not proceed to the next task without asking the waitress for directions to the markets. The correct language uses for requesting instructions needed to be negotiated. A similar need for teacher support occurred as some students attempted to haggle over pricing when they bought food at the market, a cultural application of knowledge that was not appropriate to the purchase situation. High levels of student-student interaction also occurred during the payment exchange in the markets. Some students required teacher support as the students attempted to make use of the settings in Chinese Island for financial transactions.

During the lesson student avatars were not always active and mobile. Students were required to make extensive use of support materials to make language selections based on prior lessons and activities and also to interact with peers using audio and text channels. In addition, both needs for support outlined previously, such as waiting (verbal/audio) and guiding (avatar movement) a student's pair, would result in periods of time in which a student avatar may be inactive.

Student pairs would sometimes be located in the same space in Chinese Island as they collaborated on various tasks. At other times and among different pairs, the approach used by students resulted in them becoming separated as one student took longer to complete a task or navigate the in-world environment. Most often, pairs attempted to and successfully remained in nearby in-world locations throughout activity.

Once students had obtained their ingredients they returned to the restaurant and entered the kitchen area to make the dumplings using the ingredients that they had purchased from the markets. The students interacted heavily with each other using text chat and audio as they worked through assembling and cooking their ingredients in the kitchen. Part of the reason for their interaction was because the tasks required the acquisition of several technical skills in Second Life navigation. As each student completed the cooking task and used their avatar to hold their dumplings to indicate the completion of the task, other students cheered and offered congratulatory input. The first-to-complete students then proceeded to assist their pair in the cooking task and other students in remote and face-to-face locations.

The duration of focused activity and the in-depth student-student and student-teacher interactions during virtual world activity provided evidence that students were highly engaged by the learning design.

Student Perceptions

Both remote and face-to-face students completed focus group sessions directly after the lesson. There were fewer than anticipated responses to the student survey as respondents had limited time after the lesson to participate in both survey completion and focus group discussion. And, with staff, student, and room commitments immediately following both classes, priority was given to focus group discussion and students were invited to complete the survey outside class time. There were a total of 13 survey respondents (n=13) two of which were removed prior to analysis as they were incomplete. The response levels gave an approximately even number of students participating face-to-face (n=5, 45.5%) and remotely (n=6, 54.5%). The responses to the student survey questions probing lesson experiences are presented in
Table 8.

While
Table 8 shows that both face-to-face and remote students generally provided positive responses to the survey questions, face-to-face students on the whole seemed more positive about their experiences. For example all face-to-face students (100%) agreed that they were able to communicate effectively with both face-to-face and remote participants; co-create, edit and share materials; and felt present with people participating remotely. Indeed very few face-to-face respondents disagreed with any statement (the exception was one felt it was difficult to share visual artefacts with others).

Remote students rarely disagreed with statements (with a total of only three "disagree" responses over the eight items). However, remote students were more inclined to be neutral in their responses. While care needs to be taken not to over-interpret these data given the small sample size, a slight difference in the perceptions between face-to-face and remote students seems evident in a number of areas indicating that face-to-face students were inclined to be more positive about their experiences.

Table 8: Summary of Case Study 5 student responses to key evaluation questions

Item	Face-to-face (n=5)			Remote (n=6)		
	Agree	Neutral	Disagree	Agree	Neutral	Disagree
I was able to communicate verbally in an effective manner with people in the face-to-face class	100.0	0.0	0.0	83.3	16.7	0.0
I was able to communicate verbally in an effective manner with people who participated remotely	100.0	0.0	0.0	60.0	40.0	0.0
In this lesson I was able to effectively share visual artefacts with others (e.g. images, photos, etc.)	50.0	25.0	25.0	50.0	50.0	0.0
In this lesson I was able to jointly create, edit, and share material with others in an effective manner	100.0	0.0	0.0	66.7	33.3	0.0
In this lesson I was able to effectively indicate my status to others (e.g. wanting attention, etc.)	66.7	33.3	0.0	66.7	16.7	16.7
In this lesson I felt like I was present with people who were participating remotely	100.0	0.0	0.0	66.7	0.0	33.3
In this lesson I felt like I was present with people who were in the same room as the teacher	50.0	50.0	0.0	50.0	50.0	0.0
The collaborative technology provided clear and accurate representation of information and people	80.0	20.0	0.0	66.7	0.0	33.3

The area that remote participants were most positive about was the ability to effectively communicate verbally with people in the face-to-face class, an item for which five of the six remote participants indicated they agreed with (83.3%). Four out of the six remote respondents favourably perceived four additional areas of blended synchronous learning in the lesson: ability to effectively co-create, edit and share materials; ability to indicate their status to others; feeling present with co-located students and the teacher; and clear representation of information and people. Some remote students felt that following instructions and discussion were challenging and somewhat less 'efficient' than in a face-to-face setting due to a combination of limited technology skills, audio clarity, and a lack of coordination among pairs for team-based tasks:

> *it's hard because the conversation you have with someone trying to buy an ingredient your partner doesn't see that and so when you're trying to ask for help they've got something else and they have different conversations and it's like it's not so synchronised.*

Face-to-face students commented on the utility of being able to share information from and through multiple channels as an outcome of using technologies and working in pairs.

Examples included: copying and pasting text from Internet sources using text chat, speaking over audio, and following or speaking to other people (avatars) because you can see what they are doing and join in. One face-to-face student observed that as a first-time user of Second Life, the available tools, lesson design and overall experience in-world learning was far richer than regular classes for language learning:

> *when I did Japanese before, ... online exercises, it's just like you're doing an exercise online and that's it, but this ... like it's actually kind of a real life, and you can get to talk to people and finish the tasks together, but not by yourself, and so like, you apply all those sentence structures, all that vocab, all ... that you learned before in like actual combo instead of just select ABCD in the online quiz. And that's what I think, it's more, different and also more practical and useful.*

A remote student similarly commented that online "access" and the limits of what you could "actually experience" in class were increased through online technologies:

> *... going out and making dumplings and buying things from a virtual market, from an NPC, you probably wouldn't be able to do that in a class to class setting. So it just increases the access to different ways that you can learn.*

Some students found the inactivity of other people's avatars disconcerting at times, because they were not sure whether the people were absent or simply working on another activity:

> *Not seeing the remote students sometimes creates a sense of doubt as to whether they are still there...whereas if I was in the same room, it would be obvious that I'm there.* (remote student)

Text chat was seen as an important communication mode because of its reliability:

> *Sometimes I had trouble indicating to my partner what I was actually doing, as was I sometimes unaware of whether or not she needed help. ...typing in chat was direct and sure to gain notice; it worked every time I used it.*

When asked about what enhanced their sense of co-presence, students indicated that the use of microphone headsets by all students made a contribution. One remote student indicated that their sense of co-presence was diminished when they were reminded that their teacher was not directly accessible and in another room:

> *When I heard the teacher's voice through the microphone of the partner in the background it made me feel less present, as I was unable to consult the teacher in the same way. For me this just means I was restricted by the lack of one resource; the teacher's physical presence.* (remote student)

When asked directly in a survey question whether students learned "less", "the same", or "more" than if the lesson had run in a normal face-to-face mode the survey results were very similar. A total of 54.5% reported they learned more than if the lesson was face-to-face, 27.3% of students reported they would have learned the same, and again two students (18.2%), both remote participants, indicated they reported they learned less by participating in this blended synchronous lesson. Several face-to-face students and one remote student felt that in-world learning was heightened through "making us more focused" and the learning process "more interesting". In particular, the visual component and use of avatar made some students feel the need to focus in a similar way to real life, such as saying that you have to "really focus on that environment you're in, rather than going off and doing other things – it's noticeable" and that:

> *with avatars, I think it makes us more like in a real life, because ... in here we can talk to other people .... So we just use what we learn from the textbook in this kind of real life, so it makes it more interesting and more – like you just ... focus, ... you're focused compared to in a formal class*

When students were asked whether they would like the approach used in the current class to be used in other subjects they studied a total of 45.5% of students agreed with this, 36.4% of students were neutral, while two students (18.2%) indicated they would not like this to be the case. Interestingly both students who indicated they would not like to see this approach used in other classes participated remotely. However, one of the co-located students in the focus group discussion stated that the reason they would not want this approach replicated in other classes was because of its utility in novelty to engagement:

> *I feel like you're learning things, and you're applying knowledge but I think what makes these classes so appealing is because it's different to what you normally do ... every now and again, I would find this very useful, but I couldn't learn everything just through it.*

Explanations as to why remote students might be less inclined to want to use virtual worlds in other classes and felt that they may have learned more in a face-to-face setting emerged in focus group discussions. Two students commented on problems relating to delays in responsiveness from peers and the teacher that resulted from computer mediated communication: one student reported an audio 'time lock' wherein delayed audio in peer interactions led to talking at the same time and needing to repeat points raised, while another student felt that access to teacher help was delayed because it required team work while the face-to-face team mate obtained teacher input:

> *it was interesting but then whenever we were confused or had problems it was sort of hard to get help straight away like you had to go through that person and that person had to talk to the teacher so it was like I took longer.*

Other students perceived the same scenario to be enjoyable and novel component of the learning task because it required increased peer-to-peer interaction:

> *It was quite fun because we could communicate with my partner downstairs with the teacher so that if I have questions and I ask my partner and then my partner ask the teacher and so it's like kind of I could ask my question through my partner so it was quite fun*

Several students reported working closely in teams and noted that teamwork was essential to completing the activities:

> *I thought it [teamwork] was better because we can both rely on each like if someone doesn't know something that person can help you and I thought it was good and I liked the team work. If I was by myself I couldn't be able to just finish the lesson.*

Some students articulated delays or drop-out of audio, but did not indicate that this was an insurmountable problem. Other students felt that it was quite difficult to navigate around in the environment and indicated that this could restrict the efficiency with which they engaged in the tasks, as exemplified by one students who commented "sometimes walking around is not easy... the view keep changed without my permission". Yet students acknowledged that these navigational overheads were inevitable in order to draw upon the advantages of virtual world activities, and also that the skills could be acquired over time. In terms of advice for teachers attempting blended synchronous learning, students emphasised the importance of making sure all technical difficulties were resolved before the class begins, providing clear instructions for the remote students (for instance through a website or using video), remembering to focus on remote students, and to try the approach because it was fun for students.

Most student survey and focus group indicated that students were highly positive about the lesson.

Teacher Perceptions

The teacher had taught in this unit since 1997 and began using a virtual world in 2008. He felt that practice in real-life situations accelerated learning based on personal experience living in China for four years and as a result of observing the language development of Monash exchange program students before and after they visited China over a six year period. Thus developing a virtual world was seen as a way to fill a gap in learning development that resulted from classroom learning where students "don't ever really use the language" in day-to-day settings that are "very ordinary sorts of situations" and "where things are a lot more spontaneous and they [students] have to think their way through it [language in use]". In terms of development, such learning situations were seen to create "a purpose for using the language" and "confidence" both of which "strengthen their communicative competence".

The teacher recognised how designing the lesson so that students drive their own learning has freed him up to provide in-depth support on core learning outcomes, as opposed to earlier iterations wherein students needed teacher support for directing the lesson and using the technology itself:

> *[the approach] has freed me up to actually then move around the classroom and not only help with technical issues but also to help them with the language content related issues and be able to sit down next to them and say okay so you just asked this question of a non-player character and you go this strange response back let's have a look at it together, why did that happen, what did you say, what did they reply, where could it have gone wrong*

Simultaneously facilitating interactions in the physical and in-world settings was seen to be challenging, and the teacher believed that under ideal circumstances a second teacher would be present:

> *[the challenge] has been trying to communicate in both environments at the same time so the ideal situation probably is where you have two instructors one who is present in the virtual environment and one who's in the physical environment to ensure that the communication is flowing well through both environments*

The teacher explained how he addressed the need to be present and give verbal input in the classroom and the virtual world:

> *doing it in little bursts so at the beginning ... going to my computer sitting down talking to the students making sure that they understand what's happening and then saying right now I've got to move away from the computer for a while. I've said on occasions to them if you have any issues tell one of the other students and then they can call me*

An additional strategy to simultaneously manage both the physical and virtual environment was to define a single focus environment for students:

> *the focus of student attention during the lesson is very definitely in the virtual environment and that's regardless of whether it's doing the task based lessons with the non-player characters or whether it's with the teachers*

Another challenge of teaching in the virtual world was the spatial nature of sound in the environment. The teacher needed to use an audio headset because sound at every point in the virtual world is different.

> *because this is also a spatial environment if a student moves away from the space where you have your avatar then they're not going to hear anything you say so you have to also at the same time be able to move the avatar as well*

This is particularly challenging if you want to use audio to address the whole class because avatar movement during activity takes students outside the teacher's audio field. The teacher recognised the utility of using a variety of communication channels:

> *we'll talk mostly in voice but if there's something that someone wants to say while someone else is talking it's very easy to type it in to general chat, it comes up it can be seen, it can be thought about without breaking the flow. There's been a number of times when I've used private I.M. [instant messenger] to support students*

Thus global text chat could be used to communicate with everyone at once to overcome disconnects caused by spatial sound fields and students being out of audio range of the teacher.

The teacher acknowledged how using the virtual environment could impose time overhead on the lesson, which meant he needed to clearly identify his learning goals.

> *things definitely happen slower than in the physical classroom for all sorts of reasons so ... you need to really prioritise more clearly with your lessons to make sure that the really important stuff is taught*

Providing adequate support for remote students was identified as vital to their successful participation in classes and to ensure that teacher time and class time are not taken up with technical issues. In particular, support for remote student's needs to include the ability to set-up and self-check systems ready to participate:

> *You to be extremely well organised to make sure that the people who are doing things remotely are in a place where they're able to handle the technical issues at their end reasonably well*

Flexibility and adaptability were seen as crucial when teaching in this mode, in order to accommodate unforseen circumstances:

> *You need to be able to handle the sudden issues like if a student's computer goes off line or .. where they're temporarily unable to continue to participate in the class ... you need to have something in the back of your mind as to how you're going to deal with that*

Students were seen to require time and instruction in order to acquire confidence and skills in using the virtual world environment. For example, the teacher pointed out that students sometimes require instruction to utilise the multiple communication channels:

> *it's not automatic that all students naturally do that so I think you do need to highlight to them, make them aware of the fact that there are a number of different channels they can communicate in and they can use those effectively and I think once they get that idea then they'll pick up on it and they'll run with it*

However students were seen to rapidly acquire the necessary technical skills over only a few lessons:

> *By now we're getting to their third lesson which if you think about it is not a lot, with all the basics they're fine... being able to move around the environment... clicking on things... adjusting some of the settings... they've commented on how much easier it is*

The interaction that took place in the virtual as well as the physical classroom was seen as being very helpful to drive student learning. Here, students spontaneously approach peers for assistance with in-world learning by using text and audio chat (virtual space) and in moving around the classroom to view each other's screens (physical space).

> *"Collaboration around and through the computer screen ... on-site / off-site pairs seemed to collaborate quite well and for the most part effectively with most pairs finishing the task. There also seemed to be quite a bit of around the screen collaboration between the on-site students with people getting up and walking around to the computer screens of their classmates on occasion to assist them."*

The lesson allowed students to "be much more in control of their own communication with their partners than in other lessons" and this was seen to be a strength in the learning design because learning was "totally student-driven". The teacher commented that the student innovation in task approach demonstrated cooperative endeavour that is essential to teamwork:

> *They were not being hands-off or dismissive of their partners as they seemed to have already assisted them with instructions on how to do certain aspects of the particular task at hand. I admired their spirit of cooperation and patience with their partners.*

In the future the teacher considers that continuing advances in technology, such as artificial intelligence, will increase the ability of virtual world settings to enhance language earning. In particular, the provision of more 'natural' and 'responsive' interactions, including adding voice communication and body language:

> *At the moment it's all text based so the students have to type in Chinese characters and there are good pedagogical reasons for them doing... but I'd also like to... develop the*

ability of the non-player characters to respond to voice and to respond in voice... body language, gestures that sort of thing.

Discussion

Using the in-world lesson design students developed their language application skills by working with their peers, interacting with the NPCs, and drawing on in-situ support from the teacher to deepen their understanding. The task components ensured that students were faced with virtual simulation of a real-world setting in which they needed to do things and go places in a foreign country. The simulation resulted in students needing to think like they would in that real-world setting, such as keeping in mind that if they wanted to make dumplings they would need to ask someone for recipe ingredients as well as directions to go to a market.

A distinguishing characteristic of this lesson was the high degree of student-centredness. The learning design incorporating pair work drove discussion, collaborative problem solving and resource sharing. The configuration of assigning one remote and one co-located student to a pair encouraged teamwork, particularly in cases where the face-to-face student became a conduit for communication between the teacher and the remote student. As the least teacher directed lesson it provided the teacher with more opportunities to work one-on-one with students.

Students appeared focused throughout the lesson, with many collaborating extensively to complete the tasks. They appeared to be enjoying the tasks, laughing, making jokes, and sometimes pointing out items on their screens to engage with co-located peers. Multiple online and physical resources were consulted and shared during the lesson. Engagement with the teacher largely related to language and culture as opposed to technology. All case data pointed to student-driven learning that was entirely focused on the tasks at hand, along with evident enjoyment and fun in doing so.

While several students felt that the virtual world learning experience was limited by their technical skills, equally, a similar number of students found the combined use of visual tools (avatar), text chat, and audio tools to be natural and comfortable (face-to-face and remote students). Despite some students commenting that aspects of the lesson were less efficient in the virtual world, or challenging due to technical issues, all students were able to see the merits of learning Chinese language application skills via designed lesson activities as these made use of some or all of the tools available in *Chinese Island*.

This learning design involved extensive development work over several semesters to develop NPCs and the virtual world scene. It also required considerable teacher expertise to manage the complex blended synchronous learning setting. It would be challenging for educators without experience in virtual worlds to implement a similar learning design, yet aspects of the lesson, including the student-centred learning task, the use of role play in a virtual world setting, and pairing of remote and face-to-face students may provide useful starting points for interested teachers.

Summary of Findings

The following is a summary of the key issues and take-home messages emerging from this case, broken up into broad themes.

Learning design/pedagogy issues

- The virtual world role-play challenge and Non-Player Characters provide students with a realistic and motivating practice situation.
- Learning outcomes were clearly defined and the corresponding tasks focused directly upon those outcomes (which the teacher saw as important because activities could take longer in the technology mediated environment).
- The extensive design of the task meant that the learning experience was more student-centred and the teacher could adopt a more facilitative role.
- Placing instructions and resources on the Learning Management System offered a valuable (fixed) reference point for the virtual world activity.
- Pairing remote and face-to-face students meant that remote students had access to teacher support via face-to-face students and thus encouraged collaboration, but could also mean remote students felt less connection with the face-to-face class and teacher.
- Having a clear focus environment (the virtual world rather than the face-to-face classroom) was seen to simplify the complexity of teaching in blended synchronous learning mode.

Technology issues

- There were sporadic technical issues during the lesson such as temporary audio failures that required a re-setting of the audio feature, and being automatically logged out of Second Life and needing to log back in during the session.
- The spatial nature of sound in the virtual world (and the fact that students were spread around the virtual environment at any one time) meant that the teacher needed to use text chat to communicate to the whole class at once.
- The technology imposed a degree of communication and time overhead, but student skills increased throughout the semester so less teacher support was required.
- Multiple channels of communication were used, depending on communication requirements and technology reliability (some students were more comfortable with this than others).
- Some students indicated that having a microphone for all students enhanced the lesson, particularly their sense of co-presence.
- Seeing a person's avatar was often not as good as seeing the actual person in cases where body language was important (for instance, at times students could not tell whether an inactive avatar meant the person was no longer there).

Setup and logistic issues

- Being well organised in terms of having all resources in place was seen as critical to the success of the lesson.

- The rigorous design of the environment and the lesson was based upon the development of an expert teacher over five years, which most likely would make it difficult for another teacher to attempt this for the first time.

Chapter 11: Case Study 6 – Web Conferencing to Enable Presence in Sexology

Brief Overview

This design involved the teacher holding an interactive lecture discussion with sexology students over two hours using the Blackboard Collaborate web conferencing system. The content matter of sexology (including sexual function, dysfunction, pleasure and emotions) is often confronting to students, and they needed to be taught to concurrently draw upon and distance themselves from their personal experience. In this context, web conferencing was used to provide more embodied presence and participation of remote students in the face-to-face lectures. The teacher presented material but frequently opened up discussion to engage the students in making links to the readings, describe their experiences and share their views. On-campus student comments could be heard through the web conferencing system, and remote students contributed to the discussion using text chat. Students in the face-to-face classroom could also add to the text-discussion thread using iPads. Activities were included to heighten student contribution, for instance a whiteboard graphing activity and a vignette/case-analysis problem discussion. The teacher, through the environment, played a critical role in fostering an open and safe atmosphere that encouraged everyone to contribute.

Institutional Context

Institution: Curtin University

Teaching team: P.J. Matt Tilley (Unit coordinator/lecturer)

Project team members involved: Matt Bower, Mark Lee, Jacqueline Kenney

Discipline: Department of Sexology, School of Public Health

Subject/unit: (311910) Sexology Opportunities and Challenges 682

Level of study: Postgraduate

Intended learning outcome(s):

- The student can investigate, analyse and synthesise information related to sexual difficulties and sexual variations.
- The student can identify and justify an evidenced based approach to assist and/or treat people presenting with sexual difficulties and/or variations

Description of the Learning Activity/Tasks (Learning Design as Intended)

This learning design involves a two hour interactive PowerPoint presentation seminar, with approximately 25% of that time involving class discussion. The design involves the following phases:

1. a broad overview of the area of sexual difficulties by the teacher;
2. a comparison of the changes from the DSM-IV-TR to the DSM-5, and associated class discussion;
3. an overview and discussion of the classifications of sexual difficulties;
4. presentation of material to briefly refresh student recollection of the relevant theories and frameworks relevant to the topic (which had been covered in a separate unit in the previous semester);
5. class discussion regarding the theories pertaining to the sexual response cycle;
6. an overview and discussion of the classifications within the DSM-5 Genito-pelvic pain/penetration disorder;
7. review of the factors assisting in case formulation ('the 4 P's'); and
8. discussion of a case vignette.

Presage Factors

Technology and environment setup/configuration

The tutorial room included groups of desks arranged to enable group collaboration, a lectern in the front corner of the room, a screen at the front of the room and two screens at the side of the room (see Figure 27).

The lectern computer used by the teacher was positioned at the front of the room. This computer was projected onto the front and side wall screens of the room (three projections in total), and displayed the Blackboard Collaborate web conferencing room that had been setup for the lesson. The lecture slides had been loaded into the Blackboard Collaborate room prior to the lesson. The teacher plugged his own microphone into the lectern computer in order to capture the audio from his presentation and the discussion in the room. The teacher also plugged his own webcam into the lectern computer in order to broadcast his image throughout the lesson.

The face-to-face classroom view is shown in Figure 28. The collaborative desk arrangement in the room enabled group work for up to six students per group. Students in the classroom were provided with iPads so that they could see and contribute to the online discussions with the remote students.

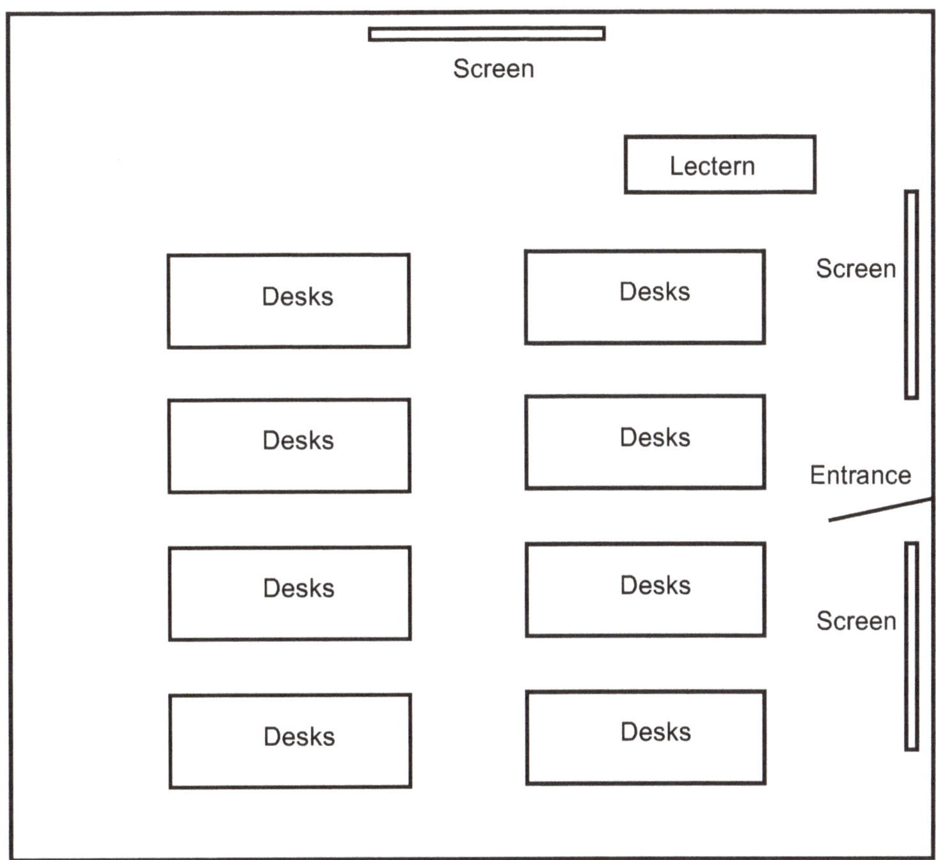

Figure 27: Case Study 6 room layout

Figure 28: Case Study 6 face-to-face room setup

Students who chose to participate remotely logged in to the web conferencing system at the start of the lesson (or a little bit earlier if they wished to check their system). The remote student view is shown in Figure 29.

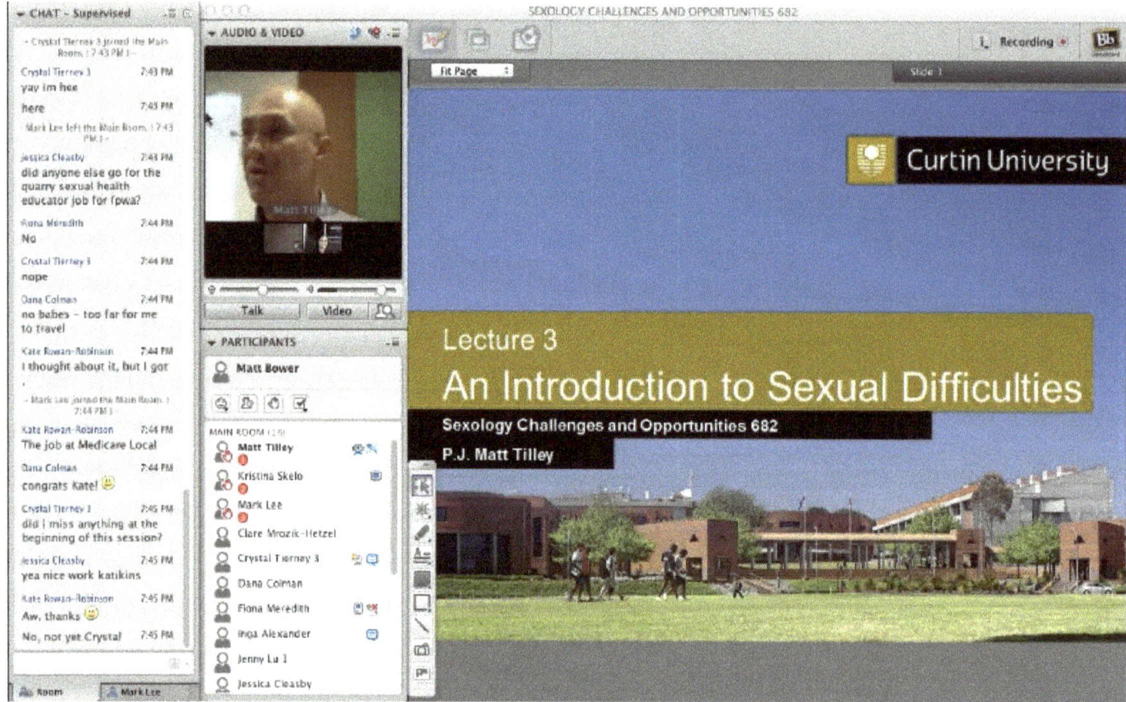

Figure 29: Case Study 6 remote student view

Remote students were encouraged to use audio headsets and their webcams when participating in the class, which was utilised by some remote students. Their audio was projected into the face-to-face classroom using the room speakers, and their webcam was visible to face-to-face participants via the web conferencing system projected onto the screens.

Resources

- PowerPoint slides (including theory, case vignette)

Support for staff

The teacher organised and setup the above resources, and ran the session on his own. A Curtin University support person provided an initial one-on-one personalised training session to help the teacher understand how the web conferencing system could be used to accomplish the desired collaborative aims. This same support person was available during office hours for ongoing support and provided weekly 'drop in' sessions for staff. The Blackboard Collaborate web conferencing system at Curtin University is supported by a 24/7 telephone support team (Blackboard Collaborate Live Help).

Support for students

Many of the students had already been exposed to the technology / teaching methods which had been used in another unit to conduct tutorial sessions for the previous semester. At the beginning of semester students were sent an announcement to provide them with an orientation of how the web conferencing system will be used throughout semester. In the first 10 minutes of the first class of semester the teacher provided an overview of the basic tools to be used and checked that students' systems were appropriately setup. The students were also provided with a link to the Curtin University's online support area for Blackboard Collaborate and a Blackboard Collaborate Getting Started for Participants Quick Reference Guide.

The teacher generally provides all in-class support for students throughout the semester.

Assessment

There was no formal assessment in this lesson. The teacher was able to formatively gauge student understanding based on their contributions to discussion and to the whiteboard.

Project Team's input into the learning design

After discussing the lesson with team members, the teacher included a whiteboard activity where people drew a graph relating to sexual arousal over time. Several iPads were also integrated into the lesson so that face-to-face students could login to the web conferencing system and make online contributions.

Class Size and Location/Distribution of Participants

For the observed lesson 7 students participated from the face-to-face classroom and 15 students participated remotely.

The Lesson as Enacted

The teacher was in the room and logged into the web conferencing system approximately 20 minutes before the lesson started. This enabled remote students to login and check that their technology setup was working correctly. Students in the room had been issued with iPads and were talking with remote students via the text chat stream. The teacher opened the class by discussing the sorts of material that they would be covering (sexual difficulties). Initially there were 19 students logged in to the web conferencing system. The lecturer's face was projected during the whole lesson in the large webcam area in the top right of the screen. At the beginning of the lesson there were two remote students who had chosen to project their webcam, but part way through the first half of the lesson one of those students turned off their camera.

The style of this class was conversational, sparked by lecturer questions, and lecturer and student responses to the themes raised by the lecture slides. A range of sexual difficulties was discussed, as well as their prevalence, varieties, explanatory models and implications. Examples included erectile dysfunction, dyspareunia and rapid ejaculation. Constructive approaches to broaching such issues as a part of clinical practice were discussed. Students were asked questions, volunteered questions, and responded to questions. Face-to-face student questions could be heard through the web conferencing system. Students used text chat to respond to the questions and contribute to discussions. At times throughout the lesson the teacher took time to read the text stream and respond to questions.

Students appeared intensely interested in the material being discussed. The teacher often related the concepts being discussed to experience garnered through his own professional practice as a clinician.

On some occasions the teacher temporarily wondered how to use the technology, but each time problems were rectified within several seconds. There was one instance of a student reporting that they were unable to see the slides, however, this appeared to be a problem with the individual's Internet connection because other students did not experience the same problem.

At one point during the lecture the teacher asked students to draw a diagram of a sexual response cycle on the whiteboard. A few students responded with enthusiasm to the opportunity, though it was hard for to them to provide high quality drawn or written responses due to difficulties using the whiteboard interface.

Because a large amount of divergent discussion had occurred, the teacher ended up skipping forward through the slides and assigned the material for students to read after the lecture.

Towards the end of the lesson the teacher placed a vignette (case study) up on some slides for students to read. They were then asked to answer questions relating to the case. Students at home were encouraged to respond via text chat, and students in the room responded via voice. There was a sense of resolution at the end of the facilitated case discussion as students were able to collectively interpret likely cause-and-effect relationships that were operating in the case.

The lesson closed with matters of housekeeping being discussed.

Student Perceptions

Of the total number of students who responded to the questionnaire about this case (n=18), one third of the class were face-to-face and two thirds took part remotely. Students' responses to the questions about their experiences are presented in Table 9. The table shows that for a number of items, all students in the face-to-face context were universally positive about their experiences. All face-to-face students felt they were able to verbally communicate effectively with others in the face-to-face class, indicate their status, shared a sense of presence both with those they were co-located with and those who were remote, and that the technology provided a clear representation of people and information. Similarly, all students who were participating remotely felt they could effectively indicate their status and felt present with other remote participants.

In post lesson surveys and focus group interviews students identified several advantages of the blended synchronous learning approach. These included the ability of everyone to share experiences, the ability to attend if you were sick or were unavoidably detained, and a much more engaging experience than just reviewing a transcript of the lesson. Both remote and face-to-face students saw advantages:

> *I absolutely love attending the classes via internet. It keeps me connected with my*

lecturer and classmates on a regular basis. Everyone is so helpful and considerate and it keeps me on track with my studies. (remote student)

enjoyed the interaction between real time and remote students - the contributions between all students are valuable. I also enjoy being able to maintain a conversation in a chat room while the lecture is going. (face-to-face student)

Table 9: Summary of Case Study 6 student responses to key evaluation questions

Item	Face-to-face (n=6)			Remote (n=12)		
	Agree	Neutral	Disagree	Agree	Neutral	Disagree
I was able to communicate verbally in an effective manner with people in the face-to-face class	100.0	0.0	0.0	80.0	0.0	20.0
I was able to communicate verbally in an effective manner with people who participated remotely	66.7	16.7	16.7	72.7	9.1	18.2
In this lesson I was able to effectively share visual artefacts with others (e.g. images, photos, etc.)	0.0	50.0	50.0	66.7	11.1	22.2
In this lesson I was able to jointly create, edit, and share material with others in an effective manner	25.0	25.0	50.0	77.8	11.1	11.1
In this lesson I was able to effectively indicate my status to others (e.g. wanting attention, etc.)	100.0	0.0	0.0	100.0	0.0	0.0
In this lesson I felt like I was present with people who were participating remotely	100.0	0.0	0.0	100.0	0.0	0.0
In this lesson I felt like I was present with people who were in the same room as the teacher	100.0	0.0	0.0	58.3	8.3	33.3
The collaborative technology provided clear and accurate representation of information and people	100.0	0.0	0.0	75.0	25.0	0.0

Suggestions for improvement included streamlining the lessons by better integrating the remote student text chat discussions and the in-class audio discussions:

I think it's really good, but I think it could be streamlined. Like for example, when we answer questions online, they're the same things that people are saying in the classroom.

One student suggested a way around this was for the teacher to say "I just want to hear from the [face-to-face] class" or "I just want people online to answer". Another on-campus student pointed out that the fact that the face-to-face conversation was often repeated by the teacher so that remote students could hear meant further doubling up of information, which could compromise the on-campus class experience.

Remote students also indicated that it was hard to hear student comments from the face-to-face class. Moreover:

> *there's sometimes a delay between what's being spoken, what's being texted and what's being shown on the slide. So you have to focus multi-times and sometimes you get a bit disorganised* (remote student)

Some students felt that it was disconcerting having so much information to attend to at once (presentation slides, teacher audio, text chat). Although the environment was seen to offer high levels of interaction, one student commented "at times it can be distracting when reading the comments online and [there is] potential to miss information". Other people enjoyed the multi-threaded nature of the learning – being able to contribute to a discussion while the teacher was presenting was seen by some to "enrich" the learning experience. One student in particular who had "hearing problems" pointed out that the text chat stream enabled them to engage in the conversation which may not have been possible if the discussion was spoken.

A remote student also pointed out that it was often "hard to type comments and questions fast enough for the lecture content". An off-campus student also expressed the view that it was hard for remote students to know when to talk because of the lack of visual cues. Another remote student felt that being able to see the face-to-face students would contribute to a sense of co-presence, which in turn could influence their propensity to interact:

> *It would be nice to see them, just to hold the camera up and show, just as you start the class or something, so we know who's there.... So I feel a disconnect and because I can't really hear them, I really can't tell who's asking questions as well, and so, I'm not sure any of us would ask questions of anyone in the classroom from here.*

The majority of the students (both face-to-face and remote) did not feel as though anything constrained their verbal communication with the face-to-face class. Any difficulties that were reported were generally technical issues for remote users, for instance "some time delay or voice distortion", and "difficult to hear people in the face-to-face class". Text chat was generally accepted as an effective mode by which to communicate with the remote students.

No face-to-face students reported being able to effectively share visual artefacts with others, while two-thirds of remote students indicated that this was possible. A similar trend existed for students' ability to jointly create, edit and share materials with others, with face-to-face students being more neutral or negative about this (75.0%) than remote students (22.2%). The face-to-face students were not able to do this because the iPads they were using to access the web conferencing environment did not have the required functionality. Remote students on the other hand were using their computer and so were able to share visual artefacts (by drawing on the whiteboard).

Remote students felt as though they could satisfactorily indicate their status using emoticons and text chat, and face-to-face students noted they had these capabilities as well as the capacity to raise their hand in class.

A notable feature of this lesson was a very strong sense of co-presence with remote students reported by participants. One student reported strong co-presence because "being able to talk continuously in the chat box is amazing". Yet co-presence was not necessarily attributed to the rich-media technologies being used. Human factors outside the realm of the technology appeared to be influential, with students volunteering reasons such as "felt supported by like-minded people", "we have a bit of a laugh doing it as we have become mates", and "we can use humour as we would in the block teaching class".

Several students indicated that completing an on-campus block session together at the beginning of semester enabled the class to conduct more cohesive group discussion during lessons. One student expressed the reason for the class repour as follows:

> *Having met all these users face-to-face already it is more like a weekly catch up... I'm not sure it would be as effective if it was a room of strangers*

While face-to-face students felt a strong sense of co-presence with their co-located peers, remote students reported lower levels of co-presence with the on-campus students (33.3% indicated they did not feel present with people who were in the same room as the teacher). The reason remote students provided for this was that they could not see or hear the face-to-face students as easily as could the other face-to-face students. One face-to-face student indicated that "It would ideally be better if we could see those online visually (not all have cameras) and hear them talk (not all have mics)." One face-to-face student noted that the use of audio would have allowed remote students to engage in more meaningful debate rather than only offering "single line thoughts".

Both remote and face-to-face students indicated that the collaborative technology provided sufficient representation of people and information, though some students pointed out there was sometimes interference caused by the unreliability of the technology. Both remote and face-to-face students were in strong agreement that the technology enabled learning to occur. One remote student explained that the technology "was able to offer up so much more than a normally recorded lecture, I did not feel at any disadvantage being online than in the room".

Most people reported no issues with having remote and face-to-face students participating in the one class. Those who did report issues raised the technology reliability, and remote students mentioned the difficulty in hearing face-to-face students. The advantages of having remote and face-to-face students in the one class included reduced isolation, the ability to have extended discussions, a greater range of perspectives from which to draw, and the ability to mutually support and network with one another.

In response to the questionnaire item relating to recommendations for people teaching in this mode, students suggested that teachers should ensure participants have good internet connections, try to avoid doubling up information, continually monitor the text box, be as interactive as possible, make sure students have the required technological capabilities, read out the text chat if not all face-to-face students are logged in, and direct the lesson so that different cohorts of students know when to contribute. One student suggested that "making sure that in class students know what's going on online and visa versa" is important. Establishing this common ground awareness seems to strike at the heart of blended synchronous learning and teaching. Another student recommended:

> *be open minded, relaxed and be prepared to respond to different channels of*

communication effectively. Have fun with it

Students were also asked whether they would like the approach used in the current class to be used in other subjects they studied, and all except one (94.4%) agreed with this statement. Remote students provided explanations such as: "all my other subjects are by distance ed and i am provided with a copy of the lecture notes... not very helpful", "Other subjects just record themselves reading the powerpoint slides - boring!!!" and "better to hear and see the lecture and be able to ask questions/ hear questions others are asking". A face-to-face student suggested that the blended synchronous learning mode "enhances a shared learning experience between all students". One student made the observation "having a consistent and confident presenter aids the process as I know what to expect from him".

The final question asked students whether they learnt "less", "the same", or "more" if the lesson had run in a normal face-to-face mode. A total of 61.1% of students reported they would have learnt the same, 38.9% reported they would have learnt more, and no students reported they would have learnt less in this mode. Several reasons for this were provided, including:

- *able to Google things at same time that I did not know;*
- *because of the conversation in the text box;*
- *all the information was there and the ability to engage;*
- *I'm more likely to be able to turn up online (rather than get to a classroom); and*
- *I would not have been able to learn from remote students if the class was only run face-to-face.*

Teacher Perceptions

The teacher had been using the web conferencing system for approximately three years to teach the unit. According to the teacher the delivery mode has been successful, and student enrolments this year were the largest ever. There are ongoing problems with using the technology-mediated approach, mainly with end user Internet speed, but also with the reliability of the platform (for instance, how the web conferencing software can change the content of PowerPoint slides). However the approach has exceeded the expectations of teaching staff for its ability to provide an inclusive environment that incorporates remote students. He believed it led to students feeling more "satisfied, engaged and connected".

In the pre-lesson interview the teacher reflected on the reasons for the approaches' utility of the approach:

> *they [students] need to be applying what we're doing to a psychotherapeutic environment, to an education environment, to a research environment, to a sexual health nurse environment. Whatever it is and the real time engagement where they can actually sit there and go, okay so I kind of get the theory but I'm struggling to see how it's going to work for me... it provides the opportunistic, or incidental learning opportunities for them to make the links between the content and their own application of that content.*

The visual modality was seen as preferable to purely audio communication in this context because it could “offer us a greater ability to connect to that student”. Although several microphones had been trialled, the teacher was still not satisfied with the ability of the microphone to capture audio in the room. That means that the teacher needed to paraphrase the audio from within the room in order for remote students to understand what was being discussed. Students also naturally and spontaneously use text chat to ask each other questions during the lesson. The teacher reflected that “when it first started I wasn’t so happy with them having their little side conversations... but I've certainly softened on that, and I actually see that as a really valuable part of their learning experience”.

The teacher describes a “mental drain” that occurs from trying to monitor so much simultaneously and still stay focused on the content of the lesson. He notes it would be great to have a second person in the room to assist with the running of the lesson, but that is not provided by the University. Sometimes he uses the students themselves to help him monitor the text chat. The teacher also observed the importance of being ‘extra’ prepared with the lesson materials, and in some cases needed to scale back the amount attempted in lessons in order to accommodate technical problems.

The ability for students to view recordings of the sessions after the lesson to some extent mitigates frustration caused by technology disruption, for instance if end user Internet connections are unreliable.

In the post lesson interview, the teacher felt that there was a good balance of structure versus open discussion to enable intended but also student directed learning. The text chat conversations that took place during the lesson were seen as positive, as they enabled students to have questions answered during the lesson (often by their peers) without feeling embarrassed. The fact that students had the opportunity to get to know each other during an on-campus residential block at the beginning of semester was seen to add to the group cohesion.

This teacher also discussed the idea that attempting blended synchronous learning required a degree of “letting go”, to be comfortable with a certain amount of chaos, and not becoming overly disheartened if the lesson did not go according to plan. Based on the extent to which it had improved the student experience in his classes, he felt that more teachers should be trying it.

Discussion

The success of this lesson was largely due to the ability of the teacher to create an open and participatory learning environment. The teacher expertly facilitated a conversational classroom, where students learned through discussion with the teacher and each other.

The teacher used voice, as well as body language, to create a relaxed and contributory atmosphere. The content of the lesson included clear explanations of concepts, engaging activities, and authentic case studies. Drawing upon industry experience and real-life examples added to the relevance of the lesson and added to the repute of the teacher.

The use of strategies such as drawing on the whiteboard and having iPads for face-to-face students meant the class was unfamiliar with some of the approaches being used in the lesson. However, both the teacher and students were able to rapidly adapt to the uses of these technologies. The approaches increased the degree of student participation.

Many of the students appeared outgoing in nature, which may have contributed to the open participation throughout the lesson. The rapport that students had with each other and the teacher was self-evident, and based on feedback from the teacher and students this was in part due to the on-campus block session that had taken place at the beginning of semester.

The highly favourable survey feedback by both remote and face-to-face participants indicates that the teacher was able to successfully unite on-campus and distance learners using the rich-media synchronous technology.

Summary of Findings

On the basis of triangulating data from the student feedback, teacher reflections and researcher observations, key findings of this case are as follows:

Learning design/pedagogical issues

- The lesson was designed for engagement, including student questioning, case study interpretation, and diagram drawing activities.
- The class was driven by the expert ability of the teacher to create a conversational classroom where open discussion was encouraged and valued.
- The teacher's body language and tone of voice were used in a way that contributed to the safe learning environment, and for remote students this was successfully mediated through the web conferencing system.
- Students were encouraged to use the text chat and respond to others while the teacher was teaching, and this student-directed discourse was seen by the teacher as a valuable aspect of the learning design.
- The highly positive student feedback was to a large extent underpinned by human factors, such as the ability to share ideas with peers and the sense of camaraderie that had been developed amongst the class.

Technology issues

- While there were some minor technological issues, the web conferencing system did enable the teacher to conduct blended synchronous learning classes that resulted in high levels of student satisfaction and a strong sense of co-presence.
- Audio transmission of comments from the face-to-face class was a perennial problem that was not yet entirely resolved, which meant that the teacher often needed to repeat the comments of on-campus students, and that remote students could miss what their peers were saying.
- Students rapidly adapted to using iPads in class to make contributions.

Setup and logistic issues

- Having students complete a residential block on campus at the beginning of the semester appeared to add to the rapport and cohesion of the class.
- Having the room setup with appropriate audio-video input facilities would decrease the burden on the teacher.

Chapter 12: Case Study 7 – Virtual Worlds For Teacher Education

Brief Overview

In this lesson the AvayaLive Engage virtual world was used to create a 'blended reality' learning environment. Students in the face-to-face classroom could see and hear remote students' avatars via a projection of the virtual world, and remote students could see and hear their face-to-face peers via a video stream into that virtual environment. The approach was used in a second year educational technology subject aimed at pre-service teachers, to help them understand how virtual worlds could be used to enable new forms of interaction and participation. The lesson incorporated teacher presentations, whole class discussions where students indicated their perceptions about the utility of virtual worlds, and group work brainstorming and design activities about the possible uses of virtual worlds in education. At times student preferences were represented using their physical placement in the virtual and face-to-face classrooms. Group work was attempted in separate breakout areas in both spaces, with face-to-face and remote group work notes shared on separate surfaces in the virtual world classroom. Network and system issues affected the quality of the student experience, however the trial served to demonstrate that blended reality classes are a feasible learning and teaching approach for uniting remote and face-to-face students. Institutional Context
Institution: Macquarie University

Teaching team: Matt Bower (Subject coordinator/lecturer)

Project team members involved: Jacqueline Kenney, Matt Bower

Discipline: Teacher Education, Department of Education

Subject/unit: EDUC261 Information and Communication Technology and Education

Level of study: Second year (undergraduate)

Intended learning outcome(s):

- the student can articulate advantages and disadvantages associated with the use of virtual worlds in education; and
- the student can create high-level designs of lessons that leverage the affordances of virtual worlds.

Description of the Learning Activity/Tasks (Learning Design as Intended)

1. The first phase of this lesson involves the teacher delivering a brief presentation (approximately 5 minute) revising the Virtual Worlds material covered in the lecture earlier in the week, including some material about features or 'affordances' of virtual worlds. The concepts of Blended reality and blended synchronous learning are also briefly introduced.
2. In the next class discussion activity (15 mins) the teacher asks students in the physical classroom and remote students in the virtual world to stand on pre-placed markers on the floor to indicate how useful and relevant they feel virtual worlds are for learning and teaching. The teacher then asks selected students in both classrooms to explain the reasoning for their perceptions, facilitating a whole class reflective discussion.
3. Students are then divided into six groups (three consisting of students in the physical classroom and three consisting of remote students who participated in the virtual classroom) and asked to brainstorm a list of the advantages and issues associated with the use of virtual worlds in schools (25 mins). One student from each group is allocated as scribe. Students in the virtual world are sent to breakout rooms to complete the task on a notes-surface, which is automatically linked to a mirrored notes-surface in the main virtual world classroom. Students in the face-to-face classroom complete the task using word-processing software and then share their screens into the virtual world main classroom via an avatar that had been logged in for them before the lesson. The teacher then leads a whole-class reflective discussion that compares and contrasts the points raised by groups.
4. In the next activity students in their same groups are challenged to design an interesting lesson idea that utilises virtual worlds, including teaching strategies they would need to employ in order to make it work well (25 mins). Students write down their ideas using the same approach as for the previous task. Students then return to the main room to share and review responses. The teacher leads the review and students vote on the best group design by raising their hands. A nominal prize is allocated to the best design.
5. In a final self-reflection task students are asked to place themselves along the marked line (in either the face-to-face or virtual classroom) in order of how useful and relevant they think virtual worlds are for learning and teaching. The teacher leads a discussion where students reflect upon whether their perceptions have changed, and if so why (10 mins).

Presage Factors

Technology and environment setup/configuration

The class was held in a computer laboratory with an interactive whiteboard at the front of the room and a separate screen on the side wall of the room (see Figure 30). The teacher presented slides and operated his avatar in the AvayaLive virtual world using the computer attached to the interactive whiteboard at the front of the room. An audio-conferencing system was attached to this computer via a USB port in order to send all of the audio from the face-to-face classroom to the virtual world, as well as to broadcast the virtual world audio into the face-to-face classroom.

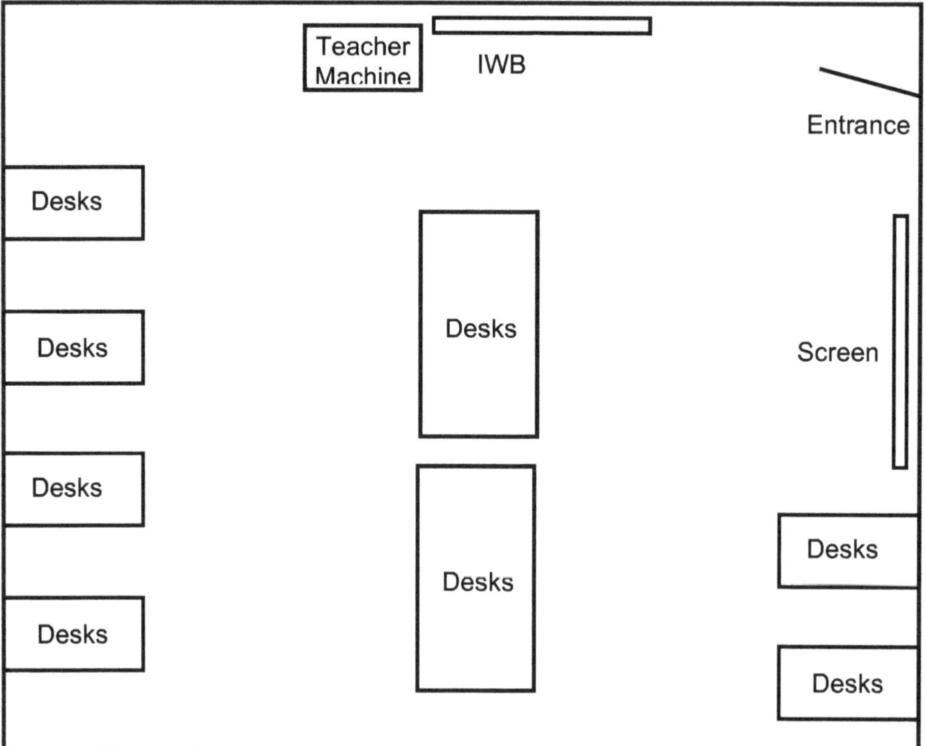

Figure 30: Case Study 7 layout of the physical room

The virtual classroom main room is shown in Figure 31.

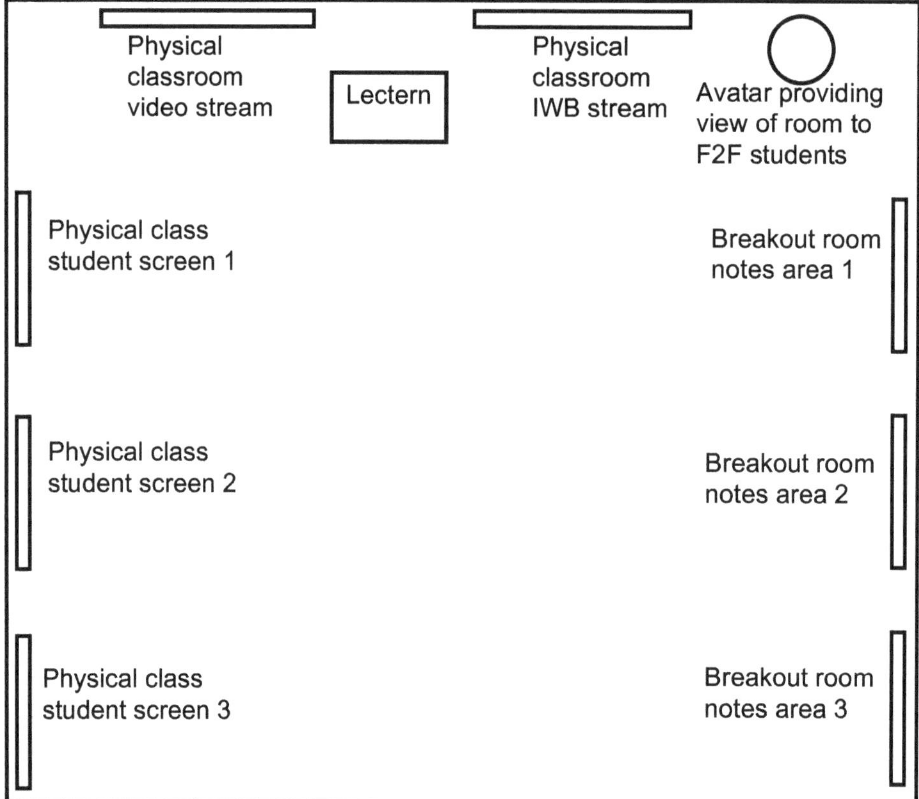

Figure 31: Case Study 7 virtual world main classroom setup

The virtual classroom consisted of the video stream of the face-to-face classroom, the stream of the interactive whiteboard (from the teacher machine), three student screens streamed from the physical classroom shown on the left hand side of Figure 31), and three notes areas linked to surfaces in the virtual world breakout rooms (shown on the right hand side of Figure 31). The virtual world breakout rooms were separate, smaller rooms outside the main classroom where groups of students had access to notes areas for writing down their responses to the group work tasks.

A second computer was used to provide the view of the virtual world for the face-to-face class. This was achieved by logging into the virtual world on that computer and having an unmanned avatar provide a viewpoint into the main virtual world classroom.

The face-to-face classroom view is shown in Figure 32. The virtual world main classroom view is shown in Figure 33.

Figure 32: Case Study 7 face-to-face student view

Resources

- The teacher presented a PowerPoint presentation about virtual worlds and blended synchronous learning.
- Circles were placed on the floor of the virtual world and face-to-face classrooms in order for students to position themselves according to their perceptions of virtual worlds in education during relevant activities.

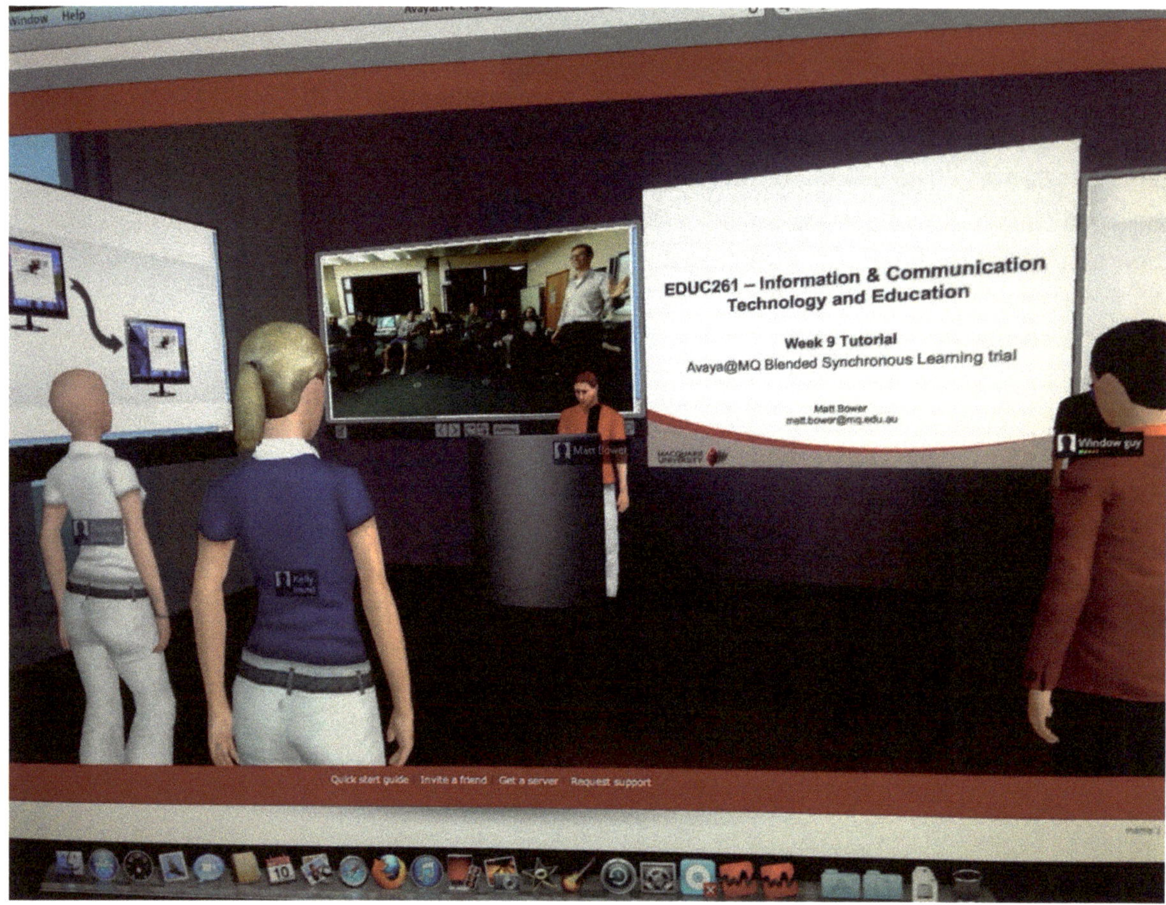

Figure 33: Case Study 7 remote student view

Support for staff

There were a considerable number of people who contributed to the setup of this environment. This included staff from Avaya to configure the virtual world and assist with technical matters, Macquarie University Informatics staff to support network performance and overall project management, staff from the Macquarie University Faculty of Human Sciences who assisted with the installation of software and setup of physical equipment, and audio-visual staff who setup the video and projection equipment. During the lesson the teacher did not receive any technical support.

Support for students

Prior to the lesson all students were asked to complete a virtual-worlds treasure-hunt using AvayaLive which was designed to help them develop all the technological skills they would need for the blended reality lesson, including the ability to navigate through the environment, communicate via audio and text, gesture, write on notes areas and share their screen. The activity also enabled them to familiarise themselves with the layout of the virtual world space.

During the lesson the face-to-face students only received support from the teacher. Remote students could also receive support from the teacher via the virtual world. Remote students who were participating in the adjacent computer lab could receive support from a lab assistant if required.

Assessment

There was no formal assessment associated with this activity. The teacher was able to formatively assess whether students were meeting the learning outcomes by reviewing their responses to the brainstorming and design activities.

Project team's input into the learning design

The project leader was also the teacher for this case. There was no extra input into the learning design from other members of the project team.

Class Size and Location/Distribution of Participants

Data for this case study was collected from the first two of seven tutorial classes EDUC261 that ran in Week 9 of classes in Semester 1 of 2013. There were 23 students who attended the first tutorial class and 22 students in the second tutorial class. Prior to the class students were invited to participate remotely, but only three students from the first class and one student from the second class accepted this invitation. For the purposes of the case study nine students from each of the face-to-face classes were invited to participate as though they were remote students by logging into the virtual world in an adjacent computer lab.

The Lesson as Enacted

When students entered the face-to-face classroom they were intrigued by the technical setup, and the teacher spent several minutes talking about how the technology enabled the face-to-face students and remote students to interact via the virtual world. The teacher then called for nine volunteers to participate in the lesson as remote students from the adjacent classroom. Several more minutes were then spent waiting for students to login to the virtual world and mute their microphone so that the audio did not create interference or feedback while the teacher was talking. The teacher then commenced with the brief presentation about virtual world affordances, blended synchronous learning and blended reality. Face-to-face students were able to see the slides on the IWB, and remote students could see and hear the avatar of the teacher presenting the same slides shared onto a surface at the front of the main virtual world classroom.

The class discussion about perceptions of virtual worlds in education progressed as intended. Students in the virtual world and face-to-face classroom faced one another while the teacher selected members in each cohort to share why they felt virtual worlds were or were not relevant in education. Remote students via their avatars were able to un-mute their microphone to have their voice broadcast into the face-to-face classroom, and face-to-face students were similarly able to express their perceptions to remote students via the audio-conferencing system. At times the audio quality was compromised by network performance, but in most cases it was possible for explanations from both cohorts to be understood.

Students were then asked to break up into groups to brainstorm the advantages and disadvantages of virtual worlds. The teacher (via his avatar) asked students in the virtual world to distribute themselves evenly into the virtual world breakout rooms, and students were able to successfully navigate to the rooms to commence the activity. The teacher then went into each virtual world breakout room to check that students understood the task and how to complete it, providing directions and encouragement where appropriate. Following this, the teacher walked around the face-to-face classroom, to provide feedback and encouragement to students in their groups. The teacher provided incidental technical support for both remote and face-to-face students, for instance by explaining to remote students how to start the notepad surface, or showing face-to-face students how to effectively share their screen into the virtual world.

After approximately 15 minutes the teacher verbally invited remote students back to the main classroom by visiting each breakout room, and reinforced this request by broadcasting a text message to all avatars. Once remote students had returned to the main virtual classroom and the face-to-face groups had shared their desktops into the virtual world the teacher attempted to facilitate a whole-class reflective discussion. While reviewing remote student group work notes (which were automatically broadcast into surfaces on the right hand side of the main virtual classroom) the teacher's browser crashed, meaning he had to restart his browser and re-login to the virtual world. It was possible to complete some reflective discussion of the remote students' group work responses, but after approximately 30 seconds the teacher's browser would crash again. This happened three times. Thus the teacher quickly moved on to reviewing the face-to-face students' responses (which were shared onto surfaces on the left hand side of the main virtual classroom). The desktop sharing was difficult to read for two out of the three groups because the desktop image was at times distorted (due to bandwidth and streaming issues).

The teacher then asked students to break up into groups again to design a virtual worlds lesson idea. This time students were able to complete the task more efficiently because they had practised group work in the previous activity. The same problems were experienced in terms of the teacher's computer crashing, and bandwidth distortion of images. However representatives from each student group were able to explain their virtual world lesson idea, with remote and face-to-face students able to see the written descriptions of other groups and hear their explanations. The teacher then asked students to vote for which design they liked best, with face-to-face and remote students raising their hand (or jumping or applauding) to nominate a winner.

Finally students were asked to line up on the floor markers according to their perceptions of the usefulness and importance of virtual worlds in education. Again the network performance at times compromised the quality of the audio, but it was possible for remote and face-to-face students to verbally share with one another how their perceptions of virtual worlds had changed throughout the course of the lesson.

Student Perceptions

Both remote and face-to-face students completed the questionnaire and focus groups directly after the lesson. This case saw the greatest number of survey respondents (n=33) with an approximately even number of students participating face-to-face (n=17, 51.5%) and remotely (n=16, 48.5%). Students' responses to the questions about their experiences are presented in Table 10.

Table 10: Summary of Case Study 7 student responses to key evaluation questions

Item	Face-to-face (n=17)			Remote (n=16)		
	Agree	Neutral	Disagree	Agree	Neutral	Disagree
I was able to communicate verbally in an effective manner with people in the face-to-face class	100.0	0.0	0.0	55.6	5.6	38.9
I was able to communicate verbally in an effective manner with people who participated remotely	33.3	20.0	46.7	77.8	5.6	16.7
In this lesson I was able to effectively share visual artefacts with others (e.g. images, photos, etc.)	86.7	13.3	0.0	68.8	25.0	6.3
In this lesson I was able to jointly create, edit, and share material with others in an effective manner	84.6	15.4	0.0	88.9	5.6	5.6
In this lesson I was able to effectively indicate my status to others (e.g. wanting attention, etc.)	76.9	23.1	0.0	72.2	5.6	22.2
In this lesson I felt like I was present with people who were participating remotely	66.7	13.3	20.0	76.5	11.8	11.8
In this lesson I felt like I was present with people who were in the same room as the teacher	71.4	14.3	14.3	61.1	11.1	27.8
The collaborative technology provided clear and accurate representation of information and people	73.3	20.0	6.7	77.8	11.1	11.1

Like other cases the majority of student responses were positive, indicating that most students had generally positive perceptions of how the collaborative technology was able to mediate the experience. A comparison between the responses of face-to-face and remote students indicated that the pattern of responses was broadly the same for many of the items. That is, approximately two thirds to three quarters of students, regardless of the site of their participation, agreed that they were able to indicate their status to others, agreed they shared a feeling of presence with people in the same room and those who were remotely located, and felt the technology provided a clear and accurate representation of information and people. While there were participants who were neutral or did not agree this was the case, they were in the minority (although close to 30% of remote students indicated they did not feel co-present with people in the classroom). Students in both locations were generally very positive about their ability to jointly create, edit and share material with others.

The clearest point of difference between students who participated face-to-face and remotely was for the first two items in Table 10. For example, while all face-to-face students agreed that they were able to effectively communicate with people in the face-to-face class, well over one third (39%) of students in the remote location indicated this was not the case. Conversely, for the second item in Table 10, the majority of the remote students (77.8%) agreed that they were able to effectively communicate with remote students, whereas almost half of face-to-face students (46.7%) indicated that they felt this was not the case.

Remote students explained that the main issue for them was the audio quality:

> *With the issues with the audio some of the conversations and instructions were missed due to drop outs*

Perceptions of the audio varied from "as a general rule it was OK" to "very flakey". Three remote students also pointed out that "it was also hard to decide when would be an appropriate [time] to talk". They indicated that this was in part caused by a slight audio delay, and in part by the "lag on the video".

Some face-to-face students appreciated the capacity to interact with remote students via their avatars:

> *I was able to talk to the remote learners from the classroom and I was also able to hear them speak to me*

But other face-to-face students felt restricted because they did not have the opportunity to interact with individuals in the virtual classroom:

> *it was difficult to talk to a certain person as the verbal message would be carried to everyone in the virtual world*

Some remote students felt that it was easier to verbally communicate with their remote peers than people in the face-to-face classroom because there was a level playing field:

> *People who were remote and by themselves had clear audio and it made it really easy to chat with them as we were both remote*

One remote student pointed out that "lack of facial cues" made it more difficult to interact with other remote students. One of the remote students felt that "text type aided slightly". Students in face-to-face and remote locations were also very positive about their ability to effectively share visual material with other students, although those in remote locations slightly less so. A face-to-face student explained:

> *Screen sharing worked quite well to be able to share things on our desktop with those in the virtual world. However, the screens in the virtual world were a little difficult to read unless you zoomed in or stood right up close.*

Students in the virtual world pointed out that latency and turn-taking were sometimes issues:

> *The text was easy to share but there was lag with typing so you'd have to wait to see if what you had typed was actually going to show up and other people could overtype your work or delete it very easily.*

Face-to-face students generally agreed that they could effectively co-create and share work with others:

> *I was participating in the face-to-face classroom, working with a group to jointly create and edit materials. We then were able to easily share these materials with the virtual class through the share screen function. I was also able to communicate our ideas verbally to the virtual class through the speakers set up in the classroom.*

Distortion of the shared screen image was identified as a factor that constrained their ability to share their ideas with other groups.

Remote students were also generally positive about how the virtual world helped them to co-create and share:

> *Typing from different people could occur simultaneously without having to wait your turn, and with different colours to help differentiate.*

Three remote students pointed out that simultaneously working on the same notepad could mean that other students' typing could interfere with their work, and one remote student pointed out that they had to "divide work and delegate jobs and roles in order for us to effectively produce any kind of work".

Survey responses from face-to-face students indicated that they were able to indicate their status in the same way as a normal classroom, using hand-raising and voice. The less than unanimous face-to-face student agreement (77%) about ability to indicate status may have been because they perceived the question to be about indicating their status using an avatar (which were not being used by individuals in the face-to-face classroom, other than the three group work machines). Though one face-to-face student did point out that they "felt that there was a great focus on the virtual world rather than face-to-face". The majority (72%) of remote students also felt they could effectively indicate their status, for instance through "gestures, they were very effective... jumping waving etc" though one student was "unsure on what keys to press". Another felt their ability to indicate their status was impeded by their understanding of what was appropriate in this new environment:

> *I didn't know if I should jump around to let the teacher know I could hear or see something. I wasn't sure of the etiquette in the on line classroom so was not able to indicate my status to others.*

Face-to-face students felt there were several features of the setup that supported a sense of being present with remote students:

> *We were able to interact successfully with the virtual world and it was as if these virtual participants were inside our classroom. The virtual participants were able to talk to us, jump, wave, type information. Giving the avatars these human qualities like the hand gestures and the verbal interaction made me feel like I was communicating with my classmates face-to-face when they were actually avatars!*
>
> *Being able to easily see their names and have them respond to requests like clapping or waving was entertaining and inclusive.*

However some face-to-face students identified impediments to their sense of co-presence, including comments like "can't really see who the avatars are in real life", "technological difficulties meant there were restrictions on interaction between the two parts of the classroom", and "only working with people in the real world made me feel like I wasn't connected to those in the virtual world".

There were 61% of remote students who felt they had a sense of co-presence with their face-to-face peers. They indicated that their ability to see what was happening via the video feed contributed to this, as did their ability to express themselves in the environment: "The use of gestures and text and voice was sufficient to make me feel that I had the same attention as others". One student who was located off campus commented:

> *Yeah I thought it was really good, I really enjoyed it; really connected us with everybody else and I think it worked well. I felt like I was engaged in it, and felt like I was in the classroom, I was there, that was me, I wasn't just like a little character on the screen, that was me.*

However another remote student identified how factors such as the lesson design and the technology (bandwidth or software) constrained their sense of co-presence with the face-to-face students:

> *didn't do any collaborative work with them, plus the uploading of their work and verbal sharing of their ideas was lost through the audio and delayed screen picture.*

Students appreciated that there were advantages to having remote and face-to-face students come together using the blended reality approach, including heightened engagement, improved access and co-presence for remote students, increased willingness of shy people to participate remotely, and access to the affordances of virtual worlds. Suggestions for running blended reality lessons included "clear concise instructions to the lesson as these type of lessons could be overwhelming or confusing for some students", and "employ the use of motion sensing cameras like Xbox Kinect so that you can gesture freely and spontaneously without having to press a key". Students also pointed out that there was a degree of difficulty introduced because "the teacher was literally in two worlds". As one student explained:

> *obviously the tasks for both groups were different it was hard as the teacher had to give two sets of instructions rather than just one, one set of instructions would have been given if we were in the virtual world as well*

Consistent with the generally positive responses, the majority of students (78.8%) indicated that they would be happy to see the approach used in the current class used in other subjects they studied. Some students were neutral on this point (12.1%) while only 3 students (9.1%; 1 remote, 2 face-to-face) indicated they would not like this to be the case. When asked whether they learnt "less", "the same", or "more" compared to a situation where the lesson was conduction in a normal face-to-face mode, 11 (33.3%) reported that they learnt more and 14 (42.4%) reported that they learnt less. Those who learnt less indicated that this was because of the interference in communication caused by the technology, that the class was slower than a normal class, and that the teacher was "in two worlds". Those who indicated that they had learnt more explained that this was because they were learning about virtual worlds through experience, because they could look around the room and see the work of others, because the novelty of the approach increased their level of engagement, and because the design of the lesson meant that they were actively involved.

Teacher Perceptions

In the pre-observation interview the teacher noted that the blended reality approach was experimental, and was meant to be pushing the boundaries of technology mediated learning. Although the concept had been tested previously (see Bower, Cram & Groom, 2010) it had never been trialled with students in live classes. The teacher felt the approach was important, as it was a step towards perfect blended synchronous learning where "remote and face-to-face students feel like they are in one physical space together". The aim was to leverage the affordances of the virtual world, such as three-dimensional space and the ability to gesture, to enable a greater range of in-class activity:

> *So often you might need to use space and movement and even gestures as ways for people to interact if they are participating remotely, but using web conferencing systems there's no real way to do that in the same way as virtual worlds. Virtual worlds provide you with more space in the class, the ability to use the affordances of virtual worlds like the ability to construct objects and to easily transfer between places, and a whole lot of things you can't do in the face-to-face classroom.*

The teacher also commented that it enabled "students in virtual worlds to share desktops or to be writing on surfaces" and for the teacher to "extend the resources available to the teacher and also the sorts of features that they [students] can use".

There was a substantial amount of work involved in setting up and testing the technology, including four 2-hour dry runs in the months leading up to the lessons. There was a range of technical issues to manage including:

> *how do you capture the audio of the room... and project the audio of the virtual world into the face-to-face classroom... there's also questions about orientation too as far as possible if you want to have a sense of co-presence developed you need to angle the screens and the cameras in the right way... [with] the ideal place for the cameras is pointing straight out of the screens.*

The teacher indicated that there was also a high level of preparation required to think through the activities, design the materials, setup the rooms (both physical and virtual), anticipate how to facilitate group work and interaction, pre-empt student problems and so on. A large amount of effort was also devoted prior the lesson building the virtual world treasure hunt that to help students acquire the virtual world operational capabilities they would need for the lesson.

Providing a somewhat equivalent experience to both cohorts, avoiding repetition, and understanding the student view, and providing technical guidance to students were all seen as issues in practice for the blended reality lesson:

> *So you need to constantly be aware of how you're appearing and how you're sounding*

to students in the face-to-face classroom and also the virtual world. As far as possible you're trying not to have to double up so that you just can say things once or represent something once and that both cohorts get to see that and have a reasonably equivalent experience. Sometimes you need to troubleshoot the technology with the students and ask them to slow down or turn off their microphone so pre-empting these problems and having students familiar with how to use the environment is really helpful.

The teacher also identified having a measured pace, teacher positioning so as to face both cohorts, and having composure in the face of problems as other important practices in the blended synchronous learning setting. He commented that "it's really about enacting general good pedagogical principles, and how to technically accomplish that using the mediating environment".

Having so many considerations to keep in mind made the teacher feel as though "it's like trying to be a good teacher but twice at once because you've got to have it pre-planned and anticipating issues not only in the face-to-face classroom but also in the virtual world and also in between those two". Elaborating, he commented "there needs to be two concurrent lines of pedagogical thinking happening at the same time, and in fact even more because you have to relate how the remote and face-to-face are going to work together".

The teacher was pleased that it was possible to run a blended reality class that involved interaction between remote and face-to-face students. The main issue that he identified was the ability of the network and software to enable high quality communication, but noted that this would improve over time as technology matured. The teacher also pointed out that in the future learning spaces and systems could be set up so that teachers could more or less walk into a room and start teaching in this mode without needing to concentrate on the technology:

one day we might walk into a room and all of this would be set up and reliable and that people would actually just be very easily able to participate with one another as though they were in the same room so that the technology became invisible. And I don't think that we're too far away from that. I think ... we're touching on something that really is going to be a large part of our learning and teaching future.

Discussion

Students were visibly excited by the setup when they first walked in the room, with laughter and occasional comments of "oh wow". The teacher also made an effort to enthuse students about the lesson by pointing out that it was a unique attempt to run a blended reality class, and students generally appeared engaged.

The teacher had to work extremely hard to simultaneously manage the content delivery, provide guidance to students and troubleshoot technology issues such as audio feedback loops caused by students who had not muted their microphones. The teacher applied several general teaching strategies during the lesson including setting tight time constraints on tasks, providing guidance and encouragement to groups (both the remote and face-to-face students), and directing questions to selected individuals so as to structure the lesson discourse. During the lesson the network and software both constrained communication at times, with choppy audio or frozen video. Performance was good enough for remote students to be able to participate in the lesson, but appeared to compromise the overall student experience.

Individual students in the face-to-face class did not interact with individual students in the virtual world (i.e. no group work with remote and face-to-face students). This was due to the fact that there was a single point of audio into and out of the face-to-face classroom. All interaction between cohorts took place through whole-of-class discussions involving both groups of students. In future iterations it would be possible for remote and face-to-face students collaborating on group tasks by having face-to-face students logged in to the virtual world using individual microphone headsets.

During the lesson many students appeared to have fun, with observed behaviours including laughing (face-to-face students), changing outfits (some remote students), and jumping up and down as part of activities (face-to-face and remote students). From this single case study it is not possible to tell whether this was a novelty effect, or whether the new way of participation would result in sustained increases in engagement.

The extensive setup and testing that was required means that substantial effort would be needed to transfer this learning design to other settings. However there are a range of interesting research possibilities relating to the sense of co-presence and the types of interactions that are possible in blended reality learning environments. For instance it would be possible to investigate how role-play and spatial design tasks could be facilitated using the blended reality mode.

Summary of findings

The following is a summary of the key issues and take-home messages emerging from this case, broken up into broad themes.

Learning design/pedagogy issues

- It was possible to conduct teacher presentations, whole class discussion, and group work activities using the blended reality approach.
- The teacher needed to work extremely hard to simultaneously teach the two cohorts of students and manage the technology under this learning design, and at times this impeded the progress of the lesson.
- Several students indicated that the affordances of the virtual world (such as the ability to gesture and move) contributed to the learning experience, though some remote students felt that it was difficult to know what sorts of behaviour was appropriate due to lack of cues from the face-to-face environment.
- Groups were selected for teamwork so that remote students were separated from face-to-face students which simplified communication, though in future it would be possible to attempt group work that involved remote and face-to-face students working in teams together.

Technology issues

- The virtual world enabled remote students to see and hear the face-to-face classroom, collaborate using voice and text with their remote peers, participate in whole-class discussions, share co-created notes with face-to-face (and remote students), and alter their location within the 3D virtual world space.
- Face-to-face students were able to see and hear remote students via the projection of the virtual world on the wall, engage in whole-class discussions with them, and share their desktop into the virtual world to share their thinking with their remote (and face-to-face) peers.
- Streaming a video feed into the virtual world was a particularly challenging undertaking because this was not a native feature of the software (though this may change in the future).
- Network and software performance compromised the quality of audio and video, which impacted on students' perceptions of co-presence, collaboration and sharing.

Setup and logistic issues

- There was a substantial amount of work involved in setting up the remote and face-to-face classroom in order to create the blended reality environment.
- Having students complete a pre-lesson 'treasure hunt' so that they could develop the required virtual world operational competencies meant that they did not need as much support during the lesson.

Chapter 13: Cross Case Analysis

Synthesising the analysis across the blended synchronous learning cases led to several emergent themes, as well as an understanding of how different approaches could lead to different outcomes. Student perceptions of blended synchronous learning as well as their views on technological competencies and how to teach well in such environments provide teachers with an understanding of blended synchronous learning issues and potentials. Student, teacher and researcher observations on how to best set up the technology, its affordances and limitations provide a basis for strategic use of rich media communication technologies in blended synchronous learning mode. Teacher perceptions on how to design and implement blended synchronous learning lessons offers fellow educators advice for attempting or enhancing blended synchronous learning and teaching. Observations on cognitive load and presence have been separated so that teachers teaching in blended synchronous learning mode can understand the key issues and adopt according strategies. Finally, reflections about how to best support blended synchronous learning have been distilled to provide recommendations for institutions.

Throughout this chapter the cases are referenced by number for brevity of identification (Case Study 1, Case Study 2,...). Table 11 below provides the full name of the seven cases to assist recall of the cases by number.

Table 11: Summary of the seven Blended Synchronous Learning cases

Case Study 1	Web conferencing to develop investment understanding (collaborative evaluation task)
Case Study 2	Room-based video conferencing to develop understanding of healthcare quality improvement approaches (collaborative evaluation task)
Case Study 3	Web conferencing to develop microscopic tissue analysis and interpretation skills (group questioning)
Case Study 4	Web conferencing for participation in statistics tutorials (collaborative problem solving)
Case Study 5	Virtual worlds to facilitate Chinese language learning (paired role-play)
Case Study 6	Web conferencing to enable presence in sexology (lecture discussions)
Case Study 7	Virtual worlds for teacher education (collaborative evaluation and design)

Student Perceptions

Student support for blended synchronous learning approaches

Remote students across the cases indicated that they preferred blended synchronous learning to learning asynchronously via online resources. This sentiment was well surmised by a Case Study 3 student who stated:

> *Although there are occasional hiccups, it's far more engaging as a DE student to be able to 'attend' class*

Remote students across the cases also appreciated how blended synchronous learning provided them with a reduced sense of isolation.

The active engagement that blended synchronous learning promoted was a common theme raised by students. For instance, when asked to identify the best aspects of the lesson one remote student commented: "applying knowledge learnt in tutorial and lectures in an interactive and stimulating environment" (Case Study 5 remote student). Remote students also valued the expedience of synchronicity:

> *I'm so much more inclined to whack my hand up and go listen yeah I need help with this I've got no idea what you're talking about whatsoever as opposed to drafting a 10 page email going what's going on here* (Case Study 3 remote student)

Face-to-face students also saw advantages of having remote students involved in their on-campus classes, particularly because it enabled "a broader range of views and ideas" to be shared and for them to hear *"a lot of questions others in class may not ask"*. As one face-to-face student in Case Study 3 put it:

> *I would not have been able to learn from remote students if the class was only run face-to-face.*

There were face-to-face students across the cases who indicated that the blended synchronous learning mode made their lessons more engaging (for instance as a Case Study 2 student put it "more interaction, and more shared thoughts"). One face-to-face student from Case Study 3 explained "This lesson is so much more engaging than your average lecture or tutorial...I find personally I'm more attentive". Often this was due to the active lesson design that the teacher employed rather than blended synchronous learning per se, where students were required to contribute to discussions, respond to polls, solve problems, co-create texts and the like. One Case Study 4 student expressed this as follows:

> *My other classes don't allow the amount of learning that this class does. We mainly listen to the teacher talk where as we are applying our knowledge in this class.*

This highlights that the attraction of blended synchronous learning for some face-to-face students may be the enhancement to learning design that occurs as teachers rethink their pedagogy. In some of the cases (for instance Case Study 3 and Case Study 6) the majority of both remote and face-to-face students reported learning more in the blended synchronous learning classes than in their normal classes. This indicates that blended synchronous learning need not compromise the learning experience for either remote or face-to-face students, and in fact if well designed and implemented it can enhance the experience for both cohorts.

Face-to-face and remote students both appreciated the flexibility of access that blended synchronous learning provided:

> *its good if you need to miss a class or cant get to the uni because you can attend online* (Case Study 4 face-to-face student)

> *I'm more likely to be able to turn up online (rather than get to a classroom)* (Case Study 6 remote student)
>
> *I'm an internal student and was unable to attend a tutorial one day as my kids were sick so I did it online whilst I was minding my kids in the comfort of my home* (Case Study 4 face-to-face student)

Other advantages of blended synchronous learning raised by both remote and face-to-face students across cases included the ability to have extended discussions, the ability to mutually support each other, and the ability to network with one another, the ability to engage in rich conversation with peers while the teacher was presenting, having all the required information organised in the one space, and the ability to engage.

Case Study 6 students also pointed out how blended synchronous learning could contribute to a sense of community and connectedness between remote and face-to-face students:

> *I absolutely love attending the classes via internet... it keeps me connected with my lecturer and classmates on a regular basis* (remote student)
>
> *it enhances a shared learning experience between all students* (face-to-face student)
>
> *love networking with class mates - it helps to you feel like you have some when you live in a rural location* (remote student)

Student issues with Blended Synchronous Learning

Both remote and face-to-face students across all seven cases raised technology reliability and performance as an issue. The main technology issue reported across cases was that the audio was not working properly. The reported impact of technology performance on learning varied greatly between cases and indeed between students within the cases. That is, the reported technology problems could range from "none" to "could not hear".

A common issue across cases was that poor audio capture in the face-to-face classroom caused a disconnect between remote students and their on-campus peers. It could mean that the teacher needed to relay in-class comments or remote students missed out on some information:

> *I only find it annoying if the teacher has to repeat questions asked by the face-to-face students so the online students can hear* (Case Study 4 face-to-face student)

In some of the cases a minority of students raised the issue of equity – questioning whether the face-to-face student experience was compromised at the expense of the remote students. A few students also pointed this out implicitly – having remote and face-to-face students together in the same class could also mean two sets of task instructions were required, which often took more time. Others commented on the challenges of group work with remote students: "it was easier to do this with the people sitting next to us rather than online with offsite students". Alternately, in other cases students felt that there was little or no interference caused by blending: *"letting the external students participate is a good idea, and I felt learning was not hindered in any way"* (Case Study 4 remote student). This once again indicates that the perceived impact of blended synchronous learning mode is more an issue of design and execution than blending itself.

Student recommendations

Across the cases students offered a range of recommendations for teachers attempting to synchronously unite remote and face-to-face students. Indicative items included (provided in the students' words):

- *provide clear instructions for the remote students before the class begins. (preferably from an external source e.g. on a website);*
- *continually check that everyone is on the same page and understands;*
- *make sure you give the right amount of time to both in class and out of class students;*
- *collaboratively involve students as though they are not online and it's one classroom; and*
- *ensure you know how to use the technology before trying to teach with it.*

Other student comments from across the cases can be summarised as follows:

- ensure participants have good Internet connections;
- provide clear and concise instructions during the lesson;
- try to avoid doubling up information;
- continually monitor the text chat area;
- be as interactive as possible;
- make sure students have the required technological capabilities;
- read out the text chat if not all face-to-face students are logged in; and
- direct the lesson so that different cohorts of students know when to contribute.

One student went further to suggest "making sure that in class students know what's going on online and vica versa". Establishing common ground awareness is an important consideration in a blended synchronous learning context where not everyone has the same view of the world.

Another student recommended: "be open minded, relaxed and be prepared to respond to different channels of communication effectively ...have fun with it". This demonstrates an awareness by the student that teaching in blended synchronous learning mode may be demanding, and that the attitude of the teacher may influence their effectiveness.

Student competencies

Perhaps surprisingly, across cases it was generally rare for students to identify their own poor technical skills or confidence as a reason for not being able to effectively participate in the blended synchronous lessons. Unsurprisingly, within any class there appeared to be a range of technical ability levels evidenced by students (based on student and teacher feedback, and researcher observations).

If students did not know how to collaborate using the environment (which tools to use and how to use them) then it could cause problems during the lesson. For example, student feedback in Case Study 1 indicated that their inexperience with using the document sharing window view meant that it was initially difficult to progress with the collaborative exam response evaluation activity: "Seems this is our first time experience, we all took sometime to understand the system before we finally realise how to use it". However, the same student pointed out the common sentiment that the skills themselves are not difficult to acquire: "It shouldn't be a big problem if we are second- or third-time user". It is important to note that after a brief period of time the teachers and students in the Case Study 1 lesson were able to overcome the difficulties caused by student unfamiliarity with the environment. That is to say, if technology and collaboration competencies are not taught pre-emptively, subsequent difficulties can often be managed during the class. This pattern of early difficulties using the environment followed by rapid skill acquisition was also observed by students and the teacher in Case Study 5.

Difficulties interacting were often less about technical skills and more about the tools that had been selected for the communication task at hand and how to establish common ground awareness, as indicated by the following student comment:

> *Only problem was the communication, and changing of slides by other students while others were writing on them. Again, if everyone had a microphone, at least they could make sure people were finished before they changed the slide.* (Case Study 3 student)

Also, some interactional issues related more to understanding what was appropriate etiquette in the environment, for instance whether it was reasonable to text chat while the teacher was presenting or jump around in the virtual world (Case Study 7).

In order to develop students' ability to collaborate in the environment teachers were often proactive, for instance by prescribing pre-lesson activities (Case Study 7) or introducing the environment to students in the first lesson of semester (all other cases).

Technology

Technology setup

When setting up the audio for blended synchronous learning classes it was important to avoid audio feedback loops caused by sound coming out of one set of computer speakers and being detected by the microphone of another computer. In most cases this was managed by having all audio into the face-to-face classroom and all audio out of the face-to-face classroom run through the one computer (the teacher's machine). Another alternative to this was to have all co-located participants use earphones so that the sound emanating from their computer was not detected by the microphone of other computers. Teachers in Case Study 1 and Case Study 3 used this technique so they could monitor the audio in the web conferencing system. In Case Study 5 all face-to-face students wore headsets. Similarly, all remote students should always be encouraged to use audio-headsets in order to avoid audio feedback loops in the system.

The main technology setup issue reported by students across all cases was that the microphone in the face-to-face classroom was unable to capture all of the student comments. This meant that the teacher needed to re-articulate student comments into the microphone in order for them to hear what was said. In each case teachers paraphrased comments or in some instances did not relay them to remote students, which led to information loss. This also led to interference with the flow of the lesson as remote students experienced periods of inaudible student commentary, and face-to-face students listened to comments twice as their teacher repeated them. The perceived impact of this problem varied from case to case and also within cases. For instance in Case Study 2 some students felt that the audio quality was a significant problem, while others felt it was "OK" or were comfortable working around it.

One important design decision for teachers is whether to let students make audio contributions as opposed to only allowing them to use text chat. The advantage of enabling audio contributions is that it can enable more rapid contribution during group work (as noted by a Case Study 1 student), it enables more extensive contributions rather than "single line thoughts" (as pointed out by a Case Study 6 student), it could enhance the sense of co-presence (as indicated by a Case Study 1 student), and it reduced cognitive overload caused by trying to work with two visual modalities such as the text chat and notes area at the same time (observed by the research team). On the other hand, text was more reliable than audio (for instance as pointed out by Case Study 1 and Case Study 5 students), and enabled many simultaneous non-interfering contributions by participants (researcher observation).

Using audio and text communication at the same time was perceived by some students to result in fragmented (disjointed) conversation that was hard to follow (for instance indicated by students in Case Study 1 and Case Study 6). A student from Case Study 6 suggested a good strategy to address this issue was to direct focus for response to either the audio or text chat channel. If audio and text comments were both being used to contribute to the same conversation there was sometimes a delay between what was typed and the current issue being discussed (as noted by a Case Study 6 student). A Case Study 1 student suggested that a good strategy to manage this was to ask students using text to send a short message indicating that they had a comment or question before typing it out in full.

Having high quality of video and audio meant it was possible for remote students to indicate their status in a natural manner (for instance by raising their hand in Case Study 2). Several students indicated that being able to see people in other locations increased their sense of co-presence (this is explained in more detail in the Presence section below). As an opposing effect, one student from Case Study 2 indicated that it could be intimidating to make a contribution when there were so many cameras pointing at them. This implies that use of video should balance the need to create connection with the need to preserve student comfort levels.

If participants need to draw or write mathematical notation on a whiteboard within the environment then it is useful to have a tablet device so people can draw naturally. In Case Study 6 it was difficult for students to draw diagrams using their mouse on the web conferencing whiteboard. In Case Study 4 working from a tablet PC enabled the teacher to annotate her slides with statistical notation within the web conferencing system.

It was evidently important to ensure students were provided with the correct permission levels to operate the environment. For instance in Case Study 1 providing students with a high level of permissions meant that some of them inadvertently change the view for their whole group. Similarly, if students do not have access to the tools they require then they will not be able to interact as intended. Face-to-face students in Case Study 4 and Case Study 7 could not easily collaborate with remote students because they were not individually logged into the environment.

When setting up audio for virtual worlds it is important to consider the implications of the spatial sound-fields (whereby avatars who are further apart may not be able to hear one another). If the lesson requires face-to-face students to collaborate with remote students on group work activities then they will each need to be logged into the environment with individual audio headsets. If they are not then the only source of audio in and out of the virtual world will be through the room or teacher's machine, meaning that as avatars move into separate spaces to complete the group work activities the remote students will only hear the audio from the location of the teacher. This effect was observed in Case Study 7.

The importance of being able to record the session was observed across cases, with students who participated in web conferencing sessions citing this as an advantage of the approach. The inability to easily record and disseminate the virtual worlds and room-based video conferencing lessons was perceived to be a limitation by both teachers and students. Also, one teacher noted that the inability to record individual breakout rooms during web conferencing sessions as a distinct weakness of the system.

Perceived advantages and affordances of the technological approach

One of the main advantages of the blended synchronous learning mode raised by students is that they could "write my questions into the text box without having to directly ask the teacher or stop the flow of the class". Face-to-face students raised this as well as remote students. Students also appreciated how they were able to simultaneously work together to compose text artefacts. Case studies 1, 2, 3, 4 and 7 all involved tasks where students co-created text documents.

The environments also afforded simple sharing of visual resources. A particularly apt example was Case Study 4 in which the teacher not only broadcast and annotated slides, but also her screen and PDF documents to demonstrate statistical analysis using Excel. This enables learning for remote students that would not have otherwise been possible, as the teacher of this case observed:

> *The initial problem was that students did not feel confident just following the written instructions on using Excel that were in the textbook and study guide. There was a proportion of students who possibly because of their learning style, they needed to be shown. And also the advantage of the [web conferencing system] meant that they could follow on using the machine that they were doing their assignment project on*

In Case Study 3 and Case Study 6 students also co-created visual artefacts by using the drawing tools of the web conferencing system. Students pointed out how the technology facilitated efficient sharing and creation of visual artefacts, for instance pointing out "I was able to work with another student to label a diagram – which in person is a much more laborious task" (Case Study 3 remote student).

Another advantage of the technology-mediated approach was the way it could encourage shy or reticent students to contribute (for instance noted by a Case Study 1 teacher and a Case Study 7 student). Using text chat means that they do not need to be as conspicuous as when they make a verbal contribution to a discussion. Responding to multiple choice questions anonymously means they do not need to feel self-conscious about answering incorrectly.

Virtual worlds enabled a range of extra possibilities for learning, due to the additional interactive features of such environments. For instance in Case Study 5 it was possible to design a whole role play environment in which students could develop their language capabilities. In Case Study 7 students were able to share their screens and notepads in the one room in a way that is impossible (or at least difficult) in a face-to-face environment. As well, the virtual world environments enabled students to move around in order to create a space for them to complete small group collaboration tasks, which is not possible in web conferencing environments.

Problems and constraints associated with the technological approach

As previously indicated, there were technological issues reported in every case, ranging from minor to substantial in impact. For instance, Internet speed and technology reliability were reported in all case studies. Effects included delayed or choppy audio, or in some cases, temporary inaudibility. Teachers indicated that they needed to monitor the system for audio feedback loops, and disable the microphone rights of other participants if feedback loops occurred.

Examples of technological problems specific to particular case studies included:

- not noticing that the teacher's microphone was muted for two minutes of the lesson (Case Study 1);
- latency on the interactive whiteboard slowing the pace of the lesson (Case Study 2);
- the web conferencing system crashing, which the teacher conjectured was because too many breakout rooms were open at once (Case Study 3);
- students experiencing temporary difficulty accessing the features of breakout rooms (Case Study 4);
- students being inexplicably logged out of the system (Case Study 5);
- inability of iPad client to allow face-to-face students to draw on the web conferencing whiteboard (Case Study 6); and
- the teacher's browser crashing during review of group work responses in the virtual world (Case Study 7).

Some difficulties with the technological approach related not to the technology itself, but conventions and etiquette relating to its use. For instance and as previously discussed, some remote students reported that it could be hard to know when to talk because of the lack of visual cues (observed in Case Study 6 and Case Study 7). Students in Case Study 3 and Case Study 7 pointed out that it was hard to know how to coordinate group work when multiple people were simultaneously creating a text. These issues relate partly to collaborative competencies and common ground awareness in rich-media synchronous learning environments. They also perhaps indicate that there is a need for additional communication tools in such environments to help coordinate group work, or a need for additional training in the use of the tools provided.

Several students who participated via virtual worlds indicated that there was an extra overhead introduced by operating in the 3D environment, for instance that it can be “quite difficult to navigate around”. This raises the question of whether the virtual world contributes to the design of the learning task, or whether it complicates access to resources and peers. In Case Study 5 the virtual world was an intrinsic part of the role-play task and so speculation about whether an alternative platform could have been used more effectively is not really appropriate. In Case Study 7, on the other hand, the task could arguably have been carried out without the use of a virtual world. Future research could compare the learning experiences of students undertaking equivalent activities using different blended synchronous platforms, such as web conferencing and virtual worlds.

Strategies for working with technology

A range of strategies for managing the technology-mediated nature of the environment emerged from the student, teacher and researcher observations. All teachers started their session at least 10 minutes before the scheduled lesson start time so that they and students could test the technology setup. The teacher of Case 2 pointed out that it was important to prompt students for contribution at regular intervals – this not only promoted engagement and learning, but also enabled the teacher to assess whether or not the technology was working as intended (as pointed out by a Case Study 2 student).

In Case Study 1 teachers also recommended micro-strategies for working with text chat. For instance it is useful to ask distance students whether or not they have any questions because it can take time for them to write, in which case the lesson might have already moved on. Asking students to use the prefix “Q” enabled the teacher to more easily distinguish text chat questions (requiring responses) from comments. If there are ever problems with audio, it is important to remember to use text chat to ask students whether they can hear.

Teachers were in general agreement that it was useful for them to develop skills in troubleshooting technological issues, because technical assistance may not always be available on demand.

Blended Synchronous Learning Pedagogy

Observations by students, teachers and researchers also provided insight into blended synchronous learning pedagogy. In particular the case studies revealed a range of presage and process considerations that impacted upon learning. Teacher reflections upon blended synchronous learning approaches offer further illumination of pedagogical and affective issues.

Presage and design factors

In terms of design, the overarching theme reported by students, teachers and researchers was how the blended synchronous learning environment could be used to increase interactivity. For instance, creating space for students to contribute (both within the web conferencing system and by providing the opportunity within the lesson) was seen to increase participation and student activity (particularly noted in Case 1, but applicable to all cases). For example, in Case Study 3 multiple choice questions and labelling tasks were incorporated into the learning design as a way to engage students and provide a catalyst for learning conversations.

Matching the tool being used to the modality of representation was important. An example of this is how an interactive whiteboard was used in Case Study 2 to enable visual sharing and interactivity across campuses.

Teachers from every case emphasised the critical need to be well prepared in advance of their blended synchronous learning classes. As the teacher from Case Study 4 put it:

> *you've got to be more prepared, more organised and, because I need PowerPoint slides, I need to know what I'm doing, setting up breakout rooms with the questions etc.*

Advanced organization was seen as essential because of the complexity and time involved in modifying the lesson during implementation. There was also a perceived risk of not anticipating what was required during the lesson and being caught without the necessary resources or tools.

Regular learning design considerations and effects were unsurprisingly identified as also being relevant for blended synchronous learning environments. For instance, designing a situated and relevant (business consultation) task appeared to engage students in Case Study 2. The teacher from Case Study 4 pointed out how they carefully "selected tutorial questions in order to bring out the main points". The teacher in Case Study 6 embedded authentic examples to heighten motivation and engagement.

Teachers from some of the cases indicated that it was discerning to build in some flexibility with timing of the lesson stages in order to account for technological issues that may be experienced (both problems, and time taken to collaborate). The teacher from Case Study 5 expressed this sentiment as follows:

> *things definitely happen slower than in the physical classroom for all sorts of reasons so you probably need to think ahead you need to plan more with your lessons, you need to really prioritise more clearly with your lessons to make sure that the really important stuff is taught.*

One teacher also illustrated the utility of having a pedagogical rationale for their learning design. For instance, the teacher from Case Study 5 the teacher pointed out that a situated role-play activity was designed because he believed confidence in language learning comes from contextualised and purposeful practice.

Process (implementation) factors

Teachers across cases exerted considerable effort to engage both remote and face-to-face students during the class. Asking questions was a primary strategy they reported using to encourage student participation. In order to encourage the participation of particular students (either face-to-face or remote) they would use directed questioning strategies (for instance *"Okay now Helen I want you to indicate with a green pencil a different structure",* Case Study 3 teacher comment). Teacher charisma was also identified as an important factor in order to enhance student engagement, for instance by presenting in an animated manner and using humour (particularly noted in Case Study 2 and Case Study 6).

The Case Study 2 teacher pointed out the importance of gauging student perceptions about the lesson in order to tailor it to their needs, and how it was more difficult to do this for remote students. Thus teachers recommend regular and explicit questioning of students. The research team also observed the importance (and skill) of responding to remote student comments during discussion, in order to cater to their needs and enhancing their sense of involvement.

As with design, teachers also applied sound pedagogical principles that they used in normal teaching environments during their blended synchronous learning lesson. For instance, teachers set tight time constraints on tasks in order to increase student productivity, moved between groups during collaborative activities, focused on providing clear explanations, and used hints and leading questions in order to increase student involvement.

Many of the teachers also highlighted the need to be flexible, for instance if technology problems occur that teachers need to be able to quickly respond and adapt. The Case Study 5 teacher expressed this as follows:

> *You need to be able to handle the sudden issues like if a student's computer goes off line or ... where they're temporarily unable to continue to not participate in the class ... you need to have something in the back of your mind as to how you're going to deal with that so that student gets the same learning experience, the same access as the ones that are in the physical classroom.*

It seemed clear from observation that a teacher's ability to be flexible was underpinned by his or her familiarity with the mode of teaching and the technology. For instance, in Case Study 4 the teacher's capacity to seamlessly shift between presenting slides, sharing applications, and marking up documents, as well as engage in conversation with both face-to-face and remote students, meant that she could readily adapt the lesson to emerging pedagogical requirements. The Case Study 4 teacher could not only respond to technical problems, but provided choice to students throughout lesson (asking what they want to get out of the tutorial, shifting back and forward between slides), which is an indicator of adaptive confidence.

The research team also noticed how important it was for the teacher to create an open and cohesive learning community through tone of voice, body language, word-choice and humour. This highlights the utility of multimodal technology in order to establish positive learning environment.

Another important process consideration that teachers from Case Study 4 and Case Study 6 pointed out is that every class is different; the character and number of students in each class can lead to vastly different collaborative dynamics even though the same learning design is being implemented.

Group work activities in blended synchronous learning environments

If group work activities are being integrated into blended synchronous learning lessons then educators need to decide whether or not to form groups that mix remote and face-to-face students together. The alternative to this is to have some groups that are comprised exclusively of face-to-face students, and other groups that only contain remote students. Observations from the case studies indicated that there are advantages and disadvantages to each approach.

Grouping face-to-face students with remote students was observed to level the playing field for remote students. As one remote student in Case Study 1 commented, since both remote and face-to-face students collaborate using the rich-media synchronous technology the participants “can't really identify who is remote and who is not”. Also, grouping remote and face-to-face students together in web conferencing environments can be quickly implemented using features that randomly allocate all participants to breakout rooms (used in Case Study 1 and Case Study 3). If face-to-face and remote students are in the same group then face-to-face students can act as relay points and assist remote students if there is any information loss from the physical classroom to the online environment (a strategy that was used in Case Study 5). The increased interaction between face-to-face and remote students in the same group may also lead to a heightened sense of co-presence between the two cohorts.

However, if face-to-face students are mixed in groups with remote students they cannot communicate as naturally with their face-to-face peers, and can be more difficult for the teacher to circulate amongst groups. Face-to-face students in Case Study 1 and Case Study 3 noted that if they were allocated into groups with remote peers then they might be sitting right next to a team member in class yet need to communicate with them through the collaborative technology using text chat or audio. This reduced the ease and naturalness of their learning interactions. As well, if the teacher wants to address a whole group then they need to do so using the collaborative technology – any verbal conversation with students in the face-to-face classroom may not necessarily be heard by remote team members.

Having co-located students work together on group work tasks and then report back to remote students meant that they could communicate naturally and without technological interference during the group work task but still share findings with the rest of the class (as observed in Case Study 2 and Case Study 7). The teacher could also circulate amongst the face-to-face groups in the class and then the remote groups online without any confusion about which group students were in. If face-to-face students are mixed with remote students then the teacher could easily be talking to a student online who was also in the class.

On the other hand having remote students in separate groups to the face-to-face student groups may decrease the sense of co-presence that students experience (as observed by students in Case Study 7). Another potential disadvantage of grouping face-to-face students together in the class and remote students together in the online environment is that it can take a considerable amount of time if the teacher needs to manually select the groupings (observed in Case Study 3 and Case Study 5).

Whether remote students are grouped with face-to-face students or not, using audio rather than text chat for all online discourse enables people to communicate more fluently, and in a way that avoids the text chat drawing their attention away from other visual production that may be occurring (for instance, composing a document or drawing a diagram).

Teacher Perceptions of Blended Synchronous Learning

Despite some initial teacher apprehension about teaching in blended synchronous learning mode (for instance indicated in Case Study 1), overall teachers felt that there were several advantages of the approach. These advantages were not only for remote students but also for the flexibility and the low risk participation that could be offered to face-to-face students:

> *I've been amazed at the benefit it's had for internal students to be honest... in the flexibility it offers them, I mean, if they can't attend during the day because we all know students work three jobs now.... the interaction for the internal student's, being able to actively answer questions, even type in a text chat box, for the shy internal student that might not have raised their hand in class, I think has been really good* (Case Study 3 teacher)

The Case Study 6 teacher noted that student enrolments have increased substantially with the more flexible offering, and believed that the blended synchronous learning mode had resulted in students feeling more "satisfied, engaged and connected". The synchronicity and flexibility was seen to avail remote students with opportunities for interacting with the subject matter that asynchronous teaching could not:

> *[It] provides the opportunistic, or incidental learning opportunities for them to make the links between the content and their own application of that content.* (Case Study 6 teacher)

Teachers also identified that the effectiveness of the blended synchronous learning mode very much depended on their underlying pedagogical aims and approaches. This was aptly articulated by the teacher in Case Study 4:

> *Really what I'm trying to do here is increase the active learning of students...thinking very carefully about what you want the students to experience, or get out of this tutorial is for this sort of unit, which is really developing techniques, developing skills, that being well prepared, actually I think leads to better outcomes.*

Blended synchronous learning was seen by teachers to require a degree of "letting go", to be comfortable with a certain amount of chaos, and not becoming overly disheartened if they were not in total control of the lesson or it did not go according to plan. For instance, having students use text chat at the same time as the teacher is presenting could be initially disconcerting, as the Case Study 6 teacher commented:

> *When it first started I wasn't so happy with them having their little side conversations... but I've certainly softened on that, and I actually see that as a really valuable part of their learning experience*

Teachers indicated that over time they soon became more comfortable with the blended synchronous learning approach. Over time this comfort level could increase to confidence, which was seen to underpin more flexible, student driven and adaptive teaching:

> *being more spontaneous I think probably with asking a question, or the students asking a question of me and actually being able to quickly adapt a question or an activity around what might have been asked. But once again I think all of that comes down to the confidence with the tools, and knowing what you can and can't do with it.* (Case Study 4 teacher)

In terms of perceived drawbacks of blended synchronous learning, teachers across all cases noted the effort involved by teachers to teach using the mode. The teaching team in Case Study 1 expressed concern over whether the face-to-face student experience was being compromised by attempting to teach the remote students at the same time.

However the consensus amongst teachers across the cases was that the advantages of blended synchronous learning outweighed the limitations. Teachers believed the approach may and should become a large part of our future (explicitly articulated by teachers in Case Study 6 and Case Study 7). Teachers also had ambitions about how they might continue to improve blended synchronous learning practices, for instance by greater use of remote student audio (Case Study 4), or incorporating gestures into virtual world activities (Case Study 5).

Finally, the research team observed that one of the advantages of blended synchronous learning is that it provided a catalyst for teachers to reflect upon their pedagogy, understand it more deeply, and expand their repertoire of practices.

Cognitive Load in Blended Synchronous Learning Environments

Teachers across cases agreed that teaching in blended synchronous learning mode involved high levels of cognitive load. The teacher in Case Study 6 explained this as a "mental drain" that occurs from trying to monitor so much simultaneously and still stay focused on the content of the lesson. Technology management, attending to the needs of different cohorts of students, and attempting to facilitate class interaction all contribute to this cognitive load, as the teacher from Case Study 7 explained:

> *it's like trying to be a good teacher but twice at once because you've got to have it pre-planned and anticipating issues not only in the face-to-face classroom but also in the virtual world and also in between those two.... there needs to be two concurrent lines of pedagogical thinking happening at the same time, and in fact even more because you*

have to relate how the remote and face-to-face are going to work together

One of the main problems that teachers experienced was trying to monitor the text chat while attempting to present information, as their attention was split between the two visual modalities.

Some students found it disconcerting to have so much information to process at once, but other students enjoyed this (for instance as noted by students in Case Study 6). Some students appreciated the way that they could combine multiple sources of information when they were learning in blended synchronous mode, for example by performing a Google Translate operation to support language learning in Case Study 5.

An interesting observation in Case Study 2 appeared to indicate that the level of cognitive load may not necessarily be impacted by the number of communication channels functioning in the environment. The large number of video screens and feeds in the Case Study 2 Access Grid setup did not lead to reports of cognitive overload by either the teacher or the students. Rather, it appears to be the number of channels that participants are trying to process at once and the extent to which the modalities interfere with one another that contributes to cognitive load.

Blended synchronous learning in virtual worlds poses additional challenges, as noted by the teacher in Case Study 5. Not only did the technology-mediated communication need to be managed, but the locations of students relative to the teacher also needed to be considered:

> *it requires the use of a headset and microphone to hear in-world discussion at all times or the use of video-screen projection in-world yet, the spatial environment of virtual worlds ensures that avatar movement during activity takes students outside the teacher's audio field*

If students are spread across a virtual world environment, the only way to communicate to all of them at once may be by using 'global' text chat.

Teachers did have strategies for managing the cognitive load incurred when teaching in blended synchronous learning mode. One strategy used by the teacher in Case Study 6 was to use students to help monitor the text chat and alert the teacher about important points. The teacher in Case Study 5 eluded to another strategy to help manage cognitive load for both students and the teacher: having a clear focus on one environment ("the focus of student attention during the lesson is very definitely in the virtual environment"). Having a teaching assistant was another way in which teachers managed cognitive load, as discussed in the Institutional Factors section below.

Presence in Blended Synchronous Learning Environments

Several factors appeared to impact on the sense of co-presence experienced across the case studies, some of which were related to the effectiveness with which the technology mediated communication, and others that related to the sense of community that people otherwise felt.

The use of audio and its quality impacted upon the sense of co-presence across the cases. Remote students indicated that poor audio capture in the face-to-face classroom could impede their sense of co-presence with the face-to-face students, because communication often needed to be relayed by the teacher (for instance in Case Study 3 and Case Study 6). In a similar vein, face-to-face students in Case Study 4 suggested that the sense of co-presence with remote students would have been improved if the remote student had used audio. Validating this from the opposite perspective, students in Case Study 5 appreciated the pervasive use of student audio, as exemplified by one students' comment "everyone having a microphone and headphones is good."

Video also enhanced the sense of co-presence for some students. For instance, in Case Study 6 the remote students indicated that seeing the face-to-face students even at the start of the lesson could enhance the sense of co-presence that they felt. The teacher in that case study chose to broadcast their webcam throughout because it offered "greater ability to connect to that student". Not being able to see or hear remote students left the teacher in Case Study 1 feeling detached from them.

It should be pointed out that co-presence is not necessarily an important outcome in its own right but may be important for some activities or in some learning contexts. Thus the teacher needs to weigh up the benefits of co-presence against the ease of communication for face-to-face students and the potential learning benefits to these students if grouped together.

It is also noteworthy that there was often a great variety in the perceived sense of co-presence within a class, with some people indicating that the technology acted as a facilitator and others feeling it was at times an impediment (this effect can be observed via the mixed responses to the co-presence survey items in Case Study 2 and Case Study 7). As well as the technology, these mixed perceptions may also depend on peoples' expectations of the communication modes. For instance, in Case Study 6, even though remote students were communicating with all of their peers via text chat, all remote students felt present with their remote peers but only 58% felt present with their face-to-face peers. Because remote students expected to be able to hear students in the classroom but sometimes could not, their sense of co-presence was sometimes reduced.

Human factors and the perceptions of the individual about the modes of communication could influence the sense of co-presence. For example, in Case Study 6 the class had a noticeable sense of community that had evidently been established at an initial block residential session that all students (remote and face-to-face) attended at the beginning of the semester. As one student from this case commented, they felt a sense of co-presence because "we can use humour as we would in the block teaching class".

People's individual comfort level with communicating online may have overridden any sense of co-presence due to the particular communication modalities. This is exemplified by a student in Case Study 3 who felt a high degree of co-presence even though the student was predominantly communicating via text chat:

> *We all communicate using the chat room and we are able to have a conversation with each other. It's not a difficult task to comprehend because we do this every day over*

social media. Everyone feels comfortable in the chat room and it feels like they are in the room with us.

Combined Quantitative Summary

The data in Table 12 reports the responses to the key questionnaire items from students across all seven case studies. The table should be interpreted with caution. It has already been clearly established that the seven cases of blended synchronous learning were by no means homogenous, with different learning designs and implementations resulting in quite different student feedback. As well, there were considerable differences in the number of respondents in each case, which means that some cases have greater influence over the percentages reported in Table 12 than others. For these reasons statistical analysis has not been conducted on the combined student feedback responses above.

Table 12: Student responses to questionnaire items for all cases combined

Item	Face-to-face (n=66)			Remote (n=62)		
	Agree	Neutral	Disagree	Agree	Neutral	Disagree
I was able to communicate verbally in an effective manner with people in the face-to-face class	95.2%	3.2%	1.6%	68.4%	12.3%	19.3%
I was able to communicate verbally in an effective manner with people who participated remotely	60.9%	14.1%	25.0%	66.7%	22.8%	10.5%
In this lesson I was able to effectively share visual artefacts with others (e.g. images, photos, etc.)	63.8%	22.4%	13.8%	67.3%	20.0%	12.7%
In this lesson I was able to jointly create, edit, and share material with others in an effective manner	73.7%	17.5%	8.8%	78.9%	17.5%	3.5%
In this lesson I was able to effectively indicate my status to others (e.g. wanting attention, etc.)	81.4%	16.9%	1.7%	79.0%	9.7%	11.3%
In this lesson I felt like I was present with people who were participating remotely	73.8%	9.2%	16.9%	75.9%	13.8%	10.3%
In this lesson I felt like I was present with people who were in the same room as the teacher	83.3%	13.3%	3.3%	60.7%	18.0%	21.3%
The collaborative technology provided clear and accurate representation of information and people	84.6%	12.3%	3.1%	80.6%	11.3%	8.1%

However, Table 12 does serve to demonstrate general trends in blended synchronous learning. In particular, the majority of face-to-face students (60.9%) and the majority of remote students (68.4%) felt that they were able to effectively communicate in a verbal manner with students attending in the other mode. Approximately two-thirds of remote and face-to-face students felt they were able to share visual artefacts with others, and approximately 80% of remote and face-to-face students felt they were able to effectively indicate their status to others. Approximately 75% of both remote and face-to-face students felt a sense of co-presence with students attending in remotely. In contrast, a over 80% of face-to-face students felt co-present with other people in the face-to-face classroom as opposed to approximately 60% of remote students who felt co-present with the face-to-face class. This is generally reflective of the way in which the technology could at times constrain the flow of information from the face-to-face class to remote students (for instance, the teacher needing to repeat face-to-face student comments for them to be heard by remote students, or remote student bandwidth issues).

Nevertheless, over 80% of remote and face-to-face students felt that the technology was generally able to provide a clear and accurate representation of people and information.

Table 13 shows student responses to general feedback items in the questionnaire for all cases combined. From Table 13 it can be seen that approximately 75% of both remote and face-to-face students would like the blended synchronous learning approach to be used in other subjects that they studied, with only approximately 10% disagreeing for each cohort. This is a strong indicator that blended synchronous learning can enhance the student learning experience.

Table 13: Student responses to general feedback items for all cases combined

Item	Face-to-face (n=66)			Remote (n=62)		
I learnt ______ in this lesson than if the lesson had run in a normal / face-to-face mode	More 53.0%	Same 36.4%	Less 10.6%	More 25.8%	Same 50.0%	Less 24.2%
I would like this sort of approach to be used in other subjects that I study	Agree 73.8%	Neutral 18.5%	Disagree 7.7%	Agree 77.4%	Neutral 11.3%	Disagree 11.3%

Table 13 also shows that 53% of face-to-face students felt that they learnt more in blended synchronous learning mode than in normal face-to-face classes, with only 11% reporting that they learnt less. This indicates that generally across the cases blended synchronous learning was seen to be more likely to increase the quality of learning rather than diminish it. On the other hand approximately one quarter of remote students felt they learnt more than in regular face-to-face mode and approximately one quarter of remote students felt that they did not. Thus remote students perceived that blended synchronous learning could achieve an equivalent quality of learning experience as normal face-to-face classes in some cases (or even exceed it). Remote students were not asked whether the blended synchronous learning approach resulted in them learning more than regular online classes so it is not possible to determine their perceptions on this issue. However, given that over 75% of remote students indicated that they would like the approach to be used in other subjects that they studied, it is possible that the majority of remote students feel that they learn more in blended synchronous learning mode than in regular online mode. More research is required to determine if this is case.

Institutional Factors

Teachers and the research team concurred on five important ways that universities can support blended synchronous learning in their institution.

First, high levels of technical support were identified by teachers and researchers as being critical when teaching in blended synchronous learning mode. Technical support can mean the difference between the lesson being successful or not. Technical support was observed to be highly useful when teachers were attempting to incorporate a new technological approach for the first time. It allowed teachers to concentrate on the pedagogical aspects of their classes rather than IT management issues (for instance, as observed and noted by the teacher in Case Study 2).

Second, teaching assistants can improve lessons by assisting with student management, technology operation, and discussion facilitation. For example in Case Study 1 the teaching assistant worked with the teacher in the room to perform valuable functions such as placing students into breakout rooms, alerting the teacher about recent student contributions to the text chat, and making announcements in breakout rooms. Tutor presence at remote locations helped to encourage student contributions and keep them on task (noted by students in Case Study 2). As was the case for IT support, the teaching assistant reduces the potential for teacher cognitive overload caused by needing to manage the technology and multiple cohorts of students all at once. Having a teaching assistant means teachers who would otherwise not be comfortable teaching in blended synchronous learning mode can still teach multiple cohorts of students at once (as observed in Case Study 1). Teachers from the case studies who did not have teaching assistants expressed how it would be useful to have one.

Third, if institutions want to derive the benefits of blended synchronous learning that were observed across the cases (including more participatory learning, higher levels of student satisfaction, more flexible offerings and potentially larger student enrolments) then they need to provide professional learning opportunities for staff so that they can teach effectively in this mode. Two obvious approaches are to offer workshops on blended synchronous learning, and to provide mentoring arrangements where teachers who have taught using the mode provide guidance for inexperienced teachers (especially during initial attempts to conduct blended synchronous learning lessons).

Fourth, as pointed about by teachers in both Case Study 4 and Case Study 7, learning and teaching spaces needed to be designed with blended synchronous learning in mind. Not having spaces designed for blended synchronous learning mode imposed a considerable logistical overhead on teachers, as exemplified by the teacher comment from Case Study 4:

> *yeah even though we're in a brand new building, the fact is that I've actually got to bring a mike and things to make it feasible*

It was pointed out that in the future it should be possible for learning and teaching spaces to be set up so that teachers can automatically and by default teach in blended synchronous learning mode as soon as they walk into a room. Audio capture and broadcast in the face-to-face room is the most pressing technical matter that needs to be addressed in order for educators to seamlessly offer Blended Synchronous learning classes.

Finally, teachers agreed that designing blended synchronous learning lessons was more time consuming than designing normal lessons in either face-to-face or online mode, and that this needed to be recognized at an institutional level. Although there were efficiencies derived from having the same content matter for both cohorts, teachers needed to be well prepared for students accessing the class via either mode and also needed to plan how the remote and face-to-face students were going to interact. To that extent, it was felt that institutions needed to take workload into account for educators who teach in blended synchronous learning mode.

Cross Case Analysis Closing Remarks

By combining the observations of students, teachers and researchers across seven blended synchronous learning cases, it was possible to construct a grounded, evidence-based understanding of the key issues and potentials of learning and teaching in this mode. While some themes related to good teaching practices in general, others (for instance cognitive load and presence) related specifically to blended synchronous learning approaches.

The next chapter distils the findings of the project into recommendations for teachers, and also considers future directions for blended synchronous learning.

Chapter 14: Recommendations and Future Directions

As universities strive to offer their students more flexible access to learning and to provide them with more engaging educational experiences, using technology to enable remote and face-to-face students to seamlessly participate with one another in active learning tasks is a worthy pursuit. It provides students who may have difficulty accessing education with the ability to interact in real-time classes so that they can develop their abilities more rapidly. It also enables face-to-face students to benefit from a larger community of peers. Having remote and face-to-face students engage in the same learning tasks together directly addresses calls for students to achieve the same learning outcomes irrespective of their place or mode of study (TEQSA, 2013).

The number of academics attempting to teach in blended synchronous learning mode is perhaps larger than expected; of the 750 university educators who responded to the 2011 blended synchronous learning survey 39.2% indicated that they had used rich-media real-time collaboration tools to simultaneously teach remote and face-to-face students. Based on this, and the comparative lack of attention that this mode of teaching has received, it appears that blended synchronous learning has been a relatively under-recognised phenomenon in Higher Education. This has meant that teachers attempting to teach in blended synchronous learning mode may not have had access to the support, guidance and resources that they would like.

Based on the background literature review, and synthesis of student, teacher and project team observations from the seven case studies, this chapter presents a rationale, recommendations and future vision for blended synchronous learning.

Blended Synchronous Learning – Why Do It?

The student perspective

Across the case studies students provided compelling arguments in favour of blended synchronous learning. Remote students generally found blended synchronous learning to be beneficial because it was more engaging, provided them with faster access to support, and reduced their sense of isolation. Face-to-face students also recognised that having remote students participate in class meant they were exposed to a broader range of perspectives and questions. Blended synchronous learning contributed to an enhanced sense of community between remote and face-to-face students in many cases. Face-to-face as well as remote students appreciated the flexibility of access that blended synchronous learning afforded.

Across the cases both remote and face-to-face students valued the ability to have extended discussions, to mutually support each other, to network with one another, to engage in rich conversation with peers while the teacher was presenting, and to have all the required information organised in one space. The technology enabled students to share resources more easily, perform group work writing and diagram labelling tasks, and complete voting activities. In two of the case studies students were able to leverage the affordances of virtual worlds, including the ability to conduct role-play activities in a simulation environment and utilise space for group work activities. In some cases both remote and face-to-face students reported learning more in blended synchronous learning mode than in their usual classes because of the active learning tasks that the teacher designed and applied.

Although both remote and face-to-face students were generally positive about blended synchronous learning some negative perspectives did emerge. Technology reliability and performance was seen as an issue for a number of remote and face-to-face students. Additionally comments from some face-to-face students suggested that the involvement of remote students could at times slow down the lesson or interfere with face-to-face students' interaction opportunities. See the Challenges section below for further details.

The teacher perspective

Teachers recognised how offering remote students access to live classes in blended synchronous learning mode afforded a range of advantages for remote students. Rather than merely watching a recording or accessing static asynchronous resources, remote students could be a part of the lessons and exchange ideas with all of their peers (both face-to-face and remote). As well as reaching remote students in real-time with their presentations, the teacher could field remote student questions and provide them with an immediate response to accelerate the feedback cycle. The questions and comments posed by remote students could in turn enhance the quality of learning for all students.

Another perceived advantage of blended synchronous learning was that it enabled teachers to increase the active learning of all of their students. For instance, by providing face-to-face students with access to the technology as well as remote, all learners could contribute to collaborative authoring and whiteboard tasks. Blended synchronous learning offered all students a low-risk means of participation through voting activities, and the ability for shy students to ask questions using text chat without having to interrupt the flow of the class. When used effectively the technology was seen to raise the sense of co-presence and connectedness between remote and face-to-face students. Teaching in blended synchronous learning mode was also a catalyst for teachers to reflect upon their learning and teaching approaches, and to enhance their pedagogies.

Institutional advantages

Blended synchronous learning also affords several advantages for institutions. It can:

- Enable more flexible access to programs for both remote and face-to-face students;
- Improve the quality of learning experience for remote students;
- Increase the degree of in-class interaction for face-to-face students; and
- Enhance the overall sense of community between distance and on-campus students.

This may lead to more students accessing the programs being offered by the institution, and more students being attracted to them. For instance, the teacher in Case Study 6 attributed increased enrolments to the blended synchronous learning approach, because all students (though particularly remote students) knew that they could flexibly access classes no matter where they were located. Remote students were no longer second-class citizens who listened to recordings or solely accessed asynchronous resources – they could participate in all learning activities.

For programs with small enrolment numbers it may not be financially viable to offer separate internal and external offerings, but it may be economically feasible to offer both simultaneously using blended synchronous learning approaches.

Blended Synchronous Learning – How To Do It

The Blended Synchronous Learning Design Framework presented in Table 14 below is based upon findings from the seven blended synchronous learning case studies, which includes student, teacher and researcher observations.

Table 14: The Blended Synchronous Learning Design Framework

Presage	*Pedagogy* • Clearly define learning outcomes • Design for active learning • Determine whether to group remote with face-to-face students • Utilise general design principles	*Technology* • Match technologies to lesson requirements (see MRSTCF in Chapter 4) • Setup and test the technology in advance	*Logistic/setup* • Be highly organised in advance • Solicit the right institutional support • Prepare students • Prepare self • Establish a learning community
Process	*Pedagogy* • Encourage regular student contribution • Distribute attention between remote and face-to-face students • Identify the focus of learning and discussion • Avoid duplication of explanations • Circulate amongst groups • Draw upon existing pedagogical knowledge • Be flexible, adaptive and composed	*Technology* • Know how to use (and troubleshoot) the technologies • Appropriately utilise audio-visual modalities • Ensure students have correct permissions • Advise students how to use the technology • Use tablet devices to facilitate visual input if required	*Logistic/setup* • Start lessons 10 mins early for technology testing • Apply tactics to work with text chat contributions • Login to a second computer (to see student view) • Seek teaching assistance where possible and desirable
Product (Outcomes)	• More active learning (remote and face-to-face) • Enhanced sense of community (through co-presence) • More flexible access to learning LEADS TO • Increased student satisfaction		

Rather than being prescriptive, the Framework aims to summarise the practices from the case studies that appeared to make a positive contribution to the student experience. We acknowledge that every context is unique and not all items will be relevant or appropriate for specific educational circumstances. Nevertheless, distilling the findings into an abridged form directly supports educators to implement blended synchronous learning in their classes, and thus directly addresses the main objective of this project.

Further explanations of each of the elements in the Blended Synchronous Learning Design Framework are provided in the sections below.

Presage Factors in Blended Synchronous Learning Environments

Pedagogy presage factors

Clearly define learning outcomes

Case study partners indicated that clearly defining learning outcomes was essential, not only because this underpinned task design and technology selection, but also because activities could take more time in blended synchronous learning mode. Identifying the key learning outcomes meant that the task and the technology could be directly focused upon what students needed to achieve in each lesson.

Designing for active learning

Students and teachers throughout the case studies indicated that a major benefit of the blended synchronous learning approach was the active learning that resulted. Lessons across the cases included collaborative evaluation tasks, group report back activities, multiple choice quizzes, diagram labelling tasks, collaborative problem solving activities, role-plays, class discussions and collaborative design tasks. Of course, there are many other learning designs possible in blended synchronous learning environments. However if active learning is to occur, then the task needs to be one that requires student participation. In order for students to share their ideas and represent their conceptions, it is crucial that the learning design provides them with space (both temporal and technological) for them to make contributions.

Determine whether to group remote with face-to-face students

If group work will be attempted, the teacher should be aware that there are different ramifications of grouping remote with face-to-face students as opposed to keeping the groups separated within the two cohorts. Grouping face-to-face students with remote students during blended synchronous learning activities "levels the playing field" between remote and face-to-face students, and can increase the sense of co-presence between the two cohorts. Allowing remote students to be grouped with face-to-face students is often simpler to organise (for instance by using the random grouping function of breakout rooms in web conferencing environments), and face-to-face students can help remote students know what is happening in the physical classroom. On the other hand, grouping face-to-face students together with their co-located peers means that they can communicate naturally without needing to operate technology. It is also easier for the teacher to circulate amongst the groups, with no confusion over whether a student in an online space is actually right next to them in the face-to-face classroom. While the decision about whether to group remote and face-to-face students can be made during the lesson, it often influences technology selection and resource design so it is recommended that teachers consider the possibilities in advance.

Utilise general design principles

The case study partners drew upon general principles of good design in order to enhance the quality of their blended synchronous learning designs. Particular examples include designing authentic tasks, using relevant examples, incorporating appropriate scaffolding, and ensuring constructive alignment between intended learning outcomes, tasks, and assessment. Utilisation of these and other general principles of good learning design can increase student motivation, engagement and learning.

Technology presage factors

Match technologies to lesson requirements

The Media Rich Synchronous Technology Capabilities Framework presented in Chapter 4 provides guidance for educators attempting to match technologies to lesson requirements. In the case studies teachers selected notes areas for student to undertake collaborative writing, interactive whiteboards for students to complete tasks involving diagrams, voting tools for students to indicate factual understanding, screen sharing to demonstrate technological processes, virtual worlds for students to complete role-plays, and text chat for multiple simultaneous discussion contributions. Selecting the correct technology enables students to more efficiently collaborate and represent their conceptions, and thus the capacity for teachers and peers to offer appropriate feedback. Readers are directed to the Media Rich Synchronous Technology Capabilities Framework in Chapter 4 for a more extensive discussion of this.

Setup and test the environment in advance

Reliable and effective technology underpins the success of blended synchronous learning lessons. First and foremost teachers are advised to setup and test the audio and video capture and broadcast in the classroom well in advance of the lesson. The four critical questions to ask are:

1. How will the audio of the face-to-face class be shared with remote students?
2. How will the audio of remote students be shared with the face-to-face class?
3. How will the video of the face-to-face class be shared with remote students?
4. How will video of remote students be shared with the face-to-face class?

For the first two points above it is crucial to test that there are no audio feedback loops in the face-to-face classroom caused by the sound from the speakers being fed back into the microphone. If the room-based lectern system does not meet the audio requirements then educators may consider bringing their own audio-conferencing system (brands include Clear One, Jabra, and Polycom) and plugging it in to the lectern or their own laptop. Similarly for video output it may be necessary for the teacher to pre-test and use their own webcam.

Teachers may decide that audio and video input is not required both into and out of the face-to-face classroom for their particular context. This may be the case due to the nature of the lesson or the availability of technology, however teachers are advised to consider how lack of audio and video sharing reduced the collaborative efficiency and sense of co-presence in some of the case studies (this is explained in more detail in a later section).

As part of lesson preparation the teacher will naturally need to design the collaborative workspaces within the web conferencing environment or virtual world, and make sure that all required resources are available to students.

Logistic and setup presage factors

Be highly organised in advance

While being organised may sound like an obvious recommendation, teachers across the case studies strongly emphasised how important it was to be well prepared due to the intense nature of teaching in blended synchronous learning mode. Because blended synchronous learning involves catering to two cohorts of students at once, it is more difficult to compensate for lack of preparation during the lesson itself. Being prepared meant carefully designed lesson resources and tasks, organising all technological and logistical aspects of the lesson (as outlined in following sub-sections), and in some cases rehearsing the class in advance. The heightened need for advanced organisation concurs with previous studies of blended synchronous learning (for instance, Chakraborty & Victor, 2004; Rogers, Graham, Rasmussen, Campbell, & Ure, 2003).

Solicit the right institutional support

Because blended synchronous learning is a relatively unrecognised phenomenon many teachers attempt to offer their lessons in this mode based on their own volition instead of working with colleagues. In some cases this can lead to a sense of being unsupported, yet often within an institution assistance may be available from the central teaching centre or within the faculty. Sourcing this support from the outset can result in more efficient and higher quality blended synchronous learning offerings.

Prepare students

Preparing students with the required online competencies is an important consideration when attempting Blended Synchronous learning lessons (as observed in this and other studies, for instance White, Ramirez, Smith, & Plonowski, 2010). If students lacked the prerequisite technology collaboration skills it can constrain their ability to participate and interrupt the flow of the lesson. Ideally, educators should provide guidance in advance on how to collaborate using the technology. This may take the form of an introduction to the technology at the beginning of semester, a set of pre-class practice tasks that students are required to complete, or just-in-time instructions at the beginning of a lesson to provide students with the skills they will need. Teachers may also prepare students by explaining in advance that blended synchronous learning will be used and the ramifications for how the class will operate (refer to the ‘process’ sections below for operational strategies and suggestions).

Prepare self

Before teaching in blended synchronous learning mode for the first time it is helpful to perform a test run in order to check that all of the required resources are in place and the technology functionality is understood. Even experienced blended synchronous learning teachers (and experienced teachers generally) will rehearse lessons in order to improve implementation. Students and teachers across the case studies identified that having a relaxed and positive attitude going into the Blended Synchronous learning lesson could improve the experience for both students and the teacher.

Establish a learning community

One of the interesting findings from the Blended Synchronous Learning Project was how establishing a learning community within a subject could enhance the experience of remote and face-to-face students within lessons. For instance, in Case Study 6 both remote and face-to-face students completed an on-campus block residential session at the commencement of semester, which meant that they became familiar with each other and subsequently more comfortable contributing to the blended synchronous learning lessons. Other strategies for establishing a positive learning community may include getting-to-know-you tasks or group work activities that occur before or outside the blended synchronous learning lessons, even if they are technology mediated.

Process Factors in Blended Synchronous Learning Environments

Pedagogy Process factors

Encourage regular student contribution

Students and teachers across the case studies pointed out the benefit of inviting regular contributions. It led to remote students feeling more included in the class, and using text chat can enable face-to-face students to more actively participate in class discussions than they would in traditional lectures. Teachers and students noted how the 'backchannel' conversations that occurred between students during teacher presentations were highly beneficial as students could learn from one another as well as the teacher. Student contribution can also be encouraged by direct questioning of individuals, as well as by using voice, body language and humour to create an open and welcoming learning environment.

Distribute attention between remote and face-to-face students

When teaching in blended synchronous learning mode it is easy to forget that the remote students are part of the class, or alternately, become consumed with teaching the remote students via the technology so as to forget that the face-to-face students are in the room. One of the main recommendations from students across the case studies was to distribute time fairly between remote and face-to-face students in order to avoid one of the cohorts feeling ostracised and receiving less teacher support.

Identify the focus of learning and discussion

In blended synchronous learning classrooms there are multiple channels of communication, which can lead to student uncertainty about where to focus their attention. For instance, some students commented that they were unsure whether they should be responding to teacher questions using audio or text, and that having a conversation split across both modalities made the narrative more difficult to follow. Some remote students indicated that it was difficult to know what they should be doing as they did not have access to as many in-class visual cues as their face-to-face peers. Explicitly identifying where remote and face-to-face students should focus their attention may prevent students missing out on valuable information.

Avoid duplication of explanations

In order to create a cohesive and integrated class it is preferable to have one set of explanations for all students. For instance, explaining a task to face-to-face students and then explaining it again to remote students means that both cohorts are listening to instructions twice. In some cases it is necessary to have different explanations for remote and face-to-face students because they need to use the technology differently. In these cases it may be possible to use written explanations so that each cohort can process their instructions at the same time.

Circulate amongst groups

Group work tasks offer the teacher a valuable opportunity to provide more individualised feedback to students and take the load off the teacher as the centre of activity. While students are occupied with their group work activities they are less likely to notice if the teacher is focusing on a particular cohort of students, either face-to-face or remote students. If face-to-face students are grouped with remote students so that they are working on a task via the technology it may be necessary for the teacher to ask students in an online group whether they are attending face-to-face if they want to take advantage of the ability to hold an in-person discussion.

Draw upon existing pedagogical knowledge

It is apparent that regular pedagogical capabilities are valuable in blended synchronous learning environments. Examples from across the case studies included the provision of clear explanations and instructions, directing questions to individuals, scaffolding thinking processes, adopting conversational approaches, and imposing time constraints on tasks. Applying these and other general pedagogical strategies while teaching in blended synchronous learning mode can help to motivate students, structure activity and promote deep thinking.

Be flexible, adaptive and composed

Teachers from the case studies commented how the teacher attributes of flexibility, adaptability, and composure were crucial in blended synchronous learning environments. Classes rarely went as planned, so it was important to make rapid decisions based on emerging circumstances. This may vary from knowing how to choose an alternative course of action in light of a technological failure to adjusting the nature of the lesson to cater to student misconceptions.

Technology process factors

Know how to use (and troubleshoot) the technologies

Researching and practicing the use of the technologies in advance can avoid embarrassing delays during class. Troubleshooting student technology problems can be difficult, especially when students are located remotely, however the experience of the case study partners was that their technology support skills did develop reasonably quickly over time. Having access to good technical support (and being able to access it immediately) is also highly beneficial.

Appropriately utilise audio-visual modalities

A fundamental consideration in blended synchronous learning classes is when to use audio as opposed to text. Audio enables rapid and extensive contribution, and the ability to convey tone supports a sense of co-presence. For this reason the teacher often uses audio to deliver extended presentations. However audio only allows one contributor at a time, is more complex to setup and is less reliable. On the other hand text enables multiple simultaneous contributions, is simple to use and reliable. These factors may lead students to use text on most occasions. Text can also be rapidly processed in retrospect as opposed to audio contributions, which generally need to be replayed at one-to-one speed. On the other hand text contributions are slower and less extensive (leading to "single line thoughts"), with reduced capacity to portray tone. Thus if students intend to make elaborate contributions in class it may be best for them to use audio.

Ensure students have correct permissions

Most rich-media synchronous technologies allow different permissions to be granted to different users, in terms of which tools they can access within the system. When setting up the environment students need to be allocated correct permissions to participate in learning activities. Having too few permissions may mean that they are unable to make contributions to the activities. Having too many permissions may mean that they inadvertently interfere with the design or setup of the technology.

Advise students how to use the technology

In cases where students are using a particular toolset for the first time (for instance during a group work activity) they may benefit from specific instructions on how to use the technology. Both teachers and students from across the case studies indicated that students are able to quickly pick-up the required technology skills, and students rarely self-reported poor technology skills as a reason for inhibiting participation. Helping students to select appropriate communication modalities can improve the efficiency and quality of interaction. For instance, encouraging students to use audio rather than text chat during group work activities may increase the speed of collaboration and mean that students' hands are free to contribute to other aspects of the task (such as draw on a whiteboard or take notes).

Use tablet devices to facilitate visual input if required

Using a tablet device allows more natural and accurate drawing on a whiteboard than is possible using a mouse. When intending to annotate slides, mark-up diagrams, or draw illustrations then a tablet PC or external tablet device enables faster and higher quality visual input. Depending on the learning design this may only be required by the teacher, but as mobile interfaces for rich-media synchronous technologies improve this will more frequently become available to students.

Logistic/setup process factors

Start lessons 10 mins early for technology testing

Starting the lesson at least 10 minutes early not only allows the teacher to test that the audio, video and other system functionality is working as intended, but also enables students to test their technology setup. This may circumvent student audio problems interfering with the actual lesson. In the first lesson of semester and depending on the size of the class 30 minutes or more may be allocated to this.

Apply tactics to work with text chat contributions

It can be challenging for teachers to monitor and respond to students' text chat contributions while they are teaching because their attention is focused on their presentation. In order to avoid cognitive overload, teachers may ask students to alert the teacher of text chat comments requiring a response, ask students to respond to other students, or ask students to propend a 'Q' to text chat comments requiring teacher attention so as to support easy selection by the teacher.

Login to a second computer (to see student view)

Due to different permissions and different viewpoints, the teacher's view of the online environment may be quite different from students' view. Logging into a second computer as a student and having that visible from where the teacher is presenting can be useful to understand how students are experiencing the lesson. This is particularly advisable during initial attempts to teach in blended synchronous learning mode.

Seek teaching assistance where possible and desirable

Across the cases teachers who had teaching assistance described it as invaluable, and teachers who did not have teaching assistance indicated that it would be highly beneficial. Teachers are recommended to source teaching assistance if it is available, especially for the first lessons in which blended synchronous learning is being attempted. In the case studies teaching assistants helped to place students in groups, send announcements, provide feedback to individual students, and manage the technology. Previous studies have also found that a teaching assistant is advantageous when attempting to teach in blended synchronous learning mode in order to monitor the text chat, facilitate student interaction, and attend to technological issues (Rogers, et al., 2003; White, et al., 2010).

Product (Outcomes) of Blended Synchronous Learning Environments

More active learning (remote and face-to-face)

Both remote and face-to-face students across the cases indicated that they appreciated the more active learning approaches afforded by blended synchronous learning. Being able to participate in classes by virtue of question and answer sessions, diagram labelling tasks, collaborative evaluation activities, role-plays, whiteboard exercises and design exercises meant that students were able to apply "knowledge learnt in tutorial and lectures in an interactive and stimulating environment". This led to many students feeling that they were more engaged with their learning:

> *This lesson is so much more engaging than your average lecture or tutorial...I find personally I'm more attentive*

Accordingly, many students felt that they learnt more in Blended Synchronous mode, as explained by a face-to-face student:

> *My other classes don't allow the amount of learning that this class does. We mainly listen to the teacher talk where as we are applying our knowledge in this class.*

In fact, across the seven cases 89.4% of face-to-face students (from n=66) and 75.8% of remote students (from n=62) who responded to the lesson evaluation questionnaire felt that they learnt the at least as much or more in their blended synchronous learning class as compared to regular face-to-face classes. While the technologies being utilised in blended synchronous learning mode allowed both remote and face-to-face students to be more actively involved in lessons, a large part of the enhancement to learning was undoubtedly due to the way that teachers had rethought their pedagogy to enable more active learning.

Enhanced sense of co-presence and community

Blended synchronous learning enabled remote and face-to-face students' to feel a sense of co-presence with one another. Of the 66 face-to-face students who responded to the lesson evaluation questionnaire the majority (73.8%) felt present with remote students, and 60.7% of the 62 remote student respondents felt present with people in the face-to-face class. It should be noted that sense of co-presence varied widely between case studies, with student open-ended questionnaire responses indicating that the sense of co-presence depended on the way the technology was used as well as human factors.

Utilising the audio-visual modalities of the blended synchronous learning technologies could enhance remote and face-to-face students' sense of co-presence. Remote student feedback highlighted the importance of having an uninterrupted audio feed from the face-to-face classroom in order for them to feel co-present. Similarly a video capture of the face-to-face class or teacher could increase the sense of co-presence that remote students experienced. Several face-to-face student questionnaire responses highlighted how co-presence was enhanced (or diminished) depending on whether remote students used audio and video, and the quality of their connection.

Human factors also influenced the sense of co-presence. For instance, running a block face-to-face session at the beginning of semester meant that remote and face-to-face students in Case Study 6 felt more connected during their blended synchronous learning classes. Humour, tone of voice, body language and words were also seen to contribute to a sense of connectedness. People's individual comfort level with communicating via different modalities could also influenced their perceived sense of co-presence; for example some students indicating that they were used to interacting on social media so felt co-present even when using text.

Several students also articulated how the blended synchronous learning mode enhanced their sense of connectedness, for instance:

> *it enhances a shared learning experience between all students* (face-to-face student)

> *I absolutely love attending the classes via internet.. it keeps me connected with my lecturer and classmates on a regular basis* (remote student)

This enhanced sense of community experienced between remote and face-to-face students that is possible in blended synchronous learning environments also accords with previous research in the area (Lidstone & Shield, 2010).

More flexible access to learning

Remote students from across the cases invariably appreciated that they could participate in live classes from their home or workplace, and indicated that this increased their capacity to attend.

> *I'm more likely to be able to turn up online (rather than get to a classroom)* (Case Study 6 remote student)

Face-to-face students also valued the flexibility blended synchronous learning offered them if they were sick or were not able to attend classes in person.

> *I'm an internal student and was unable to attend a tutorial one day as my kids were sick so I did it online whilst I was minding my kids in the comfort of my home* (Case Study 4 face-to-face student)

This increased equity of access to learning concurs with previous work on blended synchronous learning (Norberg, 2012; Pope, 2010).

Increased student satisfaction

Responses to the lesson evaluation questionnaires across the seven case studies indicated that 73.8% of face-to-face and 77.4% of remote students would like blended synchronous learning to be used in other subjects that they studied. Reasons for wanting blended synchronous learning generally related to the more active learning, the flexibility of access, and the enhanced sense of community, for instance:

> *More interaction, and more shared thoughts* (face-to-face student)

> *its good if you need to miss a class or can't get to the uni because you can attend online* (face-to-face student)

love networking with class mates - it helps to you feel like you have some when you live in a rural location (remote student)

There were some students (7.7% of face-to-face students and 11.3% of remote students) who indicated they would not like blended synchronous learning to be used in other classes, typically citing a preference for face-to-face lectures or subject inapplicability. Nor is it being claimed that the blended synchronous learning cases were without their issues (as explained in the next section). Yet, the fact that a large majority of students across the cases expressed a preference for blended synchronous learning highlights the perceived value of this emerging teaching mode.

Challenges of Blended Synchronous Learning

Teaching in blended synchronous learning mode is not without its challenges. While several blended synchronous learning issues are discussed in the Blended Synchronous Learning Design Framework section, three in particular warrant explicit attention: Technology performance issues, preserving the quality of the face-to-face experience, and heightened cognitive load.

Technology performance issues

The reliability of the technology can have a critical impact on the success of Blended synchronous learning activities, as observed in this project as well as previous studies (Chakraborty & Victor, 2004; Pope, 2010; Stewart, Harlow, & DeBacco, 2011; White, et al., 2010). Technology reliability and performance issues occurred in all seven case studies, with the resulting impact ranging from minor to substantial. Particular technology challenges included reliably capturing the audio from face-to-face classroom students and projecting the audio of remote students into the classroom. Inability for students to hear their peers in the other cohort could mean that the teacher needed to repeat or paraphrase comments, potentially leading to information loss. Other technology issues across the cases included interactive whiteboard latency, breakout rooms not functioning, students losing access to online spaces, slides not progressing, software crashing, and audio feedback loops. Yet despite the technological interruptions, the blended synchronous learning classes were able to be implemented in all seven cases. Thus teacher preparation as well as teacher flexibility are critically important.

Preserving the quality of the face-to-face experience

It is possible for face-to-face students to feel as though blended synchronous learning compromises their experience if the teacher appears distracted by the presence of remote students, or if communicating via technology imposes a communication overhead such as having to repeat comments (Popov, 2009; Rogers, et al., 2003; White, et al., 2010). This was observed in some of the case studies, with a small minority of face-to-face students questioning whether the blended synchronous learning approach compromised the quality of their learning experience. A specific example of this was some students commenting that it was easier to perform group work with people sitting next to them rather than via the collaborative technology. Yet many other face-to-face students felt that their experience was not hindered and in-fact enhanced (as indicated by the large majority of face-to-face students who felt they learnt more and wanted other subjects to utilise a blended synchronous learning approach). Thus the perceived quality of blended synchronous learning may relate to individual factors, as well as the design and execution of the lessons themselves. In any case, teachers are advised to not becoming overly absorbed in teaching one cohort over another, and should avoid duplication of explanations (as outlined in the Blended Synchronous Learning Design Framework).

Heightened cognitive load

Attempting to teach remote and face-to-face students simultaneously is substantially more demanding than attempting to teach one mode alone (Norberg, 2012; Popov, 2009). One important theme that emerged from this project was the heightened levels of cognitive load that were incurred in blended synchronous learning environments. Teachers not only need to teach the face-to-face class and the remote class at the same time, but also operate the online technology and facilitate interaction between the two cohorts. For instance, attempting to monitor the text chat while presenting information to the class could often result in split attention. Some students also indicated that learning via blended synchronous learning mode could result in information overload, yet other students found the multiple channels of information kept them engaged and interested. Strategies for managing cognitive load in blended synchronous learning environments included directing communication to one particular mode (for instance, just audio or just text chat), using students to help monitor the text chat, setting group work tasks to enable the teacher more freedom to work with individuals, and consciously focusing attention to relevant channels of information. These strategies are also outlined in the Blended Synchronous Learning Design Framework.

Recommendations for Institutions

With the potential to enable more flexible access programs, to improve the quality of learning experience for remote and face-to-face students, and to enhance the sense of connectedness that students feel, blended synchronous learning has a considerable amount to offer institutions. Yet as noted by teachers from across the case studies, teaching in blended synchronous learning mode is challenging.

If institutions are to successfully leverage the potentials of blended synchronous learning they should be cognisant of the following recommendations:

- Technical support is imperative for educators teaching in blended synchronous learning mode, particularly during their initial attempts
- A teaching assistant is often critical to help place students into breakout rooms, alert the teacher about recent student contributions to the text chat, make announcements to both cohorts and so on, especially with large numbers of students
- Professional development and mentoring arrangements are important so that teachers can quickly acquire the capabilities they need to teach in blended synchronous learning mode

- Learning and teaching spaces need to be automated with the appropriate audio-video capture facilities so that teachers can more immediately and seamlessly teach using blended synchronous learning techniques
- Blended synchronous learning needs to have workload allocated appropriately to account for the extra time that it takes teachers.

While all of these items are seen as requirements for successful institutional deployment of blended synchronous learning, this last point is particularly important to promote widespread academic buy-in. As Stewart et al. (2011) note, lack of institutional recognition for the degree of effort required to teach in blended synchronous learning environments can leave some teachers feeling unsupported and discouraged in their efforts to innovate with this mode of teaching.

Given that teaching in blended synchronous learning mode is more demanding than teaching in either online or face-to-face mode, but there are some economies derived from the common content, recognising blended synchronous learning with a workload of somewhere in-between one and two times regular classroom teaching would seem appropriate.

Future Directions

Blended synchronous learning is a new concept to many educators, and it may be a daunting prospect for some. It may be reassuring to know that several of the teachers in the case studies indicated that they initially felt apprehensive about trying to teach in blended synchronous learning mode, yet over time each has developed confidence in using the approach. They saw how blended synchronous learning could transcend the asynchronous offering availed to remote students, and could at the same time enhance the degree of interactivity for face-to-face students. Blended synchronous learning was seen by case study partners as an opportunity to improve their pedagogy, by providing a more participatory and engaging learning environment. While ensuring equity to both cohorts of students was an important consideration, it was seen to be a valuable emerging practice that could lead to students feeling more "satisfied, engaged and connected" (Case Study 6 teacher). More than one of the case study partners felt the urge to encourage their peers to 'give it a try'.

Blended synchronous learning raises some big questions for institutions, perhaps in the same way that MOOCs have recently, although with possibly greater long-term impact. The ways in which technology can increase access to education and provide students with greater flexibility of participation has the potential to fundamentally change where and how students chose to learn. And, as always, a range of technologies loom on the horizon that can push and prod our educational thinking. Technologies such as Google Glass (http://www.google.com/glass/start), X-Box Kinect (http://www.xbox.com/en-US/Kinect) and String (http://www.poweredbystring.com) promise much in the area of blended synchronous learning through the use of digital overlays, digital worlds, augmented reality and wearable technologies. In the future groups of dislocated students may be able to collaborate and access three-dimensional resources in high fidelity and real-time, as if they were all in the same room.

In future technological landscapes where students have access to near-perfect emulations of real-time face-to-face interaction, educators and institutions will be challenged to ask themselves the perennial educational technology questions:

- When is it appropriate to use these technologies?
- What educational purposes are these technologies best suited to?
- How can we support educators to optimise their teaching approaches using these technologies?
- How can we tell if our new teaching and learning approaches are effective?

Concluding remarks

This project was borne out of the utopian vision that in the future with advances in Information and Communication Technology all students should have equitable access to face-to-face learning experiences no matter where they are located. Through the outstanding efforts of the case study partners in this project it is apparent that rich-media synchronous technologies such as video conferencing, web conferencing and virtual worlds makes this a possibility in today's classrooms. As technologies develop, cultures change and expectations rise we should anticipate that the ease of access to and implementation of blended synchronous learning environments will continue to improve.

However, as for any use of technology in education, it is important to not attribute the success of the learning experience to the technology itself. As was apparent in all of the case studies, the teacher and the quality of their pedagogical practices was the main determinant of the student experience. To that extent, teacher practice, development and support should be the primary focus of any blended synchronous learning initiatives. It is intended that this Handbook provide the evidential basis and guidance to effectively support teachers and institutions in this endeavour.

References

Almpanis, T., Miller, E., Ross, M., Price, D., & James, R. (2011). *Evaluating the use of web conferencing software to enhance flexible curriculum delivery.* In Proceedings of the Ireland International Conference on Education (IICE-2011), Dublin, (pp. 317-322): IICE.

Atweh, B., Shield, P., & Godat, M. (2005). *The Bumpy road of collaborative innovation in online delivery: How to negotiate it?* Paper presented at the On-Line Teaching conference Beyond Delivery. Queensland University of Technology: Garden Point.

Barkley, E. F., Cross, K. P., & Major, C. H. (2004). *Collaborative learning techniques: A handbook for college faculty.* San Francisco: Jossey-Bass Publishers.

Beltrán Sierra, L. M., Gutiérrez, R. S., & Garzón-Castro, C. L. (2012). Second Life as a support element for learning electronic related subjects: A real case. *Computers & Education, 58*(1), 291-302.

Bergin, J. (2002). Fourteen pedagogical patterns for teaching computer science. Retrieved March, 2008, from http://csis.pace.edu/~bergin/PedPat1.3.html

Biggs, J. (1989). Approaches to the enhancement of tertiary teaching. *Higher Education Research and Development, 8*(1), 7-25.

Biggs, J., & Tang, C. (2011). *Teaching for Quality Learning at University (3rd Edition)* (3rd ed.). Maidenhead, UK: McGraw-Hill.

Borokhovski, E., Tamim, R., Bernard, R. M., Abrami, P. C., & Sokolovskaya, A. (2012). Are contextual and designed student–student interaction treatments equally effective in distance education? *Distance Education, 33*(3), 311-329.

Bower, M. (2011). Redesigning a web-conferencing environment to scaffold computing students' creative design processes. *Educational Technology and Society, 14*(1), 27-42.

Bower, M., & Hellstén, M. (2010). *An institutional study of learning and teaching using web-conferencing.* In Global Learn 2010, Penang, Malaysia, (pp. 4168-4177): AACE.

Bower, M., Kennedy, G., Dalgarno, B., Lee, M. J. W., Kenney, J., & de Barba, P. (2012). *Use of media-rich real-time collaboration tools for learning and teaching in Australian and New Zealand universities.* In Australasian Society for Computers in Learning in Tertiary Education, Wellington, (pp. 133-144).

Bradley, D., Noonan, P., Nugent, H., & Scales, B. (2008). *Review of higher education in Australia, final report.* Canberra: A. Government.

Brook, C., & Oliver, R. (2003). Online learning communities: Investigating a design framework. *Australian Journal of Educational Technology, 19*(2), 139-160.

Chakraborty, M., & Victor, S. (2004). Do's and don'ts of simultaneous instruction to on-campus and distance students via videoconferencing. *Journal of library administration, 41*(1-2), 97-112.

Conole, G. (2012). *Designing for learning in an open world (Vol. 4)*: Springer.

Dalgarno, B., & Lee, M. J. W. (2010). What are the learning affordances of 3-D virtual environments? *British Journal of Educational Technology, 40*(6), 10–32.

Dalgarno, B., Lee, M. J. W., Carlson, L., Gregory, S., & Tynan, B. (2011a). An Australian and New Zealand scoping study on the use of 3D immersive virtual worlds in Higher

Education. *Australasian Journal of Educational Technology, 27*(1), 1-15.

Dalgarno, B., Lee, M. J. W., Carlson, L., Gregory, S., & Tynan, B. (2011b). *Institutional support for and barriers to the use of 3D immersive virtual worlds in higher education.* In Changing demands, changing directions Proceedings ascilite Hobart 2011, Hobart, Tasmania, (pp. 316-330): The University of Tasmania.

Dalziel, J., Conole, G., Wills, S., Walker, S., Bennett, S., Dobozy, E., et al. (2012). *The Larnaca Declaration on Learning Design*.

de Groot, M., Harrison, G., & Shaw, R. (2011). *Web conferencing for us, by us and about us – the Leeds Met Elluminate User Group.* In Proceedings of the 10th European Conference on e-Learning (ECEL 2011), Reading, UK, (pp. 156-165): Academic Conferences.

Dede, C. (2009). Immersive interfaces for engagement and learning. *Science, 323*(5910), 66-69.

Derntl, M., & Botturi, L. (2006). Essential Use Cases for Pedagogical Patterns. *Computer Science Education, 16*(2), 137-156.

Dillenbourg, P. (1999). What do you mean by collaborative learning? In P. Dillenbourg (Ed.), *Advances in Learning and Instruction Series* (pp. 1-19). Oxford: Elsevier.

Dillenbourg, P. (2008). Integrating technologies into educational ecosystems. *Distance Education, 29*(2), 127–140.

Dobozy, E. (2013). Learning design research: advancing pedagogies in the digital age. *Educational Media International, 50*(1), 63-76.

E-LEN Project (2007). E-LEN project homepage. Retrieved Jan, 2007, from http://www2.tisip.no/E-LEN/

Fullwood, C., & Doherty-Sneddon, G. (2006). Effect of gazing at the camera during a video link on recall. *Applied Ergonomics, 37*(2), 167-175.

Gilbert, S. (1995). An 'online' experience: Discussion group debates why faculty use or resist technology. *Change: The Magazine of Higher Learning, 27*(2), 28-45.

Goodyear, P., & Retalis, S. (2010). *Technology-enhanced learning*: Sense Publishers.

Gosper, M., Green, D., McNeill, M., Phillips, R., Preston, G., & Woo, K. (2008). *The impact of web-based lecture technologies on current and future practices in learning and teaching [Final project report]*. Sydney.

Haberman, B. (2006). Pedagogical Patterns: A means for communication within the CS teaching community of practice. *Computer Science Education, 16*(2), 87-103.

Harper, B., Oliver, R., Hedberg, J., & Wills, S. (2003). Information and Communication Technologies and their role in flexible learning, from http://learningdesigns.uow.edu.au

Hastie, M., Hung, I. Ä., Chen, N. Ä., & Kinshuk (2010). A blended synchronous learning model for educational international collaboration. *Innovations in Education and Teaching International, 47*(1), 9-24.

Herrington, J., Herrington, A., Ferry, B., & Olney, I. (2008). *New technologies, new pedagogies: Using mobile technologies to develop new ways of teaching and learning [Final project report]*. Sydney.

Hew, K. F., & Cheung, W. S. (2010). Use of three-dimensional (3-D) immersive virtual worlds in K-12 and higher education settings: A review of the research. *British Journal of Educational Technology, 41*(1), 33-55.

Irvine, V. (2010). *Exploring Learner Needs for Collaboration and Access.* In World Conference on Educational Multimedia, Hypermedia and Telecommunications, (pp. 1093-1097).

Irvine, V., Code, J., & Richards, L. (2013). Realigning higher education for the 21st-Century Learner through Multi-Access Learning. *MERLOT Journal of Online Learning and Teaching, 9*(2).

Jacobson, M. J., Kim, B., Miao, C., Shen, Z., & Chavez, M. (2010). Design perspectives for learning in virtual worlds. In M. J. Jacobson & P. Reimann (Eds.), *Designs for learning environments of the future: International perspectives from the learning sciences* (pp. 111-141). New York: Springer-Verlag.

James, R., Krause, K., & Jennings, C. (2010). *The first year experience in Australian universities: Findings from 1994 to 2009*. Melbourne.

Jonassen, D. H., Lee, C. B., Yang, C.-C., & Laffey, J. (2005). The collaboration principle in multimedia learning. In R. E. Mayer (Ed.), *The Cambridge handbook of multimedia learning* (pp. 247-270). New York: Cambridge University Press.

Joseph, A., & Payne, M. (2003). Group dynamics and collaborative group performance *Proceedings of the 34th SIGCSE technical symposium on Computer science education* (pp. 368-371): ACM Press.

Kan, K. H. (2011). Meeting face to face = seeing eye to eye?: Interglobal dialogue via videoconference. *International Journal of Education & the Arts, 12*(10).

Kember, D., McNaught, C., Chong, F. C., Lam, P., & Cheng, K. F. (2010). Understanding the ways in which design features of educational websites impact upon student learning outcomes in blended learning environments. *Computers & Education, 55*(3), 1183-1192.

Kennedy, G. E. (2010). *Charting the directions of e-learning: Navigating a course. Invited seminar paper presented at the Centre of Study of Higher Education, .*

Koenig, R. J. (2010). A study in analyzing effectiveness of undergraduate course delivery: Classroom, online and video conference from a student and faculty perspective. *Contemporary Issues in Education Research, 3*(10), 13-25.

Laurillard, D. (2002). *Rethinking university teaching - A framework for the effective use of learning technologies*. Oxford, UK: RoutledgeFalmer.

Laurillard, D. (2012). *Teaching as a design science - Building pedagogical patterns for learning and technology*. NY: Routledge.

Laurillard, D., Masterman, L., Magoulas, G., Boyle, T., & Manton, M. (2011). Learning Design Support Environment. Retrieved 10 October, 2013, from https://sites.google.com/a/lkl.ac.uk/ldse/people

Lidstone, J., & Shield, P. G. (2010). Virtual reality or virtually real: blended teaching and learning in a Master's level research methods class. *Cases on Online and Blended Learning Technologies in Higher Education: Concepts and Practices*, 91-111.

Lim, K. Y. T. (2009). The Six Learnings of Second Life: A framework for designing curricular interventions in-world. *Journal of Virtual Worlds Research, 2*(1).

Lowe, D., Murray, S., Li, D., & Lindsay, E. (2008). *Remotely accessible laboratories – enhancing learning outcomes [Final project report]*. Sydney.

McCue, L., & Scales, G. R. (2007). *Embracing the middle ground: Engaging on- and off-campus students within the same 'classroom'.* In Proceedings, ASEE Southeast Section Conference, Louisville, KY.

Messinger, P., Stroulia, E., & Lyons, K. (2008). A typology of virtual worlds: Historical overview and future directions. *Journal of Virtual Worlds Research, 1*(1).

Mikropoulos, T. A., & Natsis, A. (2011). Educational virtual environments: A ten-year review of empirical research (1999-2009). *Computers & Education, 56*(3), 769-780.

Moore, M. G. (1991). Distance education theory. *The American Journal of Distance Education, 5*(3), 1-6.

Munkvold, B. E., Khazanchi, D., & Zigurs, I. (2011). *Augmenting online learning with real-time conferencing: Experiences from an international course.* In Proceedings of the Norwegian Conference on Information Use in Organisations (NOKOBIT 2011), Trondheim, Norway, (pp. 221-232): NOKOBIT Foundation and Tapir Academic Press.

Naidu, S., & Järvelä, S. (2006). Analyzing CMC content for what? *Computers & Education, 46*(1), 96-103.

Norberg, A. (2012). Blended learning and new education logistics in Northern Sweden. In D. G. Oblinger (Ed.), *Game changers: Education and information technologies* (pp. 327-330). Boulder, CO: EDUCAUSE.

Parker, C., & Joyner, S. (1995). Facilitating simultaneous engineering in the automotive industry via high-speed networks, control passing and face-to-face video: Results from the CAR project. *International Journal of Industrial Ergonomics, 16*(4-6), 427-440.

Pedagogical Patterns Project (2006). Pedagogical Patterns Project homepage. Retrieved 17th November, 2007, from http://www.pedagogicalpatterns.org/

Pope, C. L. (2010). *Breaking down barriers: Providing flexible participation options for on-campus courses.* In ERGA Conference (5th: 2010: Adelaide, Australia).

Popov, O. (2009). Teachers' and students' experiences of simultaneous teaching in an international distance and on-campus master's programme in engineering. *The International Review of Research in Open and Distance Learning, 10*(3), 1-17.

Power, M. (2008). The emergence of a blended online learning environment. *MERLOT Journal of Online Learning and Teaching, 4*(4), 513-514.

Power, M., & Vaughan, N. (2010). Redesigning online learning for graduate seminar delivery. *The Journal of Distance Education/Revue de l'Vâducation √† Distance, 24*(2).

Reeves, T. C., Herrington, J., & Oliver, R. (2004). A Development Research Agenda for Online Collaborative Learning. *Educational Technology Research & Development, 52*(4), 53-65.

Retalis, S., Georgiakakis, P., & Dimitriadis, Y. (2006). Eliciting design patterns for e-learning systems. *Computer Science Education, 16*(2), 105-118.

Rogers, P. C., Graham, C. R., Rasmussen, R., Campbell, J. O., & Ure, D. M. (2003). Case 2: Blending Face-to-Face and Distance Learners in a Synchronous Class: Instructor and Learner Experiences. *Quarterly Review of Distance Education, 4*(3), 245-251.

Roseth, C., Akcaoglu, M., & Zellner, A. (2013). Blending Synchronous Face-to-face and Computer-Supported Cooperative Learning in a Hybrid Doctoral Seminar. *TechTrends, 57*(3), 54-59.

Schield, P., Atweh, B., & Singh, P. (2005). *Utilising synchronous web-mediated communications as a booster to sense of community in a hybrid on-campus/off-campus teaching and learning environment.* In ASCILITE Conference Proceedings, December 4, 2005, Brisbane, Australia.

Slavin, R. E. (1995). *Cooperative learning: Theory, research, and practice* (2nd ed.). Boston: Allyn & Bacon.

Smyth, R., Andrews, T., & Tynan, B. (2008). *Leading rich media implementation collaboratively: Mobilising international, national and business expertise.* In Proceedings of the IADIS International Conference on e-Learning, Amsterdam: AIDIS.

Spanier, G. B. (2011). Renewing the covenant: Ten years after the Kellogg Commission. *Journal of Higher Education Outreach and Engagement, 15*(3), 9-14.

Spann, D. (2012). *Five innovative ways to use virtual classrooms in higher education.* In Future challenges, sustainable futures ascilite conference Wellington, New Zealand: Massey University.

Steed, M., & Vigrass, A. (2011). *Assessment of web conferencing in teacher preparation field experiences.* In Proceedings of Society for Information Technology & Teacher Education International Conference 2011, Chesapeake, VA, (pp. 2736-2743): AACE.

Stewart, A. R., Harlow, D. B., & DeBacco, K. (2011). Students' experience of synchronous learning in distributed environments. *Distance Education, 32*(3), 357-381.

Tertiary Education Qualification Standards Agency (2013). *TEQSA and the Australian qualifications framework – questions and answers.*

Todhunter, S. P., T.-M. (2008) (2008). *VET goes virtual: Can web conferencing be an effective component of teaching and learning in the vocational education and training sector?* Adelaide: NCVER.

Valcke, M. (2004). *ICT in higher education: An uncomfortable zone for institutes and their policies.* In Proceedings of the 21st ASCILITE Conference, Perth, (pp. 20–35): The University of Western Australia.

Vu, P., & Fadde, P. J. (2013). When to Talk, When to Chat: Student Interactions in Live Virtual Classrooms. *Journal of Interactive Online Learning, 12*(2), 41-52.

Warburton, S. (2009). Second Life in higher education: Assessing the potential for and the barriers to deploying virtual worlds in learning and teaching. *British Journal of Educational Technology, 40*(3), 414-426.

White, C. P., Ramirez, R., Smith, J. G., & Plonowski, L. (2010). Simultaneous delivery of a face-to-face course to on-campus and remote off-campus students. *TechTrends, 54*(4), 34-40.

Wimba Inc. (2010). Blackboard to acquire Elluminate and Wimba. Retrieved 10 October, 2013, from http://www.wimba.com/company/newsroom/archive/blackboard_to_acquire_elluminate_and_wimba

Yin, R. K. (2009). *Case study research: Design and methods (Vol. 5)*: Sage.

Appendix A – Blended Synchronous Learning Scoping Study Questionnaire

[Note that this appendix only includes the Blended Synchronous Learning Scoping Study questions relating to the subject matter being investigated and not the initial information and consent nor the final section relating to dissemination of results.]

Part A: Background Information

This survey is intended to be completed by teaching and educational development staff of Australian and New Zealand Higher Education institutions who have been involved in applications of rich-media real-time collaboration tools.

In this survey, the term 'rich-media real-time collaboration tools' refers to technologies such as desktop videoconferencing, web conferencing and virtual worlds, as well as other technologies that facilitate synchronous (real-time) collaboration.

- Desktop videoconferencing tools enable live audio and video interactions between remote participants via the Internet using desktop programs installed on their computers. Examples of such programs include Skype, ooVoo, iChat and FaceTime.

- Web conferencing tools (sometimes referred to as 'online meeting', 'virtual classroom' or 'webinar' tools) allow groups of users to enter a shared online space where they can use features such as whiteboards, screen sharing, chat, voting, file sharing and collaborative authoring tools together in real time. The tools tend to be web browser-based; examples include Adobe Connect, WebEx, Saba Classroom and Blackboard Collaborate.
- Virtual worlds are online, synthetic representations of physical environments in which users can move around and interact with other objects and users, usually in three dimensions (3D). Examples of virtual world platforms include Second Life, Active Worlds, OpenSim and Open Wonderland.

1. Gender: [Male/Female]

2. Age group: [25 or under/26-35/36-45/46-55/56-65/Over 65]

3. Job title/position:

4. Institution:

5. Campus/location:

6. Faculty/School/Department:

7. What is/are your teaching area(s) (please be specific)?

8. How many years' experience do you have:

a) Teaching at a tertiary/Higher Education level

b) Using computers and the Internet for learning and teaching

c) Using rich-media real-time collaboration tools for tertiary learning and teaching

9. How would you rate your ability to use computers and/or the Internet for learning and teaching:

a) In general?

b) With respect to rich-media real-time collaboration tools?

10. Which of the following tools have you used/do you use to facilitate rich-media real-time collaboration in your teaching? (Please select all that apply.)

Second Life
Active Worlds
Reaction Grid
Multiverse
OpenSim
Open Wonderland
Open Cobalt
Open Croquet
realXtend
web.alive
Vastpark
There
Adobe Atmosphere
Other virtual worlds platform (please specify below)

Adobe Connect
WebEx
Cisco Unified Meeting Place
Wimba
Elluminate
Blackboard Collaborate
Dimdim
GoToMeeting
WebTrain
Saba
Microsoft Live Meeting
Microsoft SharedView
IBM Lotus Sametime / Live
Other web conferencing platform (please specify below)

Skype
ooVoo
CU-SeeMe
Microsoft NetMeeting
Microsoft Lync / Office Communicator
Google Voice and Video Chat
Windows Live Messenger
AOL Instant Messenger
(AIM) Yahoo! Messenger
iChat FaceTime
Other desktop video conferencing platform (please specify below)

Room or lecture theatre based video conferencing

Other type of rich-media real-time collaboration tool (please specify below)

If you selected one or more "other" options above, please specify the tool(s) used:

Part B: Views and beliefs about rich-media synchronous technologies for learning and teaching

11. In what situations do you think desktop videoconferencing is best used for learning and

teaching?

12. In what situations do you think web conferencing is best used for learning and teaching?

13. In what situations do you think virtual worlds are best used for learning and teaching?

14. Please indicate the various years in which you have used each of the following types of media-rich real-time collaboration tool for tertiary learning and teaching (select all years that apply within each row):

Desktop video conferencing
[2000 or earlier/2001/2002/2003/2004/2005/2006/2007/2008/2009/2010/2011]
Web-conferencing
[2000 or earlier/2001/2002/2003/2004/2005/2006/2007/2008/2009/2010/2011]
Virtual worlds
[2000 or earlier/2001/2002/2003/2004/2005/2006/2007/2008/2009/2010/2011]

15. Have you used rich-media real-time collaboration tools to simultaneously involve face-to-face and remotely located students in learning and teaching activities? [Yes/No]

Part C: Use of rich media collaboration tools for learning and teaching

The following questions ask you to provide information about one subject or unit in which you have used rich-media real-time collaboration tools for learning and teaching.

IMPORTANT: If you have used these tools in more than one instance, please describe the case that is most relevant to simultaneously supporting remote and face-to-face students.

16. Subject unit/title:

17. Subject unit/level:

18. Discipline area of the subject/unit:

19. Please indicate which years you have made use of rich-media real-time collaboration tools in this subject/unit (select all that apply):
[2000 or earlier/2001/2002/2003/2004/2005/2006/2007/2008/2009/2010/2011]

Please answer the following questions with reference to your most recent offering of this subject/unit.

20. Number of students:

a) enrolled in the subject/unit offering
b) that participated in the rich-media real-time collaboration tool activities

21. Delivery mode (select all that apply):

Conventional face-to-face, supplemented with online materials and/or optional online activities
Conventional face-to-face, blended with mandatory online activities
Distance/online, with face-to-face residential schools or workshops
Distance/online, with no face-to-face contact
Other (please specify):

22. What was the main type of rich-media real-time collaboration tool that you used in this subject/unit?

Please specify the specific technology or tool used.

23. Please provide a summary of the overall aims of the subject/unit.

24. Why did you use rich-media real-time collaboration tools for learning and teaching in this subject/unit?

25. Please describe the learning and teaching tasks/activities in the subject/unit involving the use of rich-media real-time collaboration tools.

26. Did students undertake the rich-media real-time collaboration activities (select all that apply):
[On campus/Off campus/In class time/Out of class time/Using a university computer/Using their own computer]

Please use the space below to explain and expand upon your selection(s). If applicable, elaborate on how students in different locations collaborated in real time:

27. What do you consider to be the most successful aspects of the use of rich-media real-time collaboration tools in this subject/unit?

28. What are the main problems you encountered in the use of rich-media real-time collaboration tools in this subject/unit?

29. Any other comments on the use of rich-media real-time collaboration tools in this subject/unit?

30. Do you use rich-media real-time collaboration tools in any other ways to teach your classes? [Yes/No]

If Yes, please briefly describe each instance.

31 What other emerging approaches can you identify for uniting remote and face-to-face students using synchronous collaborative technologies? Are you motivated to use these approaches in future (please explain why / why not)

Appendix B – Blended Synchronous Learning Post-Lesson Student Survey

[Note that this appendix only includes the Blended Synchronous Learning Post-Lesson Student Survey questions relating to the subject matter being investigated and not the initial information and consent nor the final section relating to dissemination of results.]

Q1. I understand that by choosing to complete the survey I give my consent as a participant in the BlendSync research project: [Yes/No]

Q2. Please select one statement that best describes your attendance mode:

I participated in this lesson remotely (e.g. online or using technology)
I participated in this lesson in the same room as the teacher

Q3. In two or three sentences, please describe your overall impression of this lesson:

Q4. I was able to communicate verbally in an effective manner with people in the face-to-face class:

[Strongly Disagree/Disagree/Mildly Disagree/Neutral/Mildly Agree/Agree/Strongly Agree/Not Required]

Q5. What supported or restricted your verbal communication with the face-to-face class?:

Q6. I was able to communicate verbally in an effective manner with people who participated remotely:

[Strongly Disagree/Disagree/Mildly Disagree/Neutral/Mildly Agree/Agree/Strongly Agree/Not Required]

Q7. What supported or restricted your verbal communication with people participating remotely?:

Q8. In this lesson I was able to effectively share visual artefacts with others (e.g. images, photos, slides, movies):

[Strongly Disagree/Disagree/Mildly Disagree/Neutral/Mildly Agree/Agree/Strongly Agree/Not Required]

Q9. What supported or restricted your ability to effectively share visual artefacts?:

Q10. In this lesson I was able to jointly create, edit, and share material with others in an effective manner:

[Strongly Disagree/Disagree/Mildly Disagree/Neutral/Mildly Agree/Agree/Strongly Agree/Not Required]

Q11. What supported or restricted your ability to joint create, edit and share materials effectively with others?:

Q12. In this lesson I was able to effectively indicate my status to others (e.g. wanting attention, agreeing, unsure, etc.):

[Strongly Disagree/Disagree/Mildly Disagree/Neutral/Mildly Agree/Agree/Strongly Agree/Not Required]

Q13. What supported or restricted your ability to effectively indicate your status to others?:

Q14. In this lesson I felt like I was present with people who were participating remotely:

[Strongly Disagree/Disagree/Mildly Disagree/Neutral/Mildly Agree/Agree/Strongly Agree/Not Required]

Q15. What supported or restricted your sense of being present with people who were participating remotely?:

Q16. In this lesson I felt like I was present with people who were in the same room as the teacher:

[Strongly Disagree/Disagree/Mildly Disagree/Neutral/Mildly Agree/Agree/Strongly Agree/Not Required]

Q17. What supported or restricted your sense of being present with people in the face-to-face classroom?:

Q18. The collaborative technology provided clear and accurate representation of information and people:

[Strongly Disagree/Disagree/Mildly Disagree/Neutral/Mildly Agree/Agree/Strongly Agree/Not Required]

Q19. Explain how the collaborative technology provided or did not provide a clear representation of information and people:

Q20. The technology enabled learning to occur:

[Strongly Disagree/Disagree/Mildly Disagree/Neutral/Mildly Agree/Agree/Strongly Agree/Not Required]

Q21. Explain your answer:

Q22. I learnt ___________ in this lesson than if the lesson had run in a normal face-to-face mode: [less/the same/more]

Q23. Explain your answer:

Q24. Were there any issues that arose by having remote and face-to-face students participating in the one lesson? If yes, explain what they were and how they impacted on the learning experience:

Q25. Were there any advantages of having remote and face-to-face students participating in the one lesson? If yes, explain what they were and how they impacted on the learning experience:

Q26. What advice would you give to people who are trying to simultaneously teach remote and face-to-face students?

Q27. Were there any technical difficulties experienced during this lesson? If yes, please explain:

Q28. I would like this sort of approach to be used in other subjects that I study: [Strongly Disagree/Disagree/Mildly Disagree/Neutral/Mildly Agree/Agree/Strongly Agree/Not Required]

Q29. Explain your answer:

Q30. What were the best things about this lesson?:

Q31. How could this lesson have been improved?:

www.ingramcontent.com/pod-product-compliance
Ingram Content Group UK Ltd.
Pitfield, Milton Keynes, MK11 3LW, UK
UKHW060024300726
14090UKWH00019B/1071

9 781743 616857